THE ISLAMIC CONCEPT
AND
ITS CHARACTERISTICS

by

Sayyid Qutb

Translated by
Mohammed Moinuddin Siddiqui

Translation of *Khasa'is us Tasawwur al-Islami wa Muqawwamatihi* (Arabic) by Sayyid Qutb.

Copyright © 1991 American Trust Publications, IN 46231, USA
ISBN 0-89259-119-6

Library of Congress Catalog Card No.: 91-46621

CONTENTS

INTRODUCTION
A WORD ABOUT THE METHODOLOGY

For a number of reasons there is a pressing need to define and elaborate the Islamic paradigm of thought, that is, to explain for a modern audience the Islamic concept.

The Muslim needs this definition because it provides him with a comprehensive explanation of all that exists, on the basis of which he relates to the world. This explanation brings him closer to an understanding of the great realities that confront him, and of the nature of the relationships and connections that exist among these realities, namely, the reality of the Creator and the reality of the created (the latter including the universe, life, and man), and their mutual relationships and interconnections.

The definition of the Islamic concept is also necessary for the Muslim so that he may understand the central position that man occupies in this universe and the ultimate purpose for which he is created. This knowledge in turn defines the role of man in the universe, the parameters and perimeters of the field of his activities, and the limits of his relationship with his Creator.

Such a definition, moreover, is essential because the understanding of this comprehensive view and the recognition of man's central position in the universe and the purpose of his existence define the Muslim's way of life and the kind of system established by this way of life. The system established in man's life is based entirely on this comprehensive view and follows logically from it. Without this base, the system would be mere patchwork, having shallow roots that will quickly disintegrate. Such a contrived system, while it lasts, is a cause of suffering and misery for people, since there exists a fundamental conflict between such a system and man's basic nature and real needs. This judgement applies to all systems current in the world today, without any exception, especially to the systems of the so-called "advanced" nations.

The definition of the Islamic concept is also needed because the Islamic *din*[1] was revealed in order to initiate a special kind of *ummah* (community), unique and distinctive, namely, an *ummah* that came to lead mankind, to establish the way of Allah on earth, and to save

---

[1] The Arabic word *din* is often translated as "religion," but this is misleading because the term "religion" in the English language is usually restricted to personal worship, whereas *din* refers to every aspect of life. (Editor).

1

people from the misery brought about by misguided leadership, erroneous ways, and false concepts. Today we see mankind in a miserable condition, despite some variations in forms and appearances. If a Muslim grasps the Islamic belief-concept and its essential constituents, he is guaranteed a role as a founding member of this dynamic *ummah*, with its special characteristics and distinguishing features, a member capable of leadership and grace. The clarity of his belief-concept is a great guiding force because the Muslim's system of life originates from this concept and is based upon it. It is this belief-concept that directs all individual and collective activities in various fields of human endeavor.

The Qur'an presents this comprehensive explanation to people in such a complete form that it takes into consideration all aspects of human nature, and satisfies its needs in every dimension. It deals with all matters, those pertaining to the senses, to feelings, to thought, to intuition, and to insight, and addresses all the elements of man's awareness, just as it deals also with his material needs in the physical world. It does so in a style that exhorts, inspires, and guides all these elements of human nature in a harmonious and natural manner, since it comes from the Originator of the universe and the Creator of man.

The first group of Muslims molded their lives according to this concept which comes directly from the Qur'an. They adapted to it in a uniquely complete way, and consequently the leadership of mankind was bestowed upon them. They led mankind in a manner unparalleled in history, either before or after. In matters related both to the heart and mind and to the world of actions and events, these first Muslims established such an exemplary system for mankind that it has not been repeated or even approached in the subsequent history of the world. The Qur'an was the foremost source for this group of people. Indeed, this group itself was a product of the Qur'an. What an amazing phenomenon in the history of mankind: a nation emerging from the text of a Book, living by it, and depending on its guidance as the prime source! The practice or the *sunnah* of the Prophet (peace be on him) reinforced this guidance as its complete, practical application. This point has been summarized by the Prophet's wife, 'Aishah. When she was asked about the character of the Messenger of Allah (peace be on him), she replied, aptly, summing up a deep truth, "His character was the Qur'an" (Al-Nasa'i).

Later generations drifted away from the Qur'an, from its particular style, its guidance, and from the milieu of values and practice similar to those found in the milieu in which the Qur'an was revealed. Only those living in such an atmosphere can truly understand the Qur'an and be inspired by it. No one can understand the Qur'an as it should be understood unless he lives amidst the toil and struggle accompanying the revival of the real Islamic way of life, with all its burdens, its sacrifices, its sorrows, and all the situations that arise in its confrontation with *jahiliyyah* [2] at any given time.

The real problem in grasping the significance and the spirit of the Qur'anic teachings does not lie in understanding its words and sentences, that is to say, its exegesis, as is often claimed. This does not constitute a problem at all. The problem lies in the capacity of our minds to reconstruct feelings, ideas, and experiences like the feelings, ideas, and experiences of the first generation of Muslims when they received these revelations from the lips of the Prophet (peace be upon him) in the thick of the struggle. Theirs was a struggle of jihad, of striving within oneself and striving with other people. It was a fight against temptations and a battle against enemies — exertions on behalf of others, and sacrifices, fears, and hopes. It was a constant cycle of falling down and rising up. The first Muslims experienced the exhilarating beginning of the Call in Makkah, and also the subsequent poverty and weakness, the indignities of being outcasts among the people and of being shut up in the Valley of Abu Talib, the hunger and the fear, the torments of being hunted down, and the boycott. And then they experienced the atmosphere surrounding the establishment of the Muslim *ummah* and the initiation of a social and political order, with ever present friction between feelings and policies throughout its period of construction and organization.

Such was the vibrant and pulsating atmosphere in which the Qur'an was revealed, with its words and messages full of meaning and inspiration. And without doubt, in a similar atmosphere — an atmosphere that always accompanies any new attempt at the revival of Islamic life — the Qur'an will again open its treasures to men's hearts and bestow its secrets on their minds, sending forth its fragrance in all directions and bringing guidance and light.

It was at such a time that they, the first Muslims, grasped the truth of Allah's message to them:

> They consider it to be a favor on you (Muhammad) that they
> have accepted Islam. Say: Your acceptance of Islam is not a
> favor to me. Nay, rather Allah has conferred a favor on you
> by guiding you to faith, if you are (really) truthful (*Al-
> Hujurat* 49:17).

---

[2] Lit., "ignorance." As used in the Islamic sense, *jahiliyyah* denotes ignorance or lack of awareness of Allah's guidance for mankind, whether of the ancient or the contemporary variety (trans.).

And again, the truth of His exhortation to them:

> O you who believe, respond to Allah and the Messenger
> when he calls you to what will give you life, and know that
> Allah comes between a man and his (own) heart, and that
> to Him you shall be gathered. And beware of a trial that
> shall not befall only the wrongdoers among you, and know
> that Allah is severe in retribution. And remember when you
> were few and weak in the land, fearing that people would
> do away with you, whereupon He gave refuge and
> strengthened you with His help, and provided you with
> what is good, in order that you might be thankful (*Al-Anfal*
> 8:24- 26).

And the truth of His saying to them:

> And Allah helped you at Badr[3] when you were a humble
> force, so be conscious of Allah so that you may be thankful
> (*Ale-'Imran* 3:123).

And the truth of His wisdom revealed to them:

> Do not be faint-hearted nor grieve, for you shall be the
> uppermost if you are believers. If some hurt touches you,
> a similar hurt has touched the (unbelieving) people. We
> apportion such days among mankind so that Allah may
> know those who believe and that He may take witnesses
> from among you — for Allah does not love those who do
> wrong — and so that Allah may prove those who believe
> and obliterate the unbelievers. Or did you imagine that you
> would enter the Garden (of Paradise) without Allah's know-
> ing which of you have struggled or knowing those who are
> steadfast? (*Ale 'Imran* 3:139-143).

And the truth of Allah's encouragement to them:

> You will surely be tried in your possessions and your
> persons, and you will hear much abuse from those who
> were given the Book before you and from those who
> associate others with Allah. But if you remain steadfast and

---

[3] One of the battles of the Prophet's era (trans.).

are conscious of Allah, this, behold, is something to set
one's heart upon (*Ale 'Imran* 3:186).

They grasped the truth of all these messages of Allah Most High
because He was talking about events that were occurring in their lives,
about happenings that were fresh in their memories, and about conditions surrounding them that were not remote in time and were
within the experience of that generation.

Only those who are passing through similar experiences today can
truly grasp the meanings and messages of the Qur'an. It is they alone
who appreciate the beauties of the Islamic concept as presented in the
Qur'an, because this concept is an integral part of their own feelings
and experience. They are receptive to it and see its light. But such
individuals are few. Since people have drifted away from the Qur'an
and from living in its atmosphere, it becomes incumbent on us to
present to them the truths of the Islamic concept concerning Allah,
the universe, and life and man, taken directly from the text of the
Qur'an, together with some explanations, interpretations, classification, and synthesis. This can in no way be a substitute for the richness
of the Qur'an in addressing minds and hearts, but, to the extent
possible, it is intended to bring people closer to the Qur'an. It is an
attempt at making them enjoy the Qur'an and seek in it the great truths
of the Islamic concept for themselves.

We must make it clear, however, that we do not desire to seek the
truths of the Islamic concept merely for the sake of academic
knowledge. We have no desire to add still another book to the shelves
of Islamic libraries under the heading of "Islamic Philosophy." Never!
Indeed, our purpose is not mere cold "knowledge" which deals only
with intellectual issues and adds to the stock of "culture." For us, this
sort of activity is somewhat trivial and cheap and not worth the effort.
Rather, we want to bring about that "movement" which is beyond
"knowledge." We want the knowledge of the Islamic concept to lead
people toward the realization of its contents in the real world. We
desire to awaken the conscience of the "human being" so that he may
fulfill the purpose of his creation as delineated by this divinely-
revealed concept. Our concern is that people return to their Lord, to
the path He intends for them, and to the sublime way of life consonant
with the nobility bestowed upon them by Allah, as it was once
actualized in history when an *ummah* came into being based on this
concept and led mankind toward what is good, wholesome, and
constructive.

There came a time in the history of Islam when the original Islamic
way of life, based on the pure Islamic concept, came in contact with

other lifestyles and cultures prevalent in the lands that had newly joined the Islamic fold and in lands still more distant.

The early days of struggle for the propagation of the Faith and of jihad had given way to a period of ease and comfort. At the same time, certain political occurrences, harking back to the disputes between 'Ali and Muawiyah, had raised various thorny philosophical and religious issues and caused the contending parties to support their position by rational argument. People residing in the Islamic territories studied Greek philosophy and involved themselves in the theological issues that had plagued Christianity earlier, and which were now accessible to Muslims through translations into the Arabic language. Such involvement in metaphysical speculation, which no doubt gave intellectual pleasure to those who engaged in it during the Abbasid period and likewise in Andalusia, introduced deviations and foreign elements into the original Islamic concept, which had come originally to rescue mankind from such deviations and speculations. This all-encompassing concept was revealed to restore mankind to the dynamic and practical Islamic belief system that directs all human energies toward building and construction, sublimity and purity, and living and sharing, while protecting this human energy and intellectual power from being dissipated through meaningless pursuits in the wilderness of philosophical speculation.

Many Muslim scholars thought it necessary to respond to the controversies and issues concerning the person of Allah Most High and His attributes, will, and power, and concerning man's actions, and such topics as reward, punishment, sin, and repentance, with rational arguments, intellectual debate, and polemics. As a consequence of such debates, which soon degenerated into polemics, various sects came into being, such as the Kharijiyyah, Shi'ah, Mu'tazilah, Qadariyah, and Jabriyah. Among Muslim thinkers, there were some who adored Greek philosophy, especially the commentaries on Aristotle, to whom they fondly referred as "the first teacher," and they loved scholastic theology or metaphysics. They presumed that "Islamic thought" could not reach maturity and perfection, or greatness and glory, unless it were clothed in this garment, the cloak of rational philosophy, and unless volumes were written about it. Just as nowadays some people admire Western modes of thought, they admired the modes of thought of their era and attempted to develop "Islamic philosophy" on the pattern of Greek philosophy. Others initiated the *Science of Kalam* to address theological issues through Aristotelian logic.

They abandoned the Islamic concept and its own pure and independent format, which suits its nature so perfectly since both concept and format address the total nature of man with all his faculties and concerns, and not merely his intellect in cold logical terms. Instead they took the mould of philosophy and tried to pour the Islamic concept into it. They borrowed various philosophical concepts and tried to demonstrate that the Islamic concept agrees with them. Even their terminology was almost entirely borrowed.

In general, there exists a genuine disharmony between the methodology of philosophy and the methodology of belief, between the style of philosophy and the style of belief, and, in particular, between the great and sublime truths of the Islamic faith and the petty, artificial, and confused efforts that go under the headings of metaphysical philosophy and scholastic theology. The so-called "Islamic philosophy" was nothing more than a discordant note in the harmonious melody of the Islamic belief. Such intellectual gymnastics merely produced confusion in people's minds and polluted the purity of the Islamic concept, narrowing its scope and rendering it superficial, dry, complicated, and incomprehensible. The whole corpus of "Islamic philosophy" and of the *Science of Kalam* was and is completely foreign to Islam — to its nature, method, style, and teachings.

This statement will come as a shock, of course, to a great number of people who indulge in what they term "Islamic philosophy" and, in general, to those who enjoy any kind of philosophical discussion. But the Islamic concept cannot be purified of distortions and deviations unless we remove from it everything to which the label of "Islamic philosophy" applies, discard every issue relating to the *Science of Kalam*, and sweep away all the differences of various sects that have come to us from times past. We can then return to the Qur'an and take the Islamic concept, with all the characteristics that distinguish it from every other concept, directly from the Qur'an. There is, of course, no harm in making comparisons with other concepts in order to clarify its characteristics, but the constituents of this concept must be taken directly from the Qur'an and presented entirely in their own format and terminology.

In order to understand our method of presenting the Islamic concept, we must bear in mind three important facts.

First, the heritage received by the Islamic world from Greek philosophy and Christian theology can be traced in the disputes among various sects. Their disputations consisted of nothing more than latter-day commentaries on the original works, conveyed in a polemical and argumentative style. To reproduce them now would cause only confusion and disturbance in the minds of sincere people.

Second, the attempt to reconcile these commentaries on Greek philosophy with the Islamic concept was simple-minded to the extreme, because it demonstrated ignorance of the nature of Greek philosophy, its deeply-rooted pagan elements, and its lack of a unified system and a unified method, all of which are quite the antithesis of the Islamic concept as revealed in its original sources. Greek philosophy originated in the midst of an idolatrous society burdened with mythology. Its roots were nourished by the same myths and pagan concepts, and it was never free of such pagan mythological influences. What greater naivete and futility can there be than to try to reconcile such a philosophy with the Islamic concept, which is based entirely on the pure, absolute, and uncompromising belief in the Oneness of Allah, Most High. But, under the influence of latter-day Christian commentaries, Muslims who engaged in philosophical discussions held the erroneous view that "the Philosophers" (by which they meant the Greek philosophers) could not have been pagan nor could they have strayed from the Oneness of Allah. Under this illusion, they took upon themselves the impossible task of reconciling the Philosophers' discourses with the Islamic belief. Unfortunately, a major portion of "Islamic philosophy" consists of such attempts.

Third, after the murder of 'Uthman (may Allah be pleased with him), the Islamic world faced many practical problems. People began to interpret the verses of the Qur'an to suit their own purposes, giving them far-fetched meanings. Moreover, arguments were put forward for and against various sectarian views, each seeking support for its opinions from philosophy and scholastic theology. Most such arguments were biased. Consequently, such sources, biased as they are, cannot be relied upon to present the pure Islamic thought. Its characteristics and constituents must be derived from the fixed text of the Qur'an and must be free of such pollutants from the legacy of history. Indeed, it is better to set aside this entire legacy. For our understanding of the genuine teachings of Islam, however, and for the study of Islamic history in a proper perspective, we should study the various aspects of deviations and their causes in order to avoid similar pitfalls today in delineating the meaning of the Islamic concept and in formulating a blueprint of the Islamic system of thought and action.

Western modes of thought developed in their own particular fashion. In the beginning they were based on Greek thought with all its pagan elements, while in the end their main concern was to oppose the Church and its teachings.

Since the Renaissance, the general trend of the Western mode of thought was criticism of the Catholic Church and its doctrines, and, with the passage of time, to object to all religion and religious doctrines per se. But the doctrines of the Church, by and large, did not, at any point, represent the true teachings of the Prophet Jesus (peace be upon him). Christianity was born in the shadow of the pagan Roman Empire. Later, when the Roman Empire adopted Christianity as the state religion, it did great violence to the true teachings of Jesus, distorting them beyond recognition. In the beginning, the distortions came from the influence of Roman paganism, but later the Church and its councils added many alien concepts to the divinely-revealed teachings. Religious passions were exploited to keep the Empire together, expositions of faith were intended to halt disputes between the contending factions, and doctrines were propounded to unite heretics to the orthodox Church and to the central government[4]. Thus, the "Christianity" expressed in the teachings of the Church had very little relationship to what came down from Allah to Jesus, the Messiah (peace be upon him).

As a result of these compromises, the Church adopted many distorted concepts and a great deal of information concerning the universe that was incorrect and faulty, since error is a part of all human research, study, and experiment. When the astronomers and physicists started to correct the errors contained in these "facts," the origin of which was human rather than divine, the Church took a very harsh stand against them. Not content with mere verbal attacks, the Church fathers employed their temporal power to torture people for their heresies, whether religious or scientific.

From that time to the present, "European thought" has taken an inimical stand not merely against the doctrines of the Church prevalent at that time, but against all religious ideas and concepts in general. Indeed, its enmity extended beyond religious ideas and concepts to the very essence of religious thought. The European thinkers originated modes and schools of thought whose basic purpose was to oppose the essence of religious thought itself. In order to get rid of the authority of the Church, they eliminated the God of the Church, sweeping away all ideas and ways of thought related to Him. The enmity of European thought to religion and to the methodology of religion consists not simply in the philosophical system, schools of thought, and subjects of study that were established in opposition to religion, but rather lies at the very heart of European thought and its method of acquiring knowledge.

Accordingly, it is not possible to find a basis for Islamic thought in the modes and products of European thought, nor to reconstruct Islamic thought by borrowing from Western modes of thought or its products. As the reader will see toward the end of our discussion, such attempts have been made by some Muslim thinkers who desired to

---

[4] T. W. Arnold, *The Preaching of Islam,* p. 53.

reconstruct Islamic thought by borrowing the methodology of European thought.

Our methodology of researching the characteristics and con-stituents of the Islamic concept is to derive inspiration directly from the Qur'an, after having lived a lifetime under its shade, and to present, insofar as possible, the atmosphere and the religious, social, and political conditions of mankind at the time when Allah Most High revealed His Word for the guidance of humanity, as well as to point out the errors that have crept in as a result of deviating from this divine guidance.

Our method in seeking inspiration from the Qur'an is not to con-front it with pre-conceived criteria. We shall not apply to the text of the Qur'an either intellectual or rational criteria borrowed from the remnants of cultures that did not flow from the Qur'an itself, nor shall we interpret the verses of the Qur'an in such a way as to make them conform to such pre-established norms.

Indeed, the Qur'an came to establish the correct norms and criteria that Allah desires for the life of mankind. Consequently, the least human beings can do in response to this favor of their Creator, who shows us His mercy and indulgence, though He is independent of His creation, is to receive it with gratitude and with minds clear of all impure and alien elements, so that this new concept may be purified from the remnants of ignorance, old or new, and conform solely to the instructions of Allah and not to the errant speculations of man.

How can there be any room for pre-established criteria in referring to the Book of Allah, the Most High, for judgement? At the outset, we must adapt our criteria to accord with the Book of Allah and base our concepts and standards of reference upon it. This alone is the correct methodology for dealing with the Qur'an and for deriving from it the Islamic concept and its characteristics and constituents.

We must avoid the style of philosophy in presenting the Islamic concept, because there is a close relationship between subject and style of presentation. The style of philosophy can only change and distort the Islamic concept, because its nature and historical develop-ment are foreign and discordant, even inimical, to the nature of the Islamic concept. This fact is well-established. One who has grasped the Islamic concept will enjoy its truth and beauty only as expressed in the sublime text of the Qur'an.

We disagree with Iqbal[5] in his attempt to present Islam in the

------

[5] Muhammad Iqbal (1873-1938), poet and philosopher from the Punjab (Pakistan). The reference here is to Iqbal's book, *The Reconstruction of Religious Thought in Islam* (Trans).

philosophical framework that he borrowed from the well-known systems of Hegel's Idealistic Rationalism and August Comte's Materialistic Objectivism. Indeed, a creed in general, and the Islamic creed in particular, has its own style of addressing the total nature of man. It is characterized by liveliness, harmony, and a direct appeal to intuition. It inspires the human soul with great truths, truths which cannot be fully expressed in words, although the words can point to them. The Qur'anic style of presenting Islamic belief has the distinctive characteristic that it appeals to all the elements constituting human nature, leaves no aspect untouched and no avenue of knowledge ignored, and does not merely address man's intellect alone. Philosophy, on the other hand, has a different style. It tries to capture reality in words. But, there are some aspects of reality that cannot be formulated in words and phrases. Furthermore, there are other aspects of reality that cannot be comprehended by human "thought" because they are outside the realm of its operation. If the philosophical style were adopted to express the truths of religion, these truths would be rendered complicated, dry, and lifeless.

It may also be observed that philosophical systems have rarely, if ever, played a significant role in the daily lives of human beings. Religious beliefs have always motivated people to action, propelling them toward definite goals through the wilderness of time and the darkness of the way, whereas philosophical systems have not.

A creed must be presented in its own particular style. Expressing it in the style of philosophy kills it, extinguishes its light and inspiration, and restricts it to only one aspect among the many aspects of man's being. Distortions, complexities, deviations, and dryness are introduced in any exposition of a belief system when a style is adopted that is foreign to its nature and has too narrow a framework.

We should not hail the existence of "Islamic philosophy" with eagerness, nor should we feel any eagerness whatsoever to suppose that Islamic thought must possess such a branch or such a style for its exposition. Its absence is no loss to Islam or to "Islamic thought." On the contrary, its absence is a proof of Islam's strength, genuineness and great uniqueness.

Another important aspect of our method of presentation is its constructive approach. We will not focus on this or that particular deviation in Islamic thought or practice. Our effort to clarify the characteristics and constituents of the Islamic concept is not in response to a specific deviation or situation in order to correct it. Rather, we want to present the truths of Islam in their entirety in the way the Qur'an contains them — complete, all-inclusive, balanced, and harmonious. There is a danger inherent in focusing one's attention on a specific deviation or defect and in trying to refute or to correct it by employing the total force of the truths of the Islamic concept. This danger is that one may go to the other extreme and introduce a new deviation in the process of trying to remove the old one — and a deviation is after all a deviation, whether it be old or new.

We may find many examples of this danger in works produced for the "defense" of Islam by well-meaning Muslim thinkers who wanted to reply to the objections raised by the Orientalists and the atheists, both old and new. Similarly, we find examples of this in works written to correct a particular situation at a particular time and place.

As an example, some Christian missionaries and some Zionist authors have accused Islam of being a religion of the sword, asserting that it was spread by the sword, whereupon some defenders of Islam from among us immediately rose up to remove this "blemish" from Islam. In their zeal to "defend" Islam against these vicious attacks, they downgraded the place of jihad in Islam by narrowing its sphere of application and by apologetically stating that jihad is permitted only for "defensive" purposes, in the narrow current technical sense of the word. They also lost sight of the fact that Islam, in its role as the last divinely-revealed guidance for mankind, has a natural duty, and therefore the right, to establish its particular system as preeminent on earth in order that the whole of mankind may benefit from its just, balanced, and humane laws, and so that every individual living under this system may enjoy freedom of belief. "There is no compulsion in religion" is a part of this faith. The effort expended in establishing the Islamic system for the benefit of all people, both Muslims and non-Muslims alike, is termed jihad. Jihad is thus struggle for the initiation and establishment of this system which aims at securing freedom of conscience and belief for every person on earth. And this freedom can only be attained by establishing a just government and a just legal and social system, which calls to account anyone who tries to abolish freedom of speech and freedom of belief from the land.

This is merely one example of how the Islamic concept can become corrupted by the very zeal of its defenders against the shrewd attacks of Islam's enemies.

Deviations introduced into the Islamic concept by works written to correct a particular situation, may be illustrated in the writings of Imam Sheikh Muhammad 'Abduh and in the lectures of Muhammad Iqbal published as *The Reconstruction of Religious Thought in Islam*.

As Imam Sheikh Muhammad 'Abduh surveyed the Muslim world, he found that ideas were stagnant and the door of *ijtihad* closed, and that "reason" was denied its role in understanding the Shari'ah of Allah and in deducing judgements from it. He observed that Muslim people were satisfied with books written by latter-day scholars who were a product of the period of stagnation of thought and whose books, reflecting popular religious lore, incorporated many nonsensical concepts. Looking abroad, he noted that, with the advent of the Age of Reason in Europe, "reason" was being worshipped there as a god, especially after the marvelous discoveries and achievements of science and the ascendancy of rationalist philosophies which ascribed to "reason" unlimited powers. At the same time, Orientalists of various hues were busy attacking the Islamic concept, the belief in the Will and Power of Allah and the apportionment of good and evil (*qada wa qadar*), and were blaming Islam for the lethargy and intellectual inactivity of Muslims. Consequently Sheikh Muhammad 'Abduh decided to address himself to this particular situation.

He confirmed the value of "reason" in relation to the "revealed text" by reviving the principle of *ijtihad*, and fought against the nonsense that had become popular religion. He argued that Islam gives human reason great value and a significant role in religion as well as in the practical affairs of life, and that, contrary to the allegations of certain outsiders, Islam does not teach absolute "predestination" devoid of "freedom of choice." However, caught between the two extremes of the intellectual inertia in the Muslim world and the deification of reason in Europe, he propounded the theory that human reason and divine revelation are of equal importance for the guidance of man, and that it is impossible that knowledge acquired through rational thought should come in conflict with divinely-revealed truths. He did not stop at saying merely that reason can comprehend what is within its grasp but must admit to what is beyond its grasp. Indeed, neither reason nor any of the other faculties of man are absolute and all-powerful but are bounded by the limits of space and time, whereas divine revelation (*wahy*) may deal with absolute realities such as the reality of God and the relationship of the will of God to created events. Reason has no choice but to accept these absolute principles which are beyond its grasp[6]. Thus Sheikh Muhammad 'Abduh presented arguments that appeared logical, but which were, in fact, a product of his desire to correct that deviation of his time which denigrated and neglected the role of reason. He says (may Allah have mercy on his soul) in his treatise on the Oneness of Allah, "Divine revelation through messengers is an act of God, while human reason is also an act of God in this world, and acts of God are

---

[6] For further clarification of this point, see the chapter entitled "The Divine Origin of the Islamic Concept" in the present volume.

necessarily in harmony with each other, never at variance with each other.''

While this statement is true in a general sense, nevertheless divine revelation and human reason are not at the same level, the former being greater and more all-embracing than the latter. Divine revelation came down to be a source to which human reason must refer, and to be the criterion to which human reason must refer in judging norms, standards, and concepts, and in removing errors and shortcomings. While there is undoubtedly agreement and harmony between the two, it rests on the basis of the ultimate superiority of divine revelation and not on the basis of their being equal to each other in all respects. Moreover, "reason" as an abstract "ideal," free of the influences of cultural biases and personal opinions, does not exist in the actual world of human beings.

The Sheikh's commentary on Juz *'Amm* (the thirtieth part of the Qur'an) clearly shows the influence of this viewpoint. The commentary on the Qur'an by his pupil, Sheikh Rashid Rida, and the commentary on *"Tabarak"* (the twenty-ninth part of the Qur'an), by another pupil, Sheikh Al-Maghribi, are other examples of far-fetched interpretations of the Qur'anic text in an attempt to bring it into conformity with "reason." Therein lies the danger because the word "reason" does not refer to anything in existence. There is of course nothing which may be called "reason" in the abstract, free from the influence of personal desires, passions, biases, errors, and ignorance, to which the text of the Qur'an may be referred. If we were to interpret the verses of the Qur'an according to all these various examples of "reason," we would end up in chaos.

All this came about due to concentration on a single, specific deviation. But if the matter is considered on its own, we can easily understand the role of reason and its scope of action without either over- or under-estimating it, as well as the scope of Divine revelation and the correct relation between the two.

Indeed, "reason" is not abandoned, discarded, or neglected in Divine revelation. In fact, it is human reason which is the recipient of Divine revelation. Its task is to receive this revelation, to understand what it receives, to grasp what lies within its scope, and to accept what is beyond its scope. But it cannot be the final "judge." Where a clear text exists, its content, without any far-fetched interpretation, is indisputable. The task of reason is to accept the standards and criteria established by this clear text and apply them in practical life. In our subsequent discussions we will provide ample details on this topic, delineating the correct Islamic position.

Muhammad Iqbal surveyed the climate of thought in the East and found it "hazy." People were absorbed in what he called "*ajami*" (alien) mysticism, seeking "illuminations." It distressed him to see the pursuit of "annihilation" of self, in which there was no place for man's personality. The "passivity" of so-called mystic ways, which negate human endeavor and participation in worldly activity, shocked him because it is, indeed, contrary to the nature of Islam. On the other hand, he saw that, in the West, the objectivists and the pragmatists rely totally on sensory experiences. He also came across the proclamation of the birth of Superman and the death of God in Nietzsche's *Thus Spake Zarathustra*, a collection of Nietzsche's insane ejaculations which some call "philosophy."

He decided to cleanse Islamic thought and Islamic practice from negativism and passivity, and to affirm on their behalf "experimentation," the method on which the pragmatists and the objectivists relied.

But he went too far in glorifying the human "self," which, in turn, forced him to interpret certain verses of the Qur'an in a manner contrary to its temperament, as well as to the temperament of Islam. He stated that death, and even the Day of Resurrection, do not end experimentation. Experimentation and progress, according to Iqbal, will continue even in the Garden and the Fire. But the Islamic concept states decisively that this world is for trial and action, while the Hereafter is for reward and punishment. Man has no scope for action except in this world, nor is there room for new action after the final accounting and recompense. This exaggeration of his was brought about by a strong desire to affirm "life" and its perpetuity, or the perpetuity of the "self," as Iqbal borrowed the term from Hegel's philosophy.

On the other hand, he was also forced to expand the meaning of "experimentation" from its technical meaning in Western thought and its history. He included in its meaning the concept of "spiritual experience," which the Muslim realizes in his contact with the Great Reality, though in Western philosophy the term "experiment" is never applied to the spiritual, since, in its origin, the term "experimentation" was coined to exclude any source of knowledge not based on sensory experience.

Furthermore, Iqbal's borrowing of Western terminology led him to this prosaic work, which is difficult, terse as well as dry, while his poetry is alive, dynamic, and vibrant.

Our aim here is not to find fault with the great and fruitful efforts for the revival and awakening of Islamic thought made by Imam Muhammad 'Abduh and his pupils and by the poet Iqbal (may Allah have mercy on their souls), but is only meant to provide a warning that an over-enthusiastic attempt at confronting a particular deviation initiates another deviation. It is therefore best, in the course of presenting the Islamic concept, to express its truths in a complete, all-encompassing, and harmonious fashion, taking into consideration its particular nature and particular style.

Finally, this book is not a work on "philosophy," "theology," or "metaphysics." It is dictated by practical considerations and deals with practical matters.

Islam came to deliver mankind from the rubbish heaps of philosophies and religions under whose ideas, systems, and burdens it was groaning and from the wilderness of speculation in which its beliefs and ways of life had gone astray. It came to initiate for mankind a unique and distinct concept and to introduce a new life, running smoothly according to Allah's prescribed way. Unfortunately, however, mankind has again reverted to the rubbish heaps and the wilderness.

The revelation of Islam came to initiate a new ummah and then handed over to it the leadership of mankind, thus bringing man out of the wilderness and the rubbish. But this very ummah has now abandoned its position of leadership and its method of leading, and is panting after the nations that are lost in the wilderness and wallowing in refuse.

This book is an attempt to define the Islamic concept, and its characteristics and constituents, from which are derived the way of life prescribed by Allah and the principles of thought, science, and the arts, that follow from a comprehensive exposition of this original concept. Any research in any aspect of Islamic thought or of the Islamic system must be founded primarily on the Islamic way of thinking. This way of thinking is needed by the hearts and minds of man and by life and by the world. It is needed by the Muslim ummah and by the whole of mankind!

This is the first part of a two part book. It deals with "The Characteristics of the Islamic Concept." Later, Allah willing, we will present the second part, "The Constituents of the Islamic Concept."

And Allah is our Guide and Helper.

CHAPTER I

The Wilderness and the Intellectual Rubbish

Then is he who goes along with his face close to the ground [like a worm] better-guided than he who walks upright upon a straight path? (*Al-Mulk* 67:22).

At the advent of Islam there were in the world huge quantities of beliefs, concepts, philosophies, myths, superstitions, traditions, and customs in which falsehood was mixed with truth, wrong with right, nonsense with religion, and mythology with philosophy. Under the burden of this rubbish, the conscience of man was groping in obscurities and speculations without finding any certainty. The life of mankind, under the influence of this welter of confusion, was ground down by corruption and chaos, tyranny and oppression, and hardship and misery It was a life unfit for human beings, unfit even for a herd of cattle!

Life was a trackless wilderness without a guide, devoid of guidance and light, and devoid of rest and certainty. Man was groping helplessly and hopelessly to understand his God and God's attributes, man's relationship with the universe, the ultimate purpose of his existence, the way to attain this purpose, and in particular, the connection between God and man. As a consequence of being lost in this wilderness and drowned in intellectual rubbish, man's life and systems were full of evils and injustices.

It is not possible for the conscience of man to settle issues concerning the universe, his own self, the purpose of his life, his role in the universe, and the relationship between the individual and society, without first settling the issues of his belief, and his concept of his deity, and doing so in a manner that produces certainty in his heart by

17

painstakingly threading his way through that stark wilderness and by sifting through those heaps of refuse.

This matter of religious belief is not merely a medieval mode of thought, as some Western thinkers, parroted by their Eastern imitators, have made it appear to be. Never! The matter of belief is based on two fundamental realities of the human situation, both independent of time and place.

First, man, by his very nature, cannot live in this world as a detached, free-floating particle of dust. He must relate to the world in a definite manner by formulating an idea concerning his place in the scheme of things. In the final analysis, it is his belief-concept, that is to say his world-view, which in his own eyes determines his place in his surroundings. This is an intellectual necessity, natural to all human beings, and is independent of the particulars of time and place. In the course of our discussion, we will elaborate how the arrogance of people in their confusion misleads them to misunderstand this basic relationship and its importance in human affairs.

Second, a strong tie exists between the nature of the belief-concept and the nature of the social system. This bond cannot be broken, is not related to the particular circumstances of a given time or place, and is stronger than any other bond. A social system is a product of a comprehensive concept that includes an explanation of the origin of the universe, of man's place in it, and of his role and the ultimate purpose of this existence. Any social system not founded on a concept will be artificial and will not last long, and while it lasts it will bring untold suffering and misery upon the people, since there will of necessity be a conflict between this system and human nature, because a harmony between belief and the social system is both an organizational necessity and an intellectual imperative.

From Nuh (Noah) to 'Isa (Jesus), the Messengers of Allah expounded this truth to people, imparted to them correct knowledge of their Creator, and elucidated for them the position of man and the purpose of his existence. But in every case, deviations from their teachings, due to political circumstances and lusts and passions and other human weaknesses, obscured the truth, burying it under the garbage heaps of false concepts and ideas, and led mankind astray from the straight path. It would not have been possible to remove the rubbish from the minds of people except through a new messenger, a messenger who would cut through the rubbish, dispel the darkness, and blaze a path through this wilderness, by proclaiming the truths of the Islamic concept in its purest form and by building a society on the firm foundation of this sound belief. Those people who were entrenched in their deviant beliefs and corrupt practices would not have abandoned them, nor would they have separated themselves from the conditions prevailing among them, except through this Message and through the Messenger. Allah Most High proclaimed the truth in saying:

> Never would the unbelievers from among the People of the book and the polytheists have abandoned their ways until there came to them the clear evidence: a Messenger from Allah reciting from purified pages (*Al-Bayyinah* 98:1-2).

Man could not have grasped the need for this Message, the need for abandoning the falsehoods and the errors in which humanity was lost, and the need for arriving at a clear decision in the matter of belief until he was informed about the enormity of those mountains of rubbish. Never could he have grasped this Message until he had rejected that tangled welter of beliefs and concepts, myths and philosophies, ideas and superstitions, customs and traditions, and morals and manners which, at the time of the advent of Islam, had blackened the conscience of man in every place. Never could he have seen the truth until he had grasped the nature of the babble, the confusion, and the complexities that had entered into the remnants of the earlier Divine revelations. It was necessary to expose the deviations, distortions, and interpolations that were mixed in with what had been previously revealed by Allah, as well as to expose the influences of the philosophies and myths, and the paganism contained in them.

Our aim in writing this book, however, is not to present these concepts, but to present the Islamic concept and its characteristics. We shall confine ourselves therefore to giving a few examples from the religious concepts of Judaism and Christianity in the form in which they had reached the Arabian Peninsula, as well as a few examples from the days of pre-Islamic ignorance, with which Islam had to contend.

Judaism, the religion of the Children of Israel, was full of pagan concepts and was also greatly affected by their ethnic chauvinism. Many Messengers of Allah had come to the Children of Israel, among them their ancestor Israel, that is Y'aqub (Jacob), who was the son of Ishaq (Isaac), the son of Ibrahim (Abraham), may Allah's peace be on them all. Israel was one of the earliest bringing the Message of the Oneness of God in the pure form taught to them by their ancestor Ibrahim. Then came the greatest of their Prophets, Musa (Moses), may Allah's peace be on him, who, together with the Message of the Oneness of God, brought the Mosaic Law based upon this belief. But, with the passage of time, the Israelites deviated, and descended to the

level of idolators in their concepts. In their religious books, even in
the very heart of the Old Testament, they included tales and notions
concerning Allah Most High that are no higher than the lowest concepts of the Greek and other idolatrous people who had never
received any divinely-revealed book or message.

On the authority of the Qur'an, we know that their ancestor,
Ibrahim (may Allah's peace be on him), expounded to his children the
belief in the Oneness of Allah in a pure, luminous, complete, and
comprehensive form in contrast to the prevalent paganism of the
times. Similarly, his grandson, Y'aqub, prior to his death, imparted to
his children the same beliefs. Allah says:

> And narrate to them the story of Ibrahim, when he said to
> his father and his people, "What are you worshipping?"
> They said, "We worship idols, and are always devoted to
> them." He said "Do they hear you when you call or do they
> benefit or harm you?" They said, "No, but we found our
> forefathers doing this." He said, "Do you see what you
> have been worshipping, you and your forefathers? For
> truly, they (all deities) are my enemy, except the Lord of the
> Worlds, Who created me and Who then guided me, Who
> gives me to eat and to drink, and whenever I am ill it is He
> who heals me, the One Who causes me to die and thereafter
> restores me to life, and Who, I ardently hope, will forgive
> me my sins on the Day of Judgement. My Lord, bestow
> wisdom upon me, and unite me with the righteous, and
> grant me a tongue that testifies to the truth among the
> people of later times, and place me among the inheritors of
> the Garden of Bliss, and forgive my father, for he is among
> those who have gone astray, and do not abase me on the
> day when all shall be raised up, the day when neither wealth
> nor sons will be of avail but only that one should bring to
> Allah a pure heart" (*Al-Shu'ara* 26:70-89).

> And who would abandon the religion of Ibrahim, except
> one who fools himself? We assuredly chose him in this
> world, and truly in the Hereafter he shall be among the
> righteous. When his Lord said to him "Submit," he said, "I
> have submitted myself to the Lord of the Worlds." And this
> Ibrahim gave as a legacy to his sons, so likewise did Y'aqub:
> "My sons, truly Allah has chosen for you the *din* (the eternal
> and universal religion). Then do not die without having
> submitted yourselves to Him." Were you witnesses when

death approached Y'aqub? and he said to his sons, "What will you worship after me?" They said, "We will worship your God and the God of your fathers, Ibrahim, and Isma'il, and Ishaq, the One God and to Him do we submit! (*Al-Baqarah* 2:130-133).

But their descendants retrogressed from this pure concept of Oneness, this sublime faith, and this belief in the Hereafter. They remained in this state of retrogression until Prophet Musa came to revive the pure faith. The Qur'an speaks of this creed brought by Musa to the Children of Israel and it also speaks of their deviating from it:

And recall when We made a covenant with the Children of Israel: "Worship no one except Allah and be good to parents and to relations and to orphans and to the needy, and speak kindly to people and establish worship and pay the poor-due." After that all of you except a few turned back and you are backsliders. And recall when We made a covenant with you: "Do not shed the blood of your people nor turn your people out of your dwellings." Then you affirmed this and you were witnesses thereto. Yet you are the ones who kill one another and drive out a party of your people from their home, assisting one another against them by sin and oppression (*Al-Baqarah* 2:83-85).

And assuredly Musa came to you with clear evidence, but even after that you took the Golden Calf (for worship) and you became transgressors. And when We made a covenant with you and caused Mount Sinai to tower above you saying, "Hold fast to what We have given you and hearken unto it," they said, "We hear but we disobey," for their hearts were filled to overflowing with love of the [golden] calf because of their refusal to acknowledge the truth. Say, "Vile is what this false belief enjoins upon you, if indeed you are believers" (*Al-Baqarah* 2:92-93).

Thus their deviation began while Musa was yet among them, with their worship of the Calf which the Samiri had fashioned for them out of golden jewelry from the Egyptian women they had brought with them. This is the Calf referred to in the verses quoted above. Yet earlier during their exodus from Egypt, upon encountering people who worshipped idols, they had already demanded of Musa that he make an idol for them to worship.

And We brought the Children of Israel across the sea. And
they came upon a people who were devoted to their idols.
They said, "O Musa! Fashion for us a god, even as they have
gods." He said, "Truly, you are ignorant people. As for these
people their way of life will be destroyed, and all they are
doing is in vain" (*Al-A'raf* 9:138-139).

The Qur'an talks a great deal about their deviations, their blas-
phemies in relation to Allah, their associating partners with Him, and
their idolatry.

The Jews say, "Ezra is the son of God" (*Al- Tawbah* 9:30).

The Jews say, "Allah's hand is fettered." But in fact it is their
hand that is fettered, and they are accursed for what they
have said. Nay, rather His hands are spread out wide in
giving bounty (*Al-Ma'idah* 5:67).

Assuredly, Allah has heard the speech of those who said,
"Truly Allah must be poor, while we are rich." We shall
record what they say and their killing of the prophets
against all right, and We shall say, "Taste the punishment of
fire" (*Ale'Imran* 3:181).

And when you (the Children of Israel) said, "O Musa! We
will not believe in you until we see Allah plainly," then the
lightning seized you even as you looked on (*Al-Baqarah*
2:55).

Their ethnic mania was such that they believed that God was their
tribal deity! This god of theirs does not call them to account concerning their moral behavior except when they deal with each other. As
far as strangers, that is, non-Jews, are concerned, he does not hold
them accountable for their shameful behavior toward them.

And among the People of the Book is the person who, if
you entrust him with a hoard of gold, will repay it, and
among them is the one who, if you entrust him with a piece
of gold, will not return it to you unless you keep standing
over him. That is because they say, "we have no obligation
on us to these ignorant people," but they knowingly tell a
lie concerning Allah (*Ale'Imran* 3:75).

In their distorted scriptures matters are attributed to their God which are not much above what the Greeks in their paganism ascribed to their gods.

In Chapter 3 of the Book of Genesis, after Adam had committed the sin of eating the forbidden tree, which according to the author of "Genesis" was the tree of good and evil, we read:[1]

> The man and his wife heard the sound of the Lord God walking in the Garden at the time of the evening breeze and they hid from the Lord God among the trees of the Garden. But the Lord called and said to him, "Where are you?" He replied, "I heard the sound as you were walking in the Garden and I was afraid, because I was naked and I hid myself." God answered, "Who told you that you were naked? Have you eaten from the tree of which I forbade you?" ("Genesis" 3:8-11).

> He said, "The man has become like one of us, knowing good and evil; what if he now reaches out his hand and takes fruit from the tree of life also, eats it, and lives forever?" So the Lord God drove him out of the garden of Eden to till the ground from which he had been taken. He cast him out, and to the east of the Garden of Eden he stationed the cherubim and a sword whirling and flashing to guard the way to the tree of life" ("Genesis" 3:22-24).

Again, in the "Book of Genesis," the reason for the Flood is described as follows:

> When mankind began to increase and to spread all over the earth and daughters were born to them, the sons of the gods saw that the daughters of men were beautiful, so they took for themselves such women as they chose. But the Lord said, "My lifegiving spirit shall not remain in man forever; he for his part is mortal flesh; he shall live for a hundred and twenty years." In those days, when the sons of gods had intercourse with the daughters of men and got childen by them, the Nephilium (or giants) were on earth. They were the heroes of old, men of renown. When the Lord saw that man had done much evil on earth and that his thoughts

---

[1]Quotations from the Bible are from *The New English Bible*, corrected impression (1972), Cambridge University Press, New York.

and inclinations were always evil, he was sorry that he had made man on earth and he was grieved at heart. He said, "This race of men whom I have created I will wipe off the face of the earth — man and beast, reptiles, and birds. I am sorry that I ever made them." But Noah had won the Lord's favor ("Genesis" 6:1-8).

In chapter 11 of "Genesis," after a description of how the world was populated by the descendants of Noah, we read:

Once upon a time all the world spoke a single language and used the same words. As men journeyed in the east, they came upon a plain in the land of Shinar and settled there. They said to one another, "Come, let us make bricks and bake them hard." They used bricks for stone and bitumen for mortar. "Come," they said, "let us build ourselves a city and a tower with its top in the heavens, and make a name for ourselves; or we shall be dispersed all over the earth." Then the Lord came down to see the city and tower, which mortal men had built, and he said, "Here they are, one people with a single language, and now they have started to do this. Henceforward nothing they have a mind to do will be beyond their reach. Come, let us go down there and confuse their speech, so that they will not understand what they say to one another." So the Lord dispersed them from there all over the earth, and they left off building the city ("Genesis" 11:1-8).

In the second Book of Samuel, chapter 24, it is stated:

Then the angel stretched out his arm toward Jerusalem to destroy it; but the Lord repented of the evil and said to the angel who was destroying the people, "Enough! Stay your hand" (2 Samuel 24:16).

Christianity was no better than Judaism, and, in fact, was even worse and more bitter. Christianity appeared when the Roman Empire was steeped in paganism and corruption. It spread quietly until Constantine ascended the throne in 305 A.C.[2] The Roman Empire subsequently adopted Christianity not in order to conform to it but to make Christianity conform to the dominant paganism. In this

---

[2]After Christ

connection, the American author, Draper, in his book, *History of the Conflict Between Religion and Science,* says:

> Place, power, profit—these were in view of whoever now joined the conquering sect. Crowds of worldly persons, who cared nothing about its religious ideas became its warmest supporters. Pagans at heart, their influence was soon manifested in the paganization of Christianity that soon ensued. The Emperor, no better than they, did nothing to check their proceedings. But he did not personally conform to the ceremonial requirements of the Church until the close of his evil life in A.D. 337.[3]

> Though the Christian party had proved itself sufficiently strong to give a master to the Empire, it was never sufficiently strong to destroy its antagonist, paganism. The issue of struggle between them was an amalgamation of the principles of both. In this, Christianity differed from Mohammedanism which absolutely annihilated its antagonist and spread its own doctrines without adulteration.[4]

> To the Emperor, a mere worldling and a man without any religious convictions, doubtless it appeared best for himself, best for the Empire, and best for the contending parties, Christian and pagan, to promote their union or amalgamation as much as possible. Even sincere Christians do not seem to have been averse to this; perhaps they believed that the new doctrines would diffuse most thoroughly by incorporating in themselves ideas borrowed from the old, the Truth would assert herself in the end, and the impurity be cast off.[5]

But the impurity was not cast off, as the sincere Christians had hoped, and the new religion continued to be enwrapped in pagan concepts and myths, political, ethnic, and sectarian controversies, and mythological and philosophical speculations. Under all these contending influences its concept splintered into uncountable pieces. ''Christ is a mere man,'' one sect stated. ''The Father, the Son, and the

---

[3] William Draper, *History of the Conflict Between Religion and Science*, pp. 34-35.
[4] Ibid, p. 40.
[5] Ibid. pp. 40-41.

Holy Ghost are three persons in which God appears to mankind,''
another proclaimed. According to this sect, God, in the form of the
Holy Ghost, descended into Mary and was born from her as Christ.
Yet a third sect said, ''The Son is not co-eternal with the Father, but
was created before the creation of the universe, he is less than the
Father and is subservient to Him.'' Another sect denied that the Holy
Ghost was a part of the Trinity. In the Council of Nicaea, held in 325
A.C., it was decided by a majority vote that the Son and the Holy Ghost
are equal with the Father in Divinity. As to the Son, he had been born
since pre-eternity, while the Holy Ghost proceeds from the Son as
well. The Eastern and the Western Churches differed on this point and
continued on their separate ways. In the Latin Church, there were
some sects that deified Mary as the ''The Mother of God,'' as a
consequence of deifying Jesus, and so on, ad infinitum.

Dr. Alfred Butler in his book, *The Arab Conquest of Egypt*, says:

> This is not the place for a discussion upon either the facts
> for the sources of Egyptian history during the last two
> centuries of the Empire: but when that record comes to be
> fully written, it will prove a record of perpetual feud
> between Romans and Egyptians — a feud of race and a feud
> of religion — in which, however, the dominating motive
> was rather religious than racial. The key to the whole of
> this epoch is the antagonism between the Monophysites
> and the Melkites. The latter, as the name implies, were the
> imperial or the Court part in religion, holding the orthodox
> opinion about the two natures of Christ: but this opinion
> the Monophysite Copts, or native Egyptians, viewed with
> an abhorrence and combated with a frenzy difficult to
> understand in rational beings, not to say followers of the
> Gospel.'[6]

The conception of the trinity in the new faith must have seemed to
the Egyptians a mere duplication of their own triads...the most famous
of which was, of course, the triad of Osiris, Isis, and Horus.

T. W. Arnold in his book, *The Preaching of Islam*, says the following:

> A hundred years before, Justinian had succeeded in giving
> some show of unity to the Roman Empire, but after his
> death it rapidly fell asunder, and at this time there was an

---

[6]Alfred T. Butler, *The Arab Conquest of Egypt*, Oxford University (1978), p. 29.

entire want of common national feeling between the provinces and the seat of government. Heraclius had made some partially successful efforts to attach Syria again to the central government, but unfortunately the general methods of reconciliation which he adopted had served only to increase dissension instead of allaying it. Religious passions were the only existing substitute for national feeling, and he tried, by propounding an exposition of faith, that was intended to serve as an eirenicon[7], to stop all further disputes between the contending factions and unite the heretics to the Orthodox Church and to the Central government. The Council of Chalcedon (451) had maintained that Christ was "to be acknowledged in two natures, without confusion, change, division, or separation; the difference of the natures being in nowise taken away by reason of their union, but rather the properties of each nature being preserved and concurring into one person and one substance, not as it was divided or separated into two persons, but one and the same Son and only begotten, God the Word." This council was rejected by the Monophysites, who allowed only one nature in the person of Christ, who was said to be a composite person, having all attributes divine and human, but the substance bearing these attributes was no longer a duality, but a composite unity. The controversy between the orthodox party and the Monophysites, who flourished particularly in Egypt and Syria and in countries outside the Byzantine Empire, had been hotly contested for nearly two centuries, when Heraclius sought to effect a reconciliation by means of the doctrine of Monotheletism: while conceding the duality of the natures, it secured unity of the person in the actual life of Christ, by rejection of two series of activities in this one person; the one Christ and Son of God effectuates that which is human and that which is divine by one divine human agency, i.e. there is only one will in the Incarnate Word.[8]

But Heraclius shared the fate of so many would-be-peace-

[7] Eirenicon is a statement that attempts to reconcile conflicting doctrines.
[8] I. A. Dorner: *A System of Christian Doctrine*, vol. iii, pp. 215-216. (London, 1885). J. C. Robertson: *History of the Christian Church*, vol. ii, p. 226. (London 1875).

makers: for not only did controversy blaze up again all the
more fiercely, but he himself was stigmatized as a heretic
and drew upon himself the wrath of both parties."[9]

The Qur'an mentions some of these deviations, calling upon the
People of the Book to desist from them and to rectify their beliefs. It
also describes the original teachings of Jesus as revealed to him by
Allah before distortion and deviation entered into them.

They have assuredly rejected the truth who say, Truly, Allah
is the third of three, when there is no deity except Him, the
One God. And if they refrain not from what they say, a
painful punishment shall afflict those of them that reject
the truth. Will they not then turn to Allah and seek forgiveness of Him? For Allah is Forgiving, Merciful. The Messiah,
son of Mary, was nothing other than a messenger. Before
him other messengers had passed away, and his mother was
a saintly woman. Both of them ate food like mortals. See
how We make clear for them the signs, and then see how
they are turned away! Say, "Do you worship instead of
Allah what can neither harm nor benefit? Allah is the
All-Hearing, the All-Knowing. Say "People of the Book, do
not go beyond the bounds of truth in your religion, and do
not follow the errors of a people who went astray in earlier
times and who led many others astray and who have
deviated from the straight path" (Al-Ma'idah 5:723-77).

And the Jews say, "Ezra is the son of God," and the
Christians say, "The Messiah is the Son of God." That is the
utterance of their mouths in imitation of the unbelievers
who disbelieved before them. May Allah assail them! How
perverse are they! (Al-Tawbah 9:30).

And when Allah said, "O Jesus, son of Mary, did you say
unto men, 'Take me and my mother as gods, besides
Allah?,'" he said, "Glory to You! It is not mine to say what
I have no right to say. If I indeed said it, You know it,
knowing what is within my mind, and I know not what is
within Your mind. You, only You, are the Knower of the
things unseen. I said to them only what You commanded

---

[9] T.W. Arnold, *The Preaching of Islam*, Constable and Company, London
(1913), pp. 52-54.

me: 'Worship Allah, my Lord and your Lord.' And I was a witness over them while I dwelt among them; but when you took me, You were Yourself the watcher over them. You are witness of everything. If You chasten them, they are Your servants. And if You forgive them, You are the Mighty, the Wise'' (*Al-Ma'idah* 5:116-118).

Thus we see that the deviations which entered the teachings of Jesus increased due to historical circumstances with the passage of time until Christianity incorporated many pagan mythological concepts, and for centuries the Christian peoples went through cycles of theological controversies and subsequent massacres.

We turn now to the situation in the Arabian Peninsula, the place chosen by Allah for the revelation of the Qur'an. In addition to these distorted forms of the teachings of Moses and Jesus, known as Judaism and Christianity, there were other concepts carried there from the intellectual trash of Persia, and there was also their own brand of paganism. They were completely oblivious of the true religion of Ibrahim, because they had grossly distorted it. The Prophet Ibrahim taught the Oneness of Allah and surrender to Him, but they were steeped in gross idol worship. The Qur'an explicitly mentions these deviations in order to refute them.

Although hating to have daughters themselves, they held that angels are daughters of God. They worshipped angels or the idols representing them, believing that they had influence with Allah and their intercession would not be rejected by Him.

Yet they have assigned to His servants a share with Him. Indeed, man is clearly ungrateful. Or has He taken to Himself, from among His creation, daughters, and favored you with sons? And when one of them is given the news of the birth of what he has likened to the Merciful One, his face is darkened, and he chokes inwardly. Is the one who is brought up amid trinkets and is unable to reach clarity in a discussion to be likened to Allah? And they make into females the angels, who are the obedient servants of the Most Merciful. Did they witness their creation? Their testimony will be recorded and they shall be questioned. They say, ''Had the Most Merciful so willed, we would not have worshipped them.'' Of that they have no knowledge. They do nothing but speculate (*Al- Zukhruf* 43: 15-20).

Surely, the pure religion is for Allah alone. Those who

choose protectors besides Him (say), "We worship them only so that they may bring us near to Allah." Assuredly, Allah will judge between them concerning their differences. Truly, Allah does not guide the person who is a liar, an ingrate. Had Allah desired to take to Himself a son, He would have chosen whatever He willed of what He has created. Be He glorified! He is Allah, the One, the Absolute (*Al-Zumar* 39:3-6).

They worship, apart from Allah what neither harms nor benefits them, and they say, "These are our intercessors with Allah." Say, "Are you informing Allah of what He does not know in the heavens or in the earth?" Glory be to Him! High be He exalted above all that they associate with him" (*Yunus* 10:10).

They also believed that the Jinn were relations of Allah, that He had taken a wife from them and the angels are His children from this wife. Thus they worshipped the Jinn too. Al- Kalabi in *Kitab Al-Asnam* (The Book on Idols) says, "Banu Malik, a branch of Khuza'ah worshipped the Jinn" (p 34).
Concerning this myth, the Qur'an says:

Now ask them "Has your Lord daughters while they have sons?" Or did we create the angels female while they were present? Is it not assuredly from their inventions that they say, "Allah has begotten?" Truly they are liars. He has chosen daughters rather than sons? What ails you? How do you judge? Will you not then reflect? Or have you a clear proof? Then produce your divinely- revealed Book, if you are truthful. And they imagine kinship between Him and the Jinn, whereas the Jinn know very well that they will be brought before (Him). Glorified be Allah from what they attribute (unto Him)! (*Al-Saffat* 37:149-159).

On the day when He will gather them all together, He will say to the angels, "Did these worship you?" They will reply, "Glory be to You! You are our protector from them. Nay, but they worshipped the Jinn. Most of them were believers in them" (*Saba* 34:40-41).

Idol worship proliferated among them, some of the idols representing angels, others their ancestors, and yet others imaginary deities.

The Ka'bah, which had been built solely for the worship of Allah, was filled with idols, their number reaching three hundred and sixty. In addition, there were major idols of other kinds. Among them were Al-Lat, Al-'Uzza, and Manat, which are mentioned in the Qur'an, and Hubal, on whose behalf Abu Sufyan, on the day of Uhud, shouted "May Hubal be exalted!"

> Have you considered Al-Lat and Al-'Uzza, and Manat, the third, the other? Are yours the males and His the females? That was truly an unfair division. They are but names which you have named, you and your forefathers, for which Allah has revealed no authority. They follow but conjecture and what they themselves desire. And now the guidance from their Lord has come to them — or shall man have whatever he covets? But to Allah belongs the latter and the former. And however many angels there may be in the heavens, their intercession is of no avail except after Allah gives permission to whomever He desires and is pleased with. Surely it is those who do not believe in the hereafter who call the angels by feminine names, and they have no knowledge of it, merely following conjecture, and conjecture can never take the place of truth (*Al-Najm* 53:19-28).

Idol worship degenerated to the extent that they worshipped any stone. Al-Bukhari has reported that Abu Rija Al-'Utaradi said, "We worshipped stones. When we found a better stone than the one we had, we picked it up and threw away the old one. If we could not find a stone, we gathered a handful of dirt, milked a goat over it, and then worshipped it."[10]

Al-Kalabi says, "When a traveler halted at a place, he collected four stones. He worshipped the most beautiful of them and used the other three to place his cooking pot on. When he left the place he left the stones behind."[11]

They also worshipped planets and stars as the Persians also did. Sa'ed says, "The tribe of Hamir worshipped the sun, Kananah the moon, and Tamim Aldebran, Lakhm, and Judham worshipped Jupiter, Tayy the Dog-star, Qays, Sirius, and Asad, Mercury."[12]

Allah says concerning this:

---

[10] Sahih Al-Bukhari, "Kitab Al-Maghazi."
[11] *Kitab Al-Asnam*, p. 34.
[12] *Tabaqat Al-Umam* by Sa'd, p. 430.

Do not prostrate to the sun or to the moon, but prostrate
to Allah who created them, if you worship him (*Fussilat*
41:37).

He it is who is Lord of Sirius (*Al-Najm* 53:49).

Many other verses in the Qur'an likewise point to the creation of
the planets and stars, emphasizing Allah's sovereignty over them as
over the rest of His other creation in order to deny the divinity of stars
and to prohibit their worship.

In general, polytheistic beliefs permeated their lives. Many of their
nonsensical customs pointed out in the Qur'an were based on such
beliefs, such as consecrating some produce and some newborn
animals to their gods, with no share for Allah, making the eating of
some animals taboo for themselves or for women but not for men, or
making it taboo to ride on or slaughter certain animals. Sometimes
they even sacrificed their sons to propitiate their deities. For example,
it is reported that 'Abdullah, the Prophet's father, was saved from
death by the sacrifice of one hundred camels in his place. Soothsayers
played a prominent role in deciding such matters. In this regard the
Qur'an says,

And they assign Allah, of the crops and cattle that He
multiplied, a portion saying, "This is for Allah" — so
they assert — "and this is for Our 'partners!'" But the
share of their partners reaches not Allah, whereas the
share of Allah reaches their partners. Evil, indeed, is their
judgement! And, likewise their belief in beings or powers
that are supposed to have a share in Allah's divinity
makes [even] the slaying of their children seem good to
many of those who ascribe divinity to others than Allah,
thus bringing them to ruin and confusing them in their
faith. Yet, unless Allah had so willed, they would not
have done so; so leave them to their devices. They say,
"Such cattle and crops are sacrosanct; none shall eat
them except those whom we wish" [to do so] — so they
assert, and [they declare that] it is forbidden to put
burdens on the backs of certain kinds of cattle; and there
are cattle over which they do not pronounce Allah's
name — falsely attributing [the origin of these customs]
to Him. But He will requite them for these forgeries. And
they say, "What is within the bellies of these cattle is
reserved for our males and is forbidden to our wives; but

if it be born dead, then they will all share in it.'' He will surely recompense them for their attributing (these ordinances to Allah), surely He is All-Wise, All-Knowing. Lost are those who slay their children in folly, without knowledge, and have forbidden what Allah has provided them. Inventing a lie against Allah, they have gone astray and are not guided (*Al-An'am* 6:136-140).

The idea of the absolute Oneness of Allah was quite foreign to them, as were also the ideas of revelation and resurrection. Although they believed in Allah, the Creator of the heavens and the earth and whatever is between them, they did not want to acknowledge the consequences of this belief. They did not want to admit that the decision concerning their ways of living and moral behavior belongs to Allah alone, that what is prohibited and what is permissible must be taken from Him alone, that all their affairs pertaining both to this world and the hereafter return to Him alone, and that they should judge among themselves according to His Shari'ah and His prescribed Law. Without these, there can be neither faith nor religion.

The Qur'an mentions their strong objections to these truths, thus:

They marvel that a warner has come to them from among them, and the unbelievers say, ''This is (only) a lying sorcerer. What, has he made the gods One God? That is an astounding thing.'' The chiefs among them go away saying, ''Go! Be steadfast to your gods. Surely this is a thing to be desired. We heard nothing of this in the latter-day religion. Truly, this is nothing but an invention'' (*Sad* 38:3-7).

The unbelievers say, ''Shall we show you a man who will tell you that, when you have been utterly dispersed in the dust, still even then you will be created anew? He has forged a lie against Allah, or is there in him a madness?'' Not so; but those who do not believe in the hereafter are in torment and deeply in error (*Saba* 34:7-8).

Such was the repulsive collection of concepts in the Arabian Peninsula. We may pile this refuse on top of the distorted beliefs remaining from the Divinely-revealed religions to form some idea of the enormity of the conceptual rubbish heaps that were present in the East and the West at the time of the advent of Islam. Everywhere on earth the conscience of man was weighed down under these heavy loads, and on such concepts were based the systems, manners, customs, and morals of peoples.[13]

This is why the main effort of Islam was directed toward the correct formulation of belief concerning the reality of the Creator, the reality of His creation, and the mutual relationships between these two realities. Only when men have a clear concept and certainty of this belief, do their consciences have a solid foundation; and only then will their systems, morals, manners, and laws, and their social, economic, and political relationships also have a solid foundation. It is not possible to establish all these things except through a clear conception of the reality of Allah and His attributes.

Islam's particular concern was to clarify the nature of the Divine attributes and characteristics that are related to creating, willing, governing, and administering, and then the reality of the connection between Allah and man. Undoubtedly, the biggest rubbish heap in this wilderness of thought, in the midst of which religions and philosophies were stumbling blindly, was related to this matter of the Divine attributes and of the relationship between man and Allah. Yet precisely the nature of Allah and of His relationship to each individual person has a decisive impact on man's conscience and on man's system of life in all of its aspects.

The pristine religion of Islam was restored through the final Revelation — and this requires proper emphasis and due thought — to remove all kinds of confused ideas that had arisen in the many distorted religions and speculative philosophies of the time, and to eliminate all these deviations and errors for all time, whether they originated before the advent of Islam or afterwards. This astounding aspect of Islam is one of the proofs of its source, because this source comprehends all that has passed through human minds and anticipates all that is yet to pass through them, and then corrects and criticizes all errors and deviations to be found either in the past or in the future.

Many people are amazed at the great emphasis in the Qur'an and the great effort expended by it on the exposition of the Person of Allah Most High and His relationship with His creation and that of the creation with Him. This effort is apparent in a great many, prominent verses of the Qur'an, especially in the Makkan surahs but generally throughout the Qur'an. One can appreciate this great effort only if one is first aware of the great welter of concepts and the vast wilder-

---

[13] The concepts, philosophies, and religions that were found after Islam, especially the ones on which Western thought and life are based, and which are current in Eastern as well as Western countries today, are no better than the rubbish heaps of earlier times. We will discuss some of these at some other place.

ness of ideas in which mankind was stumbling blindly, even among such peoples as had previously received guidance from Allah but who had deviated from the straight path. A person who contemplates this effort without surveying these piles of intellectual rubbish cannot understand why in the Qur'an Allah found this exposition necessary with so much repetition and emphasis, and with such a detailed concern for the workings of the human conscience and peoples' way of life.

Since all of man's life, both personal and social, depends on a concept, i.e., on an underlying belief-concept, we can then understand the immense role that this sublime faith in Allah, played in liberating man's conscience, thought, and life, from the conceptual strait-jackets and intellectual quicksands of the pre-Islamic cultures. Only after studying this cultural wilderness can we grasp the value of the freedom Islam brought for the building of life in a sound and strong fashion, unburdened by persecution, oppression, injustice, and degradation. Only then can we grasp the significance of the saying by the second caliph, 'Umar (r.a.), that ''The one who is born in Islam not knowing the pre-Islamic Ignorance will unfasten the robes of Islam button by button.'' Only the one who has known *jahiliyyah*, the state of ignorance bereft of Divine guidance, can truly grasp the value of Islam and cherish the mercy of Allah embodied in it and the favor of Allah realized by it.

Indeed, the beauty of this faith, its perfection and harmony, and the simple but profound truth embodied in it is manifest only after studying the rubbish heaps of *jahiliyyah*, whether of the pre-Islamic period or in the world today. Then this faith appears as a mercy, a true mercy, a mercy for the heart and for the intellect, a mercy for the life of an individual and for the life of a community, and a mercy through its beauty and simplicity, its clarity and harmony, its familiarity and closeness, and its complete congruity with human nature.

Surely Allah Almighty spoke the truth in His saying:

Then, is he who goes prone upon his face [like a worm] better guided than he who walks upright upon a straight path? (*Al-Mulk* 67:22)

CHAPTER II

The Characteristics of the Islamic Concept

The hue of Allah — and whose hue is better than Allah's?
(*Al-Baqarah* 2:138).

The Islamic concept has special characteristics that distinguish it from all other concepts, giving it an independent personality and a particular temperament. This concept cannot be intermixed with any other nor can anything be added to it from other concepts.

The characteristics are numerous and varied, but all of them can be gathered together under one primary characteristic, of which all other characteristics are branches and from which they proceed, namely, the characteristic of being originated by Allah.

This concept is divinely ordained by Allah with all its constituents and characteristics not so that man may add something to it or take something away from it, but so that man may receive it whole-heartedly, adapt himself to it, and apply its corollaries to his life.

Since this concept comes directly from Allah, it is inherently unchangeable and causes mankind to evolve within its framework and to progress by understanding and applying its message. Mankind can continue to evolve, progress, grow, and advance indefinitely within the framework of this concept, because the spaciousness of this framework is very wide and the ability of this concept to set ever higher goals is unlimited. This is so because the source of this concept is the very source Who created man. He is the All-Wise Creator Who knows the nature of the human being and his changing needs through time. And to meet these needs He has endowed this concept with characteristics evolving within the vast boundaries of its framework.

The concepts, religions, and systems that men have devised for themselves outside Allah's guidance must always change, because man

37

feels constrained by them as his demands increase and his needs evolve. Accordingly man feels the need to update principles, transform rules, and, occasionally, completely overturn them. This need for constant updating results because these concepts, religions, and systems are formulated by men in response to the conditions, circumstances, and needs of a particular group of people living in a particular region of the world at a particular point in time. This parochialism is compounded by man's ignorance, shortcomings, prejudices, and selfish desires. Subsequent generations find the concepts, religions, and systems devised by earlier generations defective, erroneous, and irrelevant. Hence the need for continued updating and change. In contrast to this, the Islamic concept originating in Allah, is different in its origin and in its characteristics from all these humanly-devised perspectives. By its very nature it does not require any updating or change, for the One Who made it sees without any limitations of time and space, knows without any defect of ignorance or error, and decides without any influence of prejudice or selfish desire. He made this concept for the totality of mankind for all times and conditions as a holistic paradigm or permanent system of principles within the bounds of which mankind develops, evolves, grows, and advances without ever reaching the boundaries of its framework.

Motion, it appears, is a law of the universe and it also is a law in the life of man who is a part of the universe. But this law of motion is not free of restrictions or without some control, if only because it is a coherent system. An analogy to the life of a man is a planet with an orbit and an axis. This Divinely-revealed Islamic concept is like the sun around which the life of all mankind is to revolve. There is plenty of room for mankind to grow, progress, advance, and evolve, while still remaining in the field of attraction of this central concept.

Moreover, this concept is perfect and complete. It does not require any "spare parts" from outside or any change for completion. Since it is given by Allah, nothing from a source other than Him can fit it. Man is incapable of adding anything to it or making any corrections in it. Indeed, it has come as a gift to man in order to make him grow, correct him, and propel him forward. It has come to enrich his heart, his intellect, his life, and his world. This concept is designed to awaken all his powers and potentialities and to employ them entirely for constructive purposes under its own direction and control, so that they are not dissipated in futile pursuits. For the fulfillment of these objectives this Divinely-revealed concept does not need to borrow from outside nor does it need the infusion of foreign blood nor any methodology other than its own. Indeed, this concept demands to be the only controlling element in the life of man, because it has self-contained goals, incentives, methodology, resources, and all the necessary instruments to help translate its goals into a way of living that is harmonious with the universe in which man lives, so that his motion may not collide with the motion of the universe and be shattered and annihilated.

And this concept is comprehensive and balanced, taking into consideration all aspects of man's being and providing a balance and harmony among these aspects. Similarly, it takes into consideration all aspects of humankind, because it comes from the One Who made man and knows whom He created, namely, from the One Who is Subtle and All-Knowing.

The remote vistas and varied situations through which the life of the human race will pass are not hidden from His sight. He Himself made this concept for the human race, as a governing paradigm that is all-inclusive, providing a balance for all of mankind's constituent elements and for all aspects of every person's life. At the same time, this concept is practical and in harmony with man's social nature.

This concept necessarily is the only true standard to which man can refer in any place or at any time for judging his concepts and values, methods and systems, morals and manners, and customs and laws, in order to know whether he is right and whether he is truly close to Allah.

There is no other standard, nor any norm framed in previous or later times, to which reference can be made in this respect. Indeed, man learns his values and norms from this concept, adapts his heart and mind to it, forms his understanding and behavior in its mould, and refers to this standard in every matter he encounters:

> And if you have a dispute concerning any matter, refer it to Allah and the Messenger if you are sincere believers in Allah and the Last Day. This is better and fairer in the end (*Al-Nisa'* 4:59).

In this basic characteristic, namely, that it has come from Allah, and in all the other characteristics that proceed from it, we see clearly that the Islamic concept is unique among all paradigms of thought and life that it has its own personality and distinguishing features, and that it would be a grave methodological error to treat it like any other man-made concept by applying to it criteria borrowed from other sources or molding it to fit with man-made ways of thought prevailing on earth. Similarly, it would be a serious error to join other concepts with it or to subtract anything from it, for it is a divinely-originated and comprehensive concept perfect in itself.

We shall see all this more clearly as we proceed further. For the present, it is sufficient to state the following principle: in every research on Islam, whether in Islamic thought or Islamic methodology, this characteristic of Islam's Divine origin must be fully taken into consideration, for this is where the ways separate.

We shall now take a detailed look at this basic characteristic of the Islamic concept and at all other characteristics that proceed from it.

CHAPTER III

The Divine Origin of the Islamic Concept

Say: Surely my Lord has guided me to the straight way
(*Al-An'am* 6:151).

Divine origination is the foremost characteristic of the Islamic concept and the source of all other characteristics, for this belief-concept has been revealed by Allah Most High. The Islamic concept is confined to this one Source, not taking anything from anyone else. It is therefore entirely different from philosophical concepts, which originate in human minds, about the reality of God, the reality of existence, the reality of man, and the connections among these realities. It is also different from pagan beliefs, which originate in human emotion, imagination, and superstition.

An objective scholar can say with conviction that among all belief-concepts only the Islamic concept has remained as it was revealed by Allah, true to its origin in Allah Himself. Other Divinely-revealed concepts, with which the messengers of Allah before Muhammad came, were corrupted in some way or another, as we explained earlier. Interpolations, additions to the originally-revealed principles, far-fetched interpretations, and information from human sources are so intermingled with the texts of their scriptures that their ''Divine'' characteristic is lost. Islam alone remains with its principal sources intact, untouched by foreign pollutants, and without any mixture of falsehood in its truths. Allah's promise concerning it remains fulfilled:

Surely We have sent down the Message, and surely We are
its guardian (*Al-Hijr* 15:9).

This is an established fact, which gives this concept a unique value.

Philosophical concepts and belief-concepts, as such, have differing approaches. A philosophical concept originates in the thought of a man, the one who formulates it, in an attempt to explain the world and man's relationship with it. But such a concept remains in the cold realm of ideas. A belief-concept on the other hand, proceeds from the conscience, interacting with feelings and intermingling with practical life, because it is a living relationship between man and the world, or between man and the Creator of the world.

The Islamic concept differs further from other belief-concepts due to its Divine origin. It is not a concept originated by man, but comes directly from Allah. Mankind received it in its entirety from its Creator. No man, or men, invented it, as is the case with pagan or philosophical concepts, despite their mutual differences. Man's action concerning the Islamic concept is to receive it with gratitude, to understand it, adapt to it, and apply it to all affairs of life.

The Divine utterances constituting the Qur'an, which bring this concept to us, are all from Allah as a gift from Him and a mercy. The thought of all the Messengers of Allah is the same, since all of them received the same Islamic concept in its original form but none of them shared in its origination. Rather they received this concept as a guide for them and through them for others. This guidance is a gift from Allah by means of which minds are opened. The duty of a Messenger, any Messenger, with respect to this concept is to communicate it accurately to others and propagate it faithfully and diligently, without mixing any human ideas — referred to in the Qur'an as *ahwa* or "whims" — with Divine revelations. Whether the people are guided through his efforts and whether their minds are opened to its message are not the Messenger's concern.

> And thus have We by our command sent inspiration to you. You did not know [before] what Revelation is and what is faith, but We have made the [Qur'an] a light, whereby We guide whom we deem suitable of our servants. And truly you guide [men] onto the straight path, the path of Allah, to whom belongs whatsoever is in the heavens and on earth. Surely unto Allah all things return. (*Al- Shura* 42: 52-53).

> By the star when it sets, your comrade (Muhammad) is not astray; neither does he err, nor does he speak out of whim. This is nothing but a revelation revealed (*Al-Najm* 53:1-4).

> If he (Muhammad) were to invent any false sayings about

Us, We would surely seize him by his right hand and cut off the artery of his heart, and not one of you could have defended him (*Al-Haqqah* 69:44-47).

O Messenger, make known what has been sent down to you from your Lord, for if you do not do so, you will not have conveyed His message (*Al-Ma'idah* 5:67).

It is true that you will not be able to guide everyone you love, but Allah guides whomever He will. And He knows best those who receive guidance (*Al-Qasas* 28:56).

If Allah wishes to guide anyone, He opens his breast to Islam, and if He wishes to let anyone go astray He makes his breast closed and narrow, as if he had to climb up to the skies. Thus does Allah inflict horror upon those who do not believe (*Al-An 'am* 7:125).

We cannot overemphasize the point that it is the Source of this concept that makes it precious and great, because it is the only trustworthy Source, free of defect, ignorance, and whim. Defect, ignorance, and whim are characteristics of human ideas and actions and, as we saw, are embodied in all the conceptual paradigms molded by men, such as mythologies and philosophies, and in the concepts interpolated by men into the revealed beliefs of earlier times. This Source of the Islamic concept is a guarantee that it accords with human nature, responds to it from all directions, and provides for all its needs. Furthermore, from this concept proceeds the straightest and the most comprehensive way of life.

The fact that the Islamic concept did not originate in human thought does not mean that it is outside the domain of the human intellect or that rational thought is prohibited in Islam. Its divine origin, however, does imply that it is the task of human thought to receive it, grasp its significance, adapt to it, and then translate it into action. As was pointed out in the introductory chapter entitled, ''A Word About Methodology,'' there is a correct method of receiving it, and this is as follows.

Allah does not want humans to receive this Divinely-revealed concept within the context of previous norms, whether these come from other sources or from their own ideas, and then to judge this concept by them or measure it in their scale. Indeed, human thought should receive all its norms and standards from this very concept, rejecting all the previous norms and standards that do not conform to it. Man should not accept any norms and standards from any other source, but should correct all incompatible norms and standards by using the method prescribed by this concept, which originates from the Divine Source.

And then, whatever comes to a person's mind of feelings and ideas, values and concepts, and of the affairs of the worldly life, he should refer to the truths and standards of the Islamic concept in order to know what is true and what is false, and what is right and what is wrong.

> If you have a dispute concerning any matter, refer it to Allah
> and the Messenger (*Al-Nisa'* 4:59).

An inherent and central part of the Islamic concept is that human reason is a great and valuable faculty to which is assigned the task of understanding the characteristics and constituents of this concept originating from their Divine Source. From them it is the task of human reason to deduce values and norms, without adding to them anything from external sources and without distorting or impairing them in anyway. Furthermore, teachers of the Islamic method of training go to great lengths to sharpen and develop this great faculty of man, the intellect, to protect it from being wasted in futile pursuits, and to prompt it toward action in all the numerous fields for which it is equipped.[1]

Although the intellect has the prime responsibility to receive and absorb this concept, other human faculties also participate in this task. Due to its Divine origin, this concept is characterized by the fact that it addresses the personality of man in its entirety and is totally within man's comprehension.

Even if certain aspects of this concept relating to the ultimate questions of what, why, and how are beyond human comprehension, they are not contrary to human reason, as are the "mysteries" of other religions, and the concept itself is totally within the realm of human reason and logic. Human logic can never surrender itself to a contradiction, and there are no contradictions in the Islamic concept. But human reason knows when to surrender in the presence of a simple fact. The simple fact is that the domain of the Islamic concept includes matters, such as the Person and the attributes of Allah, the operation of Allah's will, and its connection with His creation, that are beyond the reach of human perception. This is the domain of the Ultimate,

---

[1]For a detailed discussion, refer to the chapter entitled, "Intellectual Training" in the book, *The Islamic Educational Method*, by Muḥammad Qutb.

the Free and the Absolute, whereas man, a mortal creature, is circumscribed in time and space and is impotent in perceiving the infinite and in knowing the totality of being.

> O company of jinn and of men, if you can penetrate through the regions of the heavens and the earth, then penetrate through them! You shall not penetrate through them except with authority (*Al-Rahman* 55:33).

> Vision comprehends Him not but He comprehends vision. He is the Subtle and Aware (*Al-An'am* 6:103).

In fact, man as a whole, and not merely his thought, is impotent to cross these boundaries. His task is to receive these truths gratefully from Allah, the Absolute and All-Knowing, within the limits of his nature and of his assigned task.

Man by nature is a creature, bound within the limits of his divinely-given capacities, and he is mortal. He is neither absolute nor all-knowing, nor is he from pre-eternity. Hence his perception is necessarily limited by the limits of his created nature. It is further limited by his assigned task. His task is to be the deputy of Allah on earth in order to establish therein the true worship of Allah alone, as will be explained later, and therefore he has been given a capacity of perception just sufficient, neither more nor less, to perform his task. There are numerous matters not needed to discharge his responsibility, and therefore he has not been given the power to grasp them in their what-ness and how-ness, but he is nonetheless capable of grasping their possibility. This is because he knows on the one hand that Allah's will is absolutely free, and on the other that he himself is a mortal creature, neither absolute nor all-knowing, and that therefore it is not possible for him to completely grasp the attributes of the Eternal, the One Who comprehends everything.

The Qur'an mentions some aspects of reality that man has not been given the power to understand, because either they are not within the limits of his finite nature or else their knowledge is not needed in the performance of his assigned task. The Qur'an also describes how a sincere believer receives these aspects and how a crooked mind reacts to them. Among these aspects is the Person of Allah Most High. The human being cannot comprehend His Person, nor does he know of anything in Allah's Creation with which to compare Him, or to make analogy with him.

Vision comprehends Him not but He comprehends vision (*Al-An'am* 6:103).

There is nothing like Him (*Al-Shura* 42:11).

So do not make any analogy to Allah (*Al-Nahl* 16:74).

Another aspect of reality is the relationship of Allah's will with His creation.

He (Zakariyyah) said, ''My Lord, how can I have a son when I have grown old and my wife is barren?'' (The angel) answered, ''Thus (it will be), Allah does what He wills'' (*Ale'Imran 3:40*).

She (Mary) said, ''My Lord, how can I have a child when no mortal (man) has touched me?'' (The angel) answered, ''Thus (it will be). Allah creates what He wills. When He decides a thing, He says only 'Be,' and it is'' (*Ale'Imran* 3:47).

This is stated without describing how it comes into being, because description would have been beyond our understanding. Anyone who has tried to describe how creation from nothing took place has succeeded only in being unintelligible and has had to resort to some analogy from the sphere of human action. To what extent then can one deviate?

Among other aspects of the Islamic concept relating to ultimate matters is ''the spirit'' in any of its three meanings, namely, ''life,'' ''Jibril,'' and ''revelation.''

They ask you concerning the spirit; say, ''The spirit is by command of my Lord; and of knowledge you have been given but little'' (*Al-Isra* 17:85).

A large part of the Islamic concept relates to the ''Unseen Realities'' *(Al-ghaib),* which are hidden from the perception of man, except for what Allah has deemed proper to reveal to some of His servants:

And with Him are the keys of the Unseen; none knows them but He (*Al-An'am* 6:59).

Knower is He of the Unseen, and He does not disclose the Unseen to anyone except one who is pleasing to Him among Messengers (*Al-Jinn* 72:26-27).

No soul knows what it will earn tomorrow, and no soul
knows in what land it will die (*Luqman* 31:34).

In particular, among the elements of the Unseen is the time of the
Last Hour:

Surely with Allah is knowledge of the Hour (*Luqman*
31:34).

They ask you concerning the Hour: when will it come to
pass? Why do they ask? What have you to tell about it? Unto
your Lord is the final end of it. You are only a warner to
him who fears it. On the day when they see it, it will be as
if they had tarried for only an evening, or [at most until]
the following morning (*Al-Nazi'at* 79:42-46).

Nay, but it will come upon them unawares so that it will
stupefy them, and they will be unable to repel it, nor will
they be reprieved (*Al-Anbiya* 21:40).

Allah Most High clarifies how these and similar matters beyond
human perception should be received:

He it is Who has revealed to you the Book wherein are
verses clear. They are the essence of the Book, and still
others are allegorical. As for those in whose heart is
crookedness, they pursue the allegorical part, seeking dissension, and seeking its (hidden) interpretations. But no
one knows its (hidden) interpretations except Allah. And
those of firm knowledge say "We believe in it; all of it is
from our Lord." But no one will (truly) grasp the Message
except men of understanding. Our Lord, make not our
hearts swerve after You have guided us, and bestow upon
us mercy from Yourself, indeed You are the Bestower of all
things (*Ale 'Imran* 3·7-8).

With the exception of these elements or aspects of the Islamic
concept, which man can never fully comprehend, human thought, or
human perception, in its comprehensive meaning, is called upon to
think and ponder upon all the signs (*ayat*) of Allah both in the Qur'an
and in the created universe, to see and learn, to understand and then
to apply the implications of the Islamic concept in the world of

conscience and in the world of events. This all-inclusive concept opens up before every individual numerous vistas of positive action.

No religion other than Islam shows so much concern for awakening the human faculty of perception, for nourishing it with sublime ideas, arousing it to action, liberating it from superstition and nonsense, and freeing it from the shackles of priestcraft and the occult arts, while, at the same time protecting it from being scattered in domains that are beyond its ken and from stumbling over the intellectual trash in the wilderness of speculation. No religion has done all this except Islam.

And no religion other than Islam has directed man's vision toward Allah's laws operating within the human self and in the outside world, toward the nature of the physical universe and toward the nature of man, with all its hidden potentialities and noble traits, and toward the law of Allah in the life of nations as revealed inexorably in history. No religion has directed human perception toward all these as has Islam.

For training the human mind and for keeping its perception and judgement on a straight path, the Qur'an says:

> And never concern yourself with anything of which you have no knowledge. Verily, [your] hearing, and sight, and heart will all be called to account for doing so (*Al-Isra* 17:36).

> O you who believe! Avoid suspicion as much as possible, for suspicion in some cases is a sin (*Al- Hujurat* 49:12).

> Most of them follow nothing but speculation. Assuredly speculation has nothing to do with the truth (*Yunus* 10:36).

> They have no knowledge whatsoever of that; they do merely conjecture (*Al-Zukhruf* 43:20).

And to encourage awareness of the laws of Allah evident in the history of mankind and in the rise and fall of nations, the Qur'an warns:

> Say: Travel in the land and see how He originated creation, then will Allah bring forth a later creation. Verily, Allah is able to do all things (*Al-'Ankabut* 29:20).

> Have they not travelled through the earth and seen what was the end of those who were before them? They were stronger than them in power, and they dug the earth and

built upon it more than these have built. Their Messengers came to them with clear proofs. Surely Allah did not wrong them, but they wronged themselves. Then evil was the consequence of those who dealt in evil, because they denied the revelations of Allah and mocked at them (*Al-Rum* 30:9-10).

Do they not see how We visit the land, reducing it from its borders (*Al-R'ad* 13:41).

Such examples are numerous in the Qur'an and, taken together, they provide a complete methodology for educating and training the faculties of human perception and for developing them in the right way. In the following chapters many more instances of this methodology will be presented as the occasion arises.

Surely, Allah Most High, the fashioner of the human being, knows the nature and extent of human faculties. He knows what capability man has been given to understand the laws of the physical universe and to control the forces of nature in order to carry out the tasks of his vicegerency on the earth, just as He also knows what is concealed from man of the secrets of "life," i.e what are his body and brain, how they came about, and how they function, and the secrets of his mind or soul and of his spirit. Even the connection between his intellectual and spiritual functions and his bodily functions is to a large extent still unknown to him. This point has been set forth for us in a frank, sincere manner by one of the greatest of the twentieth century's specialists, Dr. Alexis Carrel, who in his book, *Man the Unknown*, says:

> Indeed, mankind has made a gigantic effort to know itself. Although we possess the treasure of the observations accumulated by the scientists, the philosophers, the poets, and the great mystics of all times, we have grasped only certain aspects of ourselves. We do not apprehend man as a whole. We know him as composed of distinct parts. And even these parts are created by our methods. Each one of us is made up of a procession of phantoms, in the midst of which strides an unknowable reality.

> In fact, our ignorance is profound. Most of the questions put to themselves by those who study human beings remain without answer. Immense regions of our inner world are still unknown. How do the molecules of chemical substances associate in order to form the complex and temporary

organs of the cell? How do the genes contained in the nucleus of a fertilized ovum determine the characteristics of the individual deriving from the ovum? How do cells organize themselves by their own efforts into societies, such as the tissues and organs? Like the ants and the bees, they have advance knowledge of the part they are destined to play in the life of the community. And hidden mechanisms enable them to build up an organism both complex and simple. What is the nature of our duration, of psychological time, and of physiological time? We know that we are a compound of tissues, organs, fluids, and consciousness. But the relations between consciousness and cerebrum are still a mystery. We lack almost entirely a knowledge of the physiology of nervous cells. To what extent does will power modify the organism? How is the mind influenced by the state of the organs? In what manner can the organic and mental characteristics, which each individual inherits, be changed by the mode of life, the chemical substances contained in food, the climate, and the physiological and moral disciplines?

We are very far from knowing what relations exist between skeleton, muscles, and organs, and mental and spiritual activities. We are ignorant of the factors that bring about nervous equilibrium and resistance to fatigue and to diseases. We do not know how moral sense, judgment, and audacity could be augmented. What is the relative importance of intellectual, moral, and mystical activities? What is the significance of esthetics and religious sense? What form of energy is responsible for telepathic communications? Without any doubt, certain physiological and mental factors determine happiness or misery, success, or failure. But we do not know what they are. We cannot artificially give to any individual the aptitude for happiness. As yet, we do not know what environment is the most favorable for the optimum development of civilized man. Is it possible to suppress struggle, effort, and suffering from our physiological and spiritual formation? How can we prevent the degeneracy of man in modern civilization? Many other questions could be asked on subjects that are to us of utmost interest. They would also remain unanswered. It is quite evident that the accomplishments of all the sciences having

man as an object remain insufficient, and that our
knowledge of ourselves is still most rudimentary."[2]

This is how great our ignorance is concerning both the most obscure
and the most obvious aspects of the reality of "man," as elucidated
by one of the greatest scientists of the twentieth century, whose
scholarship is undisputed and whose place among scholars, old and
new, is unquestioned. All of these questions are dealt with by the
Islamic concept.

In the view of Alexis Carrel, the reasons for this ignorance are many.
His view, which we support only in part, is based on the scientific
method as known in the West and on his upbringing in Western society
and in the atmosphere of "scientific research" with its typical limitations in the context of Western thought, which are frankly admitted
by him in the "Preface."

Our ignorance may be attributed, at the same time, to the
mode of existence of our ancestors, to the complexity of
our nature, and to the structure of our mind."[3]

He elaborates on the first two reasons, with which we are not
concerned here. About the third reason, he says:

There is another reason for the slow progress of the
knowledge of ourselves. Our mind is so constructed as to
delight in contemplating simple facts. We feel a kind of
repugnance in attacking such a complex problem as that of
the constitution of living beings and of man. The intellect,
as Bergson wrote, is characterized by a natural inability to
comprehend life. On the contrary, we love to discover in
the cosmos the geometrical forms that exist in the depths
of our consciousness. The exactitude of the proportions of
our monuments and the precision of our machines express
a fundamental character of our mind. Geometry does not
exist in the earthly world. It has originated in ourselves.
The methods of nature are never so precise as those of men.
We do not find in the universe the clearness and accuracy
of our thought. We attempt, therefore, to abstract from the
complexity of phenomena some simple systems whose

---

[2] *Man the Unknown*, Harper & Brothers, 1935, pp. 4-5.
[3] Ibid., pp. 5-6.

components bear to one another certain relations suscep-
tible to being described mathematically.

This power of abstraction of the human intellect is responsible for the amazing progress of physics and chemistry. A
similar success has rewarded the physicochemical study of
living beings. The laws of chemistry and of physics are
identical in the world of living things and in that of inanimate matter, as Claude Bernard thought long ago. This
fact explains why modern physiology has discovered, for
example, that the constancy of the alkalinity of the blood
and of the water of the ocean is expressed by identical laws,
that the energy spent by the contracting muscle is supplied
by the fermentation of sugar, etc. The physicochemical
aspects of human beings are almost as easy to investigate as
those of the other objects of the terrestrial world. Such is
the task that general physiology succeeds in accomplishing.

The study of the truly physiological phenomena, that is, of
those resulting from the organization of living matter —
meets with more important obstacles. On account of the
extreme smallness of the things to be analyzed, it is impossible to use the ordinary techniques of physics and of
chemistry. What method could bring to light the chemical
constitution of the nucleus of the sexual cells, of its
chromosomes, and of the genes that compose these
chromosomes? Nevertheless, those very minute aggregates
of chemicals are of capital importance, because they contain the future of the individual and of the race. The fragility
of certain tissues, such as the serious substance, is so great
that to study them in the living state is almost impossible.
We do not possess any technique capable of penetrating the
mysteries of the brain, and of the harmonious association
of its cells. Our mind, which loves the simple beauty of
mathematical formulas, is bewildered when it contemplates the stupendous mass of cells, humors, and consciousness that make up the individual. We try, therefore,
to apply to this compound the concepts that have proved
useful in the realm of physics, chemistry, and mechanics,
and in the philosophical and religious disciplines. Such an
attempt does not meet with much success, because we can
be reduced neither to a physicochemical system nor to a
spiritual entity. Of course, the science of man has to use the

concepts of all the other sciences. But it must also develop its own. For it is as fundamental as the sciences of the molecules, the atoms, and the electrons.

In short, the slow progress of the knowledge of the human being, as compared with the splendid ascension of physics, astronomy, chemistry, and mechanics, is due to our ancestors' lack of leisure, to the complexity of the subject, and to the structure of our mind. Those obstacles are fundamental to be overcome at the cost of strenuous effort. The knowledge of ourselves will never attain the elegant simplicity, the abstractness, and the beauty of physics. The factors that have retarded its development are not likely to vanish. We must realize clearly that the science of man is the most difficult of all sciences.[4]

This exposes our ignorance about the reality of man, and about even the smallest and most obvious facts of this reality, in the view of this great Western scientist. We note that he has touched upon the main reason, that is the structure of our mind. This structure is connected with man's role, which is to be the deputy of Allah on earth, and is so designed as to facilitate the performance of this role. Hence our mind is capable of advancing in comprehending the laws of matter and in controlling it, as it is also capable of understanding many aspects of "the reality of man," most of which are already known. But the secret of man's existence, the secret of life, and the secrets of man's soul and spirit will remain beyond his comprehension, because the knowledge of these things is not essential for the performance of his basic task.

In any case, two basic facts emerge from this discussion:

First: It is Allah's mercy that He did not leave man alone in his deep ignorance, as described by a great twentieth century scientist, to construct a belief-concept on his own. Rather, He gave him a comprehensive concept, governing not merely the reality of man, but also the much greater realities of the Creator Himself, of the universe, of life, and of all the interconnections among these realities. Again, He did not leave man, with his ignorance of even his own self, to construct his way of life, the form of his system, and its laws and rules, because this requires a complete and comprehensive knowledge not merely of the nature of man, but also of the nature of the universe in which he lives, as well as the nature of life, and the reality of the great Creator of this universe and of whatever and whoever is in it.

---

[4]*Man the Unknown*, Harper & Brothers, 1935, pp. 8-10.

Second: It is sheer ignorance on the part of some people, of earlier times or of the present, even to try to devise a comprehensive explanation of the existence of life and of man and to attempt to design ways of life and systems for human beings together with rules of conduct, even though all the while they are in complete ignorance of even the rudiments of man's nature, let alone of other greater realities. They succeeded only in piling up rubbish heaps of false concepts, in devising corrupt systems and erroneous ways, and bringing misery and sorrow to the world, for all these are nothing, but natural consequences and bitter fruits of this unseemly arrogance, which is exceeded only by the deep ignorance underlying it.

Indeed, the Divinely-revealed concept that man has received from Allah is a gift from Him. It has spared this weak and ignorant creature from struggling in vain in this matter, rescuing him from trying to originate this concept on his own and thus scattering his energy in a domain for which Allah has not given him any resource or tool. People have been spared all this so that they may devote their time and effort to learning and understanding this Divine gift in order to adapt to it, to build the foundations of their lives upon it, to judge their values by its standard, and to be guided by it. If they were to deviate from this God-given concept, they would certainly fall into error and confusion and the result would be the self-same rubbish heaps of concepts and ideas, which should evoke either tears or laughter, and a repetition of the suffering and sorrow that are natural consequences of ways of life erected on this ignorance, confusion, and error.

In this respect, Professor Abul Hasan Ali Nadwi writes in his valuable work, *Islam and the World*:

> The prophets had imparted to man the true knowledge of God's existence and His attributes and actions. They had laid the foundations upon which man could erect the edifice of his own spiritual conduct without getting involved in the fruitless metaphysical discussions on ''being'' and ''knowing.'' But man heeded not. Instead of being grateful for Divine guidance, he allowed the ship of his thought to drift on uncharted seas. He behaved like an explorer who, setting aside the geographical charts and maps, tries to scale every height, fathom every depth, and measure every distance on his own initiative. The results of such endeavors can at best be a few sketchy notes and incomplete hints picked up here and there. So when the people tried to reach God with the help of reason alone and without the aid of light furnished by the Prophet's teach-

ings, the knowledge of God gathered by them consisted of little else besides random thoughts, conflicting theories, and haphazard conclusions.[5]

The situation of those who, on their own, try to invent belief systems or to construct a philosophical concept for the explanation of existence and its interconnections is worse than the situation of the lone explorer described by Professor Nadwi, and is more dangerous for the life of mankind. Still more dangerous than this is the distortion of a revealed message, and, in particular, the distortion of the message revealed to Jesus, the establishment of the Church of Europe, deriving its authority from this distorted Christianity, and the subsequent imposition of its false concepts by the use of force through the insistence on its erroneous teachings concerning the physical world and through the savage suppression of scientific research within its rightful domain by claiming religious sanction for such matters. While the true religion of Jesus is not to be blamed for it, all this persecution was carried out in the name of religion.

This whole calamity descended upon the heads of millions of people because human thought was interpolated into the original Divinely-revealed teachings of Jesus, rendering them distorted, misshapen, contradictory, and unintelligible.

All the European schools of thought, from "Idealism" to "Positivism" to "Dialectical Materialism," originated in the revolt against religion and religious thought, and came into being only because of these distortions in the teachings of Jesus. This shows the enormity of the plague brought upon mankind by the interpolation of human thought in a divinely revealed message. Such a devastating calamity has no parallel in human history.

In order adequately to clarify this important point, it seems appropriate here to present a brief review of the history of European thought as a direct consequence of distortions and interpolations of human ideas in the religious concept, of its subjugation to political exigencies, and of the influence of racial and pagan heritages.

Perhaps this summary may open our minds to the wisdom and the mercy of Allah Most High in preserving the Islamic concept from distortion by human beings. The divinely-revealed Islamic concept has remained free of such human attempts as "Reformation," "Protestantism," or "development of religious thought." This concept alone remains in its pristine purity, untouched by human ignorance and

---

[5]Nadwi, *Islam and the World,* pp. 62- 63.

error, as a secure refuge for mankind and as a source of guidance, solace, and satisfaction.

It is sufficient for our purposes to quote from Muhammad Al- Bahi's book, *The New Islamic Thought and Its Connection with Western Imperialism*, under the heading, "Is Religion a Drug?"

Under the sub-heading, *The Conflict Between Religion, Reason, and Senses In the History of Western Thought,* Al-Bahi writes:

"Since the fourteenth century, European thought has passed through four stages. These stages are related to the justification of one or another of the three sources of knowledge prevailing in the history of mankind up to modern times; religion, reason, and sensory perception or facts. At every stage, the relative 'value' of the three sources in providing positive or certain knowledge came into question. These stages are characterized by a positive or negative answer to this question of sure knowledge. Controversies relating to the importance and value of these sources of human knowledge have led to various schools of thought.

"**The Supremacy of Scripture and Religion**: During the long centuries of the medieval period, religion was predominant in directing human affairs, in organizing institutions, and in explaining the world. The religion here referred to was Christianity; Christianity meant Catholicism; and Catholicism meant Papism, that is to say, as the Vicar of Christ, the Pope was the final authority. The interpretation of the 'Holy Book' was strictly limited to the Pope and the College of Cardinals, so that 'what the Book says' meant 'what the Catholic Church says.' Thus, the Church formulated the doctrine of the Trinity and introduced confession and indulgences, and whatever else relates to the Catholic faith and practice.

"This state of affairs continued until the fifteenth century, by which time the positive ideas which the Crusaders had brought back from the Muslims to Europe had gradually changed European thinking. Martin Luther (1453-1546) stood up against the authority of the Catholic Church, castigating its teaching as 'satanic.' He opposed the sale of indulgences, which only perpetuated the enslavement of the masses. He fought against the concept of the Trinity as well as that of Papal infallibility, declaring that only the Holy Book was the final authority and demanding the freedom to study the Book. But he did not demand total freedom of thought. He stated that the Holy Book is the source of faith and that faith has priority over other matters including reason and observation.

"In the footsteps of Luther came Calvin (1509-1564), who affirmed with Luther that the Bible is the only true source for 'real Christianity' and that belief in the Trinity as defined by the popes is no part of true Christianity.

"It may be noted that what Luther and Calvin wanted to reform was Papal Catholicism. The philosophers, who began to object to religion in the wake of these reformist movements, also objected to papal authority. When they pointed to the contradictions between reason and 'religion,' they meant contradictions between common sense and the teachings of the Catholic Church such as the Trinity, the sacraments, the sale of indulgences, and so on. Anyone who defended Christianity among the philosophers, as for example, Hegel, defended its 'pure teachings' as expounded by Luther, in contrast to the teachings of the Catholic Church.

"Thus, whenever 'religion' is spoken of, whether favorably or unfavorably, in European philosophy it means this particular form of religion.

"**The Supremacy of Reason.** The supremacy of the Scriptures over other sources of knowledge continued until the mid- eighteenth century when the Age of Enlightenment dawned on the horizons of European thought. The Age of Enlightenment, which lasted for about half a century, has peculiar characteristics that distinguish it from the periods preceding and following it. These characteristics are common among the German, French, and English philosophers of the time. The thought of this period has three characteristics:

> It extols human reason, proclaiming that the future of mankind will be by its hand once it is rid of its past heritage of suppression and denigration. The line of progress will then be very clearly defined.

> It demonstrates boldness and intellectual courage in submitting every historical event to the test of reason. The same boldness is shown in applying reason to political institutions, economics, law, religion, education, and so on, in order to rest them on a rational foundation.

> It proclaims its faith in cooperative efforts for all human affairs, in the brotherhood of man on the basis of this new civilization based on reason, and in marching forward from progress to progress.

"All of this may be summarized as meaning the supremacy of 'reason' over the other source of knowledge, 'religion,' that is to say, both the Catholic Church and Protestantism, as the reformist movement was called:

"Reason has the right to be the supreme guide in all human affairs such as politics, law, and religion, and the ultimate goal for man is humanism.

"This period is called by such names as The Age of Enlightenment, The Age of Humanism, and occasionally as The Age of Deism. Deism is a belief in the transcendent deity postulated by the philosophers. This deity is neither the Creator of the universe nor concerned with human affairs, nor does He send down revelation. All these names signify the supremacy of human reason. 'Enlightenment' had no other purpose than to depose religion from its throne of authority and to put reason in its place. 'Humanism' existed to replace 'the pleasure of God' as the ultimate good, while 'God,' who does not create or reveal Himself, was merely an entity that conformed to the dictates of reason.

"Throughout this period there existed a conflict between the teachings of religion and the dictates of reason, and a diligent effort to subdue religion by reason. Thus this age is characterized by the supremacy of reason just as the age preceding it was characterized by the supremacy of religion. The religion here was the Christianity of the Church and the field of this conflict was all those aspects of life where the Church was dominant, such as faith and belief, knowledge and science, politics and law.

"**The Supremacy of Senses.** This Age of Enlightenment came to an end by the beginning of the nineteenth century. The subject of controversy, however, continued to be the same: the relative importance of religion, reason, and sensory perception or 'nature.' Nineteenth century Europe now inclined toward the supremacy of 'Nature' or 'facts' over both religion and reason as a sure source of knowledge. It was the Age of Positivism, signifying a philosophy of knowledge with its own climate of thought. This climate of thought came into being in the first place because of a certain abhorrence among some scientists and philosophers toward the Church. The Church had a particular kind of knowledge, the Catholic doctrine, which it had imposed for a long period of time on everyone, including scientists and researchers. The Positivist not only rebelled against this doctrine, but also against all religious knowledge, and even all metaphysical knowledge. In addition to this, the Positivist also opposed the philosophies of The Age of Enlightenment, 'Rationalism' and 'Idealism,' which, according to the Positivists, were completely bankrupt in attaining their stated goal, namely, to replace the religious objective by the objective of humanism and human welfare. Strangely enough, this philosophy in the time of Hegel tended once again to support religion and religious inspiration.

"The main objective of positivism was to oppose the Church, or to oppose its type of knowledge, that is, metaphysical and rational knowledge, in the name of 'science.' But positivism merely replaced one religion with another, with its own forms of 'worship' and its own 'priesthood,' its saints and sacred symbols, exactly paralleling the Catholic Church.

"Positivism is based on the affirmation of fact. Fact, sensory perception, natural phenomena, and reality are synonymous in the vocabulary of the positivists. According to them, any proposition that does not admit of being ultimately reduced to a simple statement of fact can make no intelligible sense. Thus, nature, that is to say sensory perception, is the only source of sure and positive knowledge. It is nature that imprints facts on the human intellect, inspires it, and provides it with clear guidelines. Indeed, the human intellect is nothing but a creation of nature. There is nothing beyond the world of phenomena that can provide knowledge to the human intellect or dictate to it nor anything within man's own self that can inform him about anything real or true. Whatever is supposed to have come from beyond nature is an illusion of reality, and not reality, while whatever is produced by the human intellect on its own is mere imagination and a reflection of reality and not reality. Hence religion, which is the revelation from 'beyond nature,' is nothing but a deception. The theological explanation of natural facts is a mere stage in the history of ideas. Similar is the case of the metaphysical or 'ideal' approach to physical phenomena. These do not represent reality but are only products of human imagination and mere reflections of reality.

"When people talk about human personality, the rights of man, or the role of man in this world, or the nature of the world, based on religious knowledge or on philosophical reasoning, they are propounding unreal dogmas with no basis in observed fact. These are lies invented to lead people into religious deceptions or to pander to their high opinion of themselves.

"The human intellect, together with the knowledge it contains, is a product of nature, which is represented by inherited characteristics, the environment, and socio-economic conditions. The human intellect is a creature but its creator is the physical world. It thinks but only through interaction with the universe surrounding it. It is imprisoned and determined by the laws operating in the body and brain. There is no Mind prior to Matter, nor is there knowledge prior to human existence. And both mind and knowledge appear with the appearance of the human being, who himself is a product of the material world.

"Nature speaks concerning itself and the human being must listen to it. As he is constrained to live within the natural world, he must follow Nature's logic, and that logic is one — not the logic of theologians, nor of metaphysicists, nor of psychologists — but the logic inherent in human nature propelling it along a straight, narrow path, setting its goal and inexorably leading toward that goal.

"The natural path for every human being starts at the individual and ends in the group. The individual himself is not the ultimate goal of his existence, nor should he be the object of his striving. The ultimate goal of all one's striving is the annihilation of the self in 'humanity,' just as a mystic's goal is to annihilate his self in the God whom he worships. Humanity must occupy the place of God, and each individual must sacrifice himself in order that 'humanity' be preserved.

"*Marxism*. The dialectical materialism of Marx, as distinct from scientific or mechanical materialism, does not deny the existence of 'mind.' But matter precedes mind, which depends on matter for its existence and which cannot be found independent of matter. Marx not only denies that the mind (or the soul) survives the body, as religion asserts, but, in fact, denies the very basis of religious thought — belief in God, the Eternal, the Self-Subsisting Creator of the material world. In Marx's view, all religion, because of its very origin, is a curse or 'opium of the masses.'

"Hegel had centered his thought around the notion of Spirit or Mind: Mind is real and matter is its reflection. Marx inverted this by saying that the basic reality is material and mind is merely a reflection of it. Marx contended that the generating influence on men's political, social, and moral phenomena was the sum total of the material circumstances (i.e. economic) of any historic time. In the view of Marx and Engels, all human history was to be seen as a movement brought about by conflicts in the material order, which is to say that history is a dialectical materialistic power.

"Only change in the means of production and consequent economic development influences a society and its political structure, science, and religion. Thus, all cultural and intellectual attainments are branches of economic life. The entire course of human history is nothing but the history of the economic law of motion."

These stages in European thought, as outlined by Muhammad Al-Bahi, are the various consequences of running away from the distorted concepts of the Church and from its abuse of authority in the name of religion. In one direction lay the philosophy of Idealism, which rejected religion and the supremacy of Reason in various ways, such as the philosophy of Fichte and the support of the concept of the God of religion as the Absolute in the philosophy of Hegel. In another direction this rebellion against the Church went toward the philosophy of Positivism in the hands of Comte and Stendahl, and then toward dialectical materialism in the hands of Karl Marx and Engels.

This long detour in European thought was a direct result of tampering with the revealed religious concept and introducing human distortions into it by the Church and by a succession of Councils.

When an impartial inquirer looks into these wanderings in the wilderness of thought, in frantic attempts to run away from God in order to get rid of the yoke of the Church, he will only find that such attempts failed miserably in clarifying ideas or in coming closer to anything "concrete." After all these mental gymnastics, one cannot even say that they succeeded in getting rid of metaphysical riddles.

Take, for example, the philosophy of rationalism wherein "reason" is held to be supreme, which is supposed to guide us without reference to God or physical phenomena. Where is this ideal reason to be found? What is its nature and its laws of operation?

Again, take the philosophy of Idealism, either as expounded by Fichte or as developed into a metaphysical system by Hegel or as later transformed by Karl Marx into dialectical materialism. Let us look at the "Principle of Contradiction," which Fichte introduced. One of its arguments runs somewhat as follows:

"Every person has a concept of his own Self. The Self is sharply distinguished from the rest of the universe, the Not-Self, which it knows, but which is other than it. Thus the self is also the Not-Self. But the existence of Not-Self is entirely dependent on the existence of Self and has no independent existence. Thus Self, which contains in itself Not-Self, is both Self and Not-Self.

"But the Not-Self has no reality. Whenever the human being looks into himself he is conscious of Self, and the things which are outside the Self, i.e. the Not-Self, which are perceived by us as a separate reality, are but a product of mind.

"Hence, to start with, Self exists by itself and Not-Self does not exist. The Self (or mind) imposes its categories upon experience, and every object other than Self is a product of Self."

Proceeding on this line of thought, Fichte argued that the mind has an existence completely independent of other-than-itself. Its existence is its own existence, and not of other-than-itself. There cannot be unknowable things-in-themselves. Knowledge was possible because the mind itself produced the forms of knowledge through its various categories. Thus every object of knowledge, including things, is the product of mind. To say otherwise would be to admit the existence of Not-Self which would contradict the Self, that is to say, the existence of the mind itself.

Now, this kind of an argument has nothing to do with our practical lives, and is merely an exercise in verbal jugglery. Why should the existence of Not-Self contradict the existence of Self? Why cannot there be things and objects as well as minds?

But the main purpose was to depose the God of the Church and to put in His place some other god who will have neither priests, nor Pope, nor churches. So "the Mind" became that god, needing no priests or churches, and this was the ultimate objective.

While Fichte employed the principle of contradiction to argue for the supremacy of the mind, Hegel employed it to establish the reality of the Absolute. The dialectic process of Hegel exhibits a triadic movement. This is a movement from thesis to antithesis and finally to synthesis, after which the synthesis becomes a new thesis and so on. The human mind, then, moves dialectically, constantly embracing an ever-increasing scope of reality which discovers the truth of anything only after discovering its relation to the whole, to the Idea. According to Hegel, the Idea in its wholeness, the Absolute Idea, is eternal and was self-existing before the realm of Nature or finite minds came into being. This Absolute Idea is what religions refer to as God. But Hegel was not referring to a Being separate from the world of nature. As he puts it, Nature represents the Idea "outside itself." That is to say, Nature is the rationality of the Idea in external form.

But there are not two separate entities, Idea and Nature. Ultimate reality is a single organic and dynamic whole. The distinction between the Idea as "behind" all things on the one hand and Nature on the other, is simply to distinguish between the "inner" and the "outer" aspects of the self-same reality. Nature, in short, is the antithesis of the thesis Idea. Our thought moves dialectically from the rational (Idea) to the non-rational (Nature). The concept of Nature leads our thought finally to a synthesis represented by the unity of Idea and Nature in the new concept of Spirit or Mind.

This is an example of "Idealism," which the European thinkers quickly abandoned in favor of "Positivism." Indeed, they were right in abandoning it. This kind of philosophy is purely intellectual and has nothing to do with the practical affairs of human life.

But the leaders of Positivism, in their revolt against the God of the Church and the godhead of "Absolute Idea," did not move toward anything better. They ended by making the phenomenal world, or Nature, their god. But what is this Nature, which, according to them, has created the mind and imprints reality on the mind? Is this some well-defined being? Is it the universe as a whole? Or is it the various "things" and their shapes and movements? Does it have an existence independent of the human concepts concerning it? Or is it what our senses tell us it is?

Again, did it "create" the human intellect out of nothing? How is it that it created intellect in man but not in animals or in plants? Does Nature have a will and a power to make decisions, so that it singled out human beings for the bestowal of this gift of reason?

Again, if its reality is manifested in human thought, how can we say that it does not depend on the existence of the human mind? How is it that this Nature is the "Creator" of the human mind, while it makes its appearance nowhere except in the human mind?

Thus, these philosophers present us with a thousand unanswered questions — and they point to Nature. What is this Nature? Is it matter in the universe? What is the nature of this matter? They themselves admit they do not know what this thing, which they term "matter" and consider to be something permanent, really is. When matter transforms it becomes energy. So is energy Nature because it is matter? Or is matter, in which energy expresses itself as objects possessing masses and shapes, the "Nature" of these philosophers? In which of the two states, mass or energy, does it create the human mind, since this "creator" itself remains perpetually in motion, transforming from particles to energy, from energy to objects, from objects to particles, and from particles to energy? During these transformations, at which stage does it impart life and consciousness? When did this "god" acquire the power of creation? In which of its states?

And if this Nature "imprints the reality on the human mind," why on the human mind alone? Does it not speak so that all living beings hear it? Does it imprint the reality on the minds of mules, donkeys, parrots, and monkeys, or not? And is the reality that it imprints on the mind of a parrot or a monkey the same reality that it imprinted on the minds of August Comte and Karl Marx?

Again, if Nature imprints reality on the human mind, does it imprint the correct reality? Did not this reality and this mind decide that the earth was the center of the universe, and then again that the earth is but a small planet, moving around the sun? Did not this imprinted reality and the mind assert that matter and all objects are mere sensory perceptions and that matter is nothing but a product of mind? And did it not assert that the mind is but a product of matter?

Which of these contradictory intellectual judgements are the realities imprinted on the human mind by Nature? Does one observe that it makes mistakes in its imprints? Or is it the human mind that makes mistakes? If so, is it not then an independent and active agent?

How can the positivists assert that it is nothing more than what this Nature has made it to be?

We shall leave the discussion of the origin of life, its manifestations and secrets, to a later chapter in this book, when we shall discuss this subject in the context of Islamic concepts and other concepts. Rather than discuss the origin of life and its secrets here, we merely ask: What is this "god" which the philosophers of Materialism are trying to present to us? In terms of our experiences, ideas, or point of view, we do not find in it anything solid and clear to hold on to. One wonders why anyone would adopt this "idol," seeing that it is neither concrete to the touch, fixed for the sight, nor even firm as an idea? And, praise be to Allah, we are not running away from the Church! We cannot help but shudder in utter disgust at the narrow mentality of Karl Marx and Engels in their distorted perception of the life of mankind, and of man's motivations and field of actions. They have imprisoned man's scope within the mouse-hole of the "the factors of production." Think of all the great forces of the physical universe and their miraculous harmony in producing the exact conditions suitable for human life and human endeavors, and think of the special place that human beings occupy in the scheme of existence, and then think of how Marx and Engels turned their backs upon all this greatness and beauty to hide their heads within the narrow confines of economics and factors of production, not merely as the goal and motivation for human activity, but as the First Cause, the Creator God, and the Controlling Lord. One can only throw up one's hands in utter contempt and disgust at the pettiness of their mentality.

After mentioning all this, we return to the point that this entire calamity, from beginning to end, befell the peoples of Europe only because the Church and the Councils deviated from the divinely-revealed concept. This left no choice for the European thinkers but to try to run away from the Church and its God. We thank Allah Most High that the divinely-revealed Islamic concept has remained pure and there was no "Church" to tamper with it. The sort of conflict, which in Europe gave rise to all this metaphysical and speculative trash, never occurred in Islamic civilization, because there can be no conflict between the Islamic concept and human reason or human experience.

We proclaim that the Islamic concept leaves a vast field of activity for human reason and scientific experimentation. It does not put any obstacles in front of reason for doing research and for engaging in contemplation in order to discover the universe and its workings. Indeed, the Islamic concept encourages and inspires it to engage in such research. Again, it does not stop scientific experimentation, but counts it as a necessary function of man's role as Allah's deputy on earth. We appreciate the great blessing and favor of Allah upon us in giving us this concept and keeping it secure from human interpolation and interference.

CHAPTER IV

The Permanent Realities

And so, set your face [surrender your whole being and purpose] toward the [one, ever- true] faith, turning away from all that is false in accordance with the natural disposition that Allah has instilled into man. No change (let there be) in what Allah has created: that is the ever-true faith. But most people do not know (*Al-Rum* 30:30).

From the basic characteristic of the Islamic concept that is, its divine origin, proceed all the other characteristics. As this concept has been revealed by the Creator, man's obligation in relation to it is to receive it with an open mind, respond to it with a willing heart, adapt to it, and apply its teachings to the affairs of his life. One must realize that the Islamic concept is neither a product of human thought, nor a response to some particular environment, nor valid only for a particular period of time, nor has it sprung from any earthly cause. It is a pure gift of guidance from the Creator as a mercy for mankind.

This characteristic of divine origination implies another very important characteristic. The Islamic concept contains certain unchangeable realities, so that all development and changes in the Islamic society must be within the framework of these permanent realities.

The "constituents" and "values" of the Islamic concept are permanent and unchangeable, whereas the "styles" and "forms" of societies and ways of doing things may change. All the changes in the outward forms of practical life, however, remain under the firm and fixed fundamentals and values of this concept.

This does not mean a "freezing" of thought and action. On the contrary the Islamic concept not only permits but encourages movement and change as long as they are within its own framework and around its fixed axis.

A little observation and thought will convince anyone that this characteristic, i.e movement within an orbit around a fixed axis, is a characteristic of all of Allah's creation, not merely of the Islamic concept. Some examples of this follow.

Matter, whether in the form of particles or in the form of energy is subject to the law of conservation, yet it is always in motion and changes its form and appearance.

The atom consists of a nucleus and some electrons that revolve around it in fixed orbits.

Every planet has an orbit, and every star has a course. They all move in an orderly fashion, within a particular system.

The "humanity" of a human being with a breath of divine spirit blown into his frame, which makes him superior to all other creatures around him, is a fixed reality. "Humanity" or "human nature" is found in every human being, although each human being goes through various stages, from an embryo to an old man or woman, and through various social roles, advancing or regressing, in proportion to his nearness or distance from his "human nature." Yet none of those changes and developments take him outside the essence of his "human nature," with all the desires, powers, and capacities inherent in that nature.

The inclination of man to change the existing conditions of his environment in order to improve it is also a permanent reality. This desire is in the depth of his nature and is a product of his position as the deputy of Allah on earth because this responsibility requires the control and development of earthly resources. The expressions of this desire, however, vary according to time and place.

Thus the characteristic of "movement within a fixed boundary around a fixed axis" seems to be a deep property of all of Allah's creation, and it is also clearly exhibited in the nature of the Islamic concept.

We present here in a summary fashion a few examples of the permanent constituents and values of this concept that may be considered as the "fixed axis" around which the Islamic system revolves. The following are at least ten of such permanent realities:

1) Whatever is related to Allah — and He is the axis of the Islamic concept — has a fixed meaning, i.e there is no scope for change or development here. This relates to the existence of Allah, His eternity, His Oneness, His power and dominion over His creation, the absolute freedom of His will, and each of His attributes operating within the universe, on the earth, and among human beings.

2) The entire universe, comprised of objects and living beings, is Allah's creation and His origination. Allah Most High willed its existence and it came into being. Nothing animate or inanimate in this universe had or has any share in creating, managing or controlling any part of the universe, or a share in any of the Divine attributes.

3) All of Allah's creation, that is, the objects and living beings, including all human beings among whom are the messengers of Allah, are in a relationship of servitude to their Creator, who alone is the Master. As creatures of Allah, everything and everyone is His servant, without possessing any part of the attributes of divinity. In this relationship of servitude to their Creator, they are all equal.

4) Action without faith in Allah is just as useless as faith without action. Belief in Allah, including the attributes that He has ascribed to Himself, and in His angels, His books, His messengers, and in the Final Judgement, whereby good and evil are appropriately recompensed, is a precondition for meritorious actions. Their acceptance by Allah depends on this faith in some form. Without this faith, actions are meaningless from their very inception, incapable of acquiring any value, rejected, and neither taken into account nor accepted by Allah.

5) In the sight of Allah only Islam is the true religion and Allah does not accept any other faith or way of life from people. The meaning of Islam is to worship Allah alone, to ascribe Divine attributes to no one but to Allah alone, and then to submit to His commands and be pleased with His judgements in human affairs and with His prescribed way of life embodied in the Shari'ah. Islam and only Islam is the religion with which the Creator is pleased.

6) Man, as a species, is the noblest of all the creatures on earth, because he is the deputy of Allah on earth in the sense that to him belong the control and management of this earth and whatever it contains, and because there is no material value on earth that can be raised higher than the value of man or for which man can be sacrificed.

7) All the people on earth came from one origin, and hence, in this regard, they are all equal. They acquire merit and rank with respect to each other through their faith, consciousness of Allah, and good deeds. Other criteria of distinction among people such as place of birth, family, wealth, nationality, class, and race, have no value in the estimation of Allah and His religion.

8) The ultimate purpose of man's existence is the worship of Allah, in the sense of complete obedience to Allah alone. Among the requirements of complete obedience is to respond to His and only His commands in the affairs of life, whether these affairs are big or small, and out of love for Him to direct every intention, every vibration of one's heart, and every action toward Him and Him alone. To be His

deputy on earth is the way of life and the religion for man, because the way of life and the religion are equivalent expressions of one reality.

9) In Islam, the basis of human groupings is belief and adherence to the way of Allah, not ethnicity, or nationality, or country, or race, or class, or economic and political interests, or any other earthly cause.

10) The life of this world is a test of belief and action, and the life in the Hereafter is a product of accounting and reward. Man is tried and examined every moment of his earthly life in his movements and deeds, in his reaction to whatever reaches him of good and bad or of benefit and harm, all of which comes from Allah, Who is the final Judge.

All of these values and norms of the Islamic concept are permanent, not subject to change or evolution. They are fixed, and the appearances, manners, and modes of individual lives move within their frame of reference and evolve in connection with them. Their meanings are to be realized in developing every institution of Islamic society, in every relationship within that society, and in every organization of peoples' affairs, individual as well as collective, under all conditions and environments.

As the circumstances of a living society expand, so does the scope within which the meaning of these norms and values are expressed. And as the field of human knowledge expands, the varieties of expression for these permanent values and norms also enlarge. But the principles remain fixed, and all these varieties of expression are governed in their application by these principles.

To illustrate this point, let us consider the permanent reality that man is the deputy of Allah on earth. This reality is expressed in various forms. It is expressed when man tills the land to produce food, and it is expressed when man smashes the atom or sends satellites into space to investigate the earth's atmosphere or other planets. All such activities from one end of the spectrum to the other, as well as whatever may come in the future, are various expressions of man's vicegerency on this earth. While the varieties and scope of these expressions may increase and expand, the reality of man's vicegerency on earth remains fixed and unchanged. Its permanent nature demands that no man should be denied the dignity belonging to him of being Allah's vicegerent on earth and sharing with all other human beings this honor in the way prescribed by Allah, and that his value should not be sacrificed for the sake of increasing material production or for making spaceships. Man, every man, is the master of the satellites and the master of material production.

Or consider the reality that the purpose of man's life is to worship

Allah. This is expressed in all his actions directed toward Allah, and human actions are unlimited. The varieties of human actions grow and expand with the growing and expanding demands of his vicegerency. Similarly, the meaning of worship is attained when man implements Allah's injunctions in the affairs of his life, and such affairs are unlimited. They also expand with the growing and expanding demands of his vicegerency. But the reality of the ultimate purpose of man's existence remains fixed and does not change. If a man does not direct all his affairs toward Allah, and does not implement the injunctions of Allah in his life, he falls short of his essential duty and removes himself from the ultimate purpose of his existence, so that, in the estimation of Allah and the believers, his actions become null and void, neither acceptable nor capable of being set aright.

Thus, room for the expression and application of these values and norms expands and the forms of expression multiply, while they remain fixed and unchanged as constituents of the Islamic concept.

An advantage of this permanence in the constituents and norms of the Islamic concept is that the movement of mankind and its development remain guided rather than becoming random and chaotic, as occurred in the life of Europe when it loosened the knots of transcendent belief and ended in a miserably lost situation. With all its deceptive luster and false glamour, Europe hides within its fold bewilderment, defeat, and despair.

Another value of fixed norms and standards is that man can refer to them whatever occurs to him in feelings, thoughts, and concepts, and all that reaches him from his surroundings, changing environments, and connections. He can weigh them in the invariant balance of the Islamic concept to see whether they are near or far from the truth and from goodness. Thereby he lives always within secure boundaries, safe from temptations to wander away into the wilderness of speculations, with fixed stars to show the direction and signposts to mark the way.

Another value of a permanent "standard" for human thought is that one can organize one's ideas with reference to it and not be swayed by emotions and desires. If such a fixed standard did not exist, how would one be able to refer to anything at all? If belief and values were to change with human thought, wherever it happened to go, and with the conditions of life, whatever they might become, how would it be possible to have any control and any stability, since human thought and living conditions change continually.

For the sanity of the human mind and the security of human life the movement of our thoughts and actions must remain within the parameters of orbit established by our Creator around a fixed axis, which itself remains firm in the place created by Allah and does not move. This is how this whole universe is organized, from the atoms to the galaxies, without any exceptions to this rule.

The need for a fixed standard and unchangeable norms was never more apparent than it is today, because people have abandoned fixed principles and mankind is cut loose from its axis. Our situation resembles a planet that has broken loose from its orbit and threatens to collide with others, destroying itself as well as everything in its path.

"Had the truth followed their desires, the heavens and the earth and whoever is in them would have been corrupted" (*Al- Muminun* 23:71). Only the person not overpowered by the madness that has gripped mankind today is enlightened and wise. He looks at this miserable mankind, with its false concepts and systems, and realizes that the manners, morals, customs, and habits of people have all come off their moorings, that people are wandering aimlessly like madmen, pulling off their clothes and tearing them to pieces and moving feverishly from one hallucination to another. He observes mankind changing its concepts and beliefs in the same nonchalant manner as it changes its fashions in responding to the advertising of fashion houses. He sees mankind screaming with pain, laughing like a loon, running as if hunted, staggering about like a drunk, throwing away what is precious in its hand, and grasping at stones and dirt.

Hundreds of millions of humans have been destroyed and made into machines in order to increase production! Human norms have been sacrificed, together with the sense of beauty, morality, and higher values merely so that a handful of usurers, pornographers, producers of films, and directors of fashion houses may become rich.

Look at the faces of people and at their movements and clothes, and then peer into their minds and survey their thoughts, opinions, and desires, and you will find a people frightened, running away as if hunted down, and never stopping or resting long enough to see anything in its right and proper perspective. Indeed, they are running away, running from their own hungry, anxious, bewildered selves, unable to hold on to anything fixed or move in a permanent orbit around any stable axis. But the human soul cannot live by itself, separated from the reality of Allah's universe, nor can it be contented in such a state. Thus it becomes shattered and wanders aimlessly, finding neither rest nor peace.

Standing on the periphery of this miserable mankind is a gang of exploiters whose sole aim is to profit from other peoples' miseries and confusion. These gangsters consist of usurers, film producers, manufacturers of fashions, and publishers of pornographic books and magazines. Whenever they sense that mankind has had enough, has begun to realize its mistake, and is about to find an orbit and a fixed axis, they prod it on toward more madness and confusion. This gang, shouting slogans of progress and liberation, without bounds and limits, shoves mankind with both hands toward still greater chaos. What a crime, what a horrible crime this is against the whole of mankind and especially against the current generation!

As we explained earlier, the notion of perpetual "progress" or advancement in all values and culture is contrary to the very basis of the universe and of nature. Secondly, from this idea stems a disturbance in human affairs from which there is no refuge, because it justifies any concept, value, or system merely because it comes later in time. The sort of reasoning that whatever is more recent is ipso facto more advanced is absurd and should not be employed for judging a concept, a way of life, a value, or a system. Rather, weight should be given only to the constituents and elements of a system and way of life, and not to the epoch in which it appears.

We know that European thought, in its flight from the Church and in its intense desire to be rid of this yoke, went to an extreme in its denial of "absolutes" and in its affirmation of "change" by denying the very concept of religious faith and revealed law. This was perhaps inevitable when the "absolutes" of the time were manmade and obviously flawed.

We know the road that European thought followed and have described it in some detail in an earlier chapter. We should not be too harsh in condemning the historical course that it took, because this wrong and blameworthy course was merely a reaction to a distorted belief, which from the very first moment of its inception was mixed up with paganism and mythology. At the same time, European thinkers and scientists also had to face a corrupt and tyrannical Church which imposed conceptual nonsense, in the name of its absolute and fixed faith, on thought, science, and people generally.

Though we should not judge too harshly the course of Western thought forced upon it by the tyranny of the Church, we must be clear about its error in going to the other extreme of revolt against all fixed principles, permanent values, and absolute truths by embracing the notion of perpetual change and continual progress in a universe devoid of anything absolutely true or permanently valid. This position is not scientifically valid, but is rather a violent reaction to the tyranny of the Church.

Darwin, who introduced the idea of evolution in the development of living beings, only touched the superficial aspects of life, without penetrating into its origin in the Will that brought life into being. Even if we suppose this theory to be correct, despite the axes that already are cutting at its very roots,[1] all the supporting evidence merely indicates that evolution is following a path determined by a transcendent Will, without any role for randomness or chance. Evolution is one of the laws of motion operating in this universe, and, as we stated earlier, the natural laws governing motions within the universe are within fixed orbits around fixed axes.

In any case, neither "the scientific method" nor "factual truths" guided the thoughts of Darwin. He did not guide us toward the secret of life nor did he give a scientific explanation for its appearance. He was trying his best to avoid any reference to God. A scientific mind would immediately recognize that the existence of life implies the existence of the One who invented it. And the direction of its development in harmony with its environment implies that its Originator had a Will and a plan, was aware of what He was doing, and was capable of translating His Will into the reality of existence. But Darwin could not acknowledge this, because he had revolted against the Church and was running away from the God of the Church. He therefore ascribed the evolution of life forms to "Nature," which, according to him, has limitless powers. He then tried to give the false impression that nothing, absolutely nothing, is fixed and permanent. All his research was confined, however, to the development of life forms after they had already emerged, and so in no case could have been applied universally to everything.

The Marxist school is the most fantastic among the "objectivist" schools of philosophy in opposing the idea of "movement within a stable orbit around a fixed axis" in human affairs, although Marxism acknowledges its validity in the material world. What then is the main support of its claim of continual "progress?" Muhammad Al-Bahi answers this question in the following excerpts from his book quoted above, *The New Islamic Thought and Its Connection with Modern Imperialism* (pp. 311-315):

"Marx employed the dialectic of the principles of contradiction introduced by the German philosophers Fichte and Hegel before him. But, while they employed it in the realm of concepts and ideas, Marx employed this principle in the field of "economics" in relation to the history of societies.

"In this view every 'thing' has its opposite and thus every thing annihilates itself. This is the general principle of contradiction, but

---

[1] Refer to Julian Huxley: *The Challenges of Modern Science to Human Action and Belief*, Chatto and Windus, London, 1931. [See also *Clinging to A Myth: The Story Behind Evolution*, American Trust Publications, 1991. Editor]

Marx applies it to the annihilation of classes that support 'capitalism,' just as those classes were annihilated which pre-dated the capitalistic system. The monarchs and feudal systems collapsed, according to Marx, because of their inherent contradictions. Thus will the new capitalistic system collapse by producing its opposite or contradiction, the communistic system, which will have but one class of workers.

"According to this logic, the principle of contradiction does not stop after producing the opposite of a 'thing,' but continues onwards by a synthesis of the two, which brings about a new 'thing,' which again produces its opposite, and so on. But, contrary to its own logic, Marxism expects that after the communistic system comes into being it will not collapse by producing its opposite.

"Adopting the Hegelian principle of contradiction, Marxism explains that everything contains two opposing forces: if one of them is termed 'the thesis,' the other is 'the antithesis.' These two opposites annihilate each other; but out of this mutual destruction is produced the synthesis of the thesis and antithesis. The synthesis is again a new thing, which produces its opposite and a new synthesis, and so on, ad infinitum.

"Now Marxism takes this principle and applies it to human history, arguing that communism, as a social system, is at a higher level than any previous social system. The hierarchical system, with the king's lords on one side and the subjects on the other, produces a conflict between these two classes and is annihilated to produce the synthesis, which is the feudal system. The feudal system, with the land-lords on one side and the peasants on the other, produces a conflict between these two classes and is in turn annihilated to give birth to the synthesis, which is the capitalistic system. Now, says Marxism, the capitalistic system, with the capitalists on one side and the workers on the other, will produce a conflict between these two classes and will in its turn be annihilated to give birth to the synthesis, namely, the communistic system consisting of but one class.

"The question is why should the principle of contradiction stop its operation at this stage? Why should not the communist system, by the inexorable logic of this principle, produce its opposite, then a conflict of the two, and then a new system?

"Furthermore, according to Marxism, every new synthesis produces a superior social system. Hence, the feudal system is superior to monarchy, capitalism is better than feudalism, and finally communism is better than capitalism.

"This claim that every system is superior to its predecessor is tooted very loudly by the communist propagandists, and many simple-minded persons fall for this propaganda believing that whatever comes later in time is superior to what has gone before and that they will be working for a world that will be better than the one that they found.''

From the above it ought to be very clear that Marxism is founded on dogmatic assertions and has nothing to do with facts or historical reality. To begin with, the principle of contradiction as formulated by Fichte and Hegel is a purely intellectual construct, having no roots in fact. Marx takes this principle and applies it to history, disregarding all elements or factors of human societies except the economic, thus sparing himself the trouble of demonstrating the validity of this principle in other aspects of societal developments. Next, he takes the economic element, which despite its importance is by no means the sole factor in the development of human societies, and traces the history of a single group of people, the Europeans, in an extremely simplified fashion by emphasizing only a few aspects of it. How could this one man, living for a limited span of time in a particular place and society, comprehend the infinitely many causes and influences operating on millions of people over several centuries? But he chooses one aspect of this complex and multi-dimensional history, throwing away all other aspects, and then issues a dogmatic judgement that what came later in time is better than what came before it. Furthermore, he does not even try to be consistent with himself, but abruptly brings the historical process to a complete stop as soon as it reaches communism. Why should the historical process stop here, one may ask, depriving mankind of better and superior systems that ought to follow communism? In addition to this obvious incoherence in the very foundation of this dogmatic system based on wishful thinking, there is a madness in the ordering of values which is not limited only to its followers but has also gripped its opponents both in Europe and in America.

This madness is the craze to discard everything from the past and to embrace everything new, to remove all restrictions in the way of fulfilling desires and passions, and to mock everything traditional whether in the moral or in any other sphere. For the Marxist regimes, this madness is pre-planned and has a definite objective.

To advocate continual change is merely an excuse for doing whatever one wants to do. In particular, when it is advocated by ''the State'' it means that the government wants an excuse to take away from people all the fixed reference points and established values against which the actions of the government may be judged. When there are no established rights or fixed constitutional guarantees, where can the people find any refuge?

While the government enjoys the freedom to deal with individuals as it pleases, it encourages individuals to indulge in their desires and to pursue bodily pleasures as a replacement for their usurped rights, usurped values, and usurped freedoms. On the one hand this madness justifies complete license for animalistic lusts, and on the other complete license for dictatorship, one in exchange for the other. And this deal is transacted between the parties, in technical jargon, the "people" and the "state."

In communist societies this deal is rooted in a discrete "philosophy" and "scientific" system, namely, the "principle of contradiction" and "dialectic materialism." And yet this "scientific" system dares to declare that religion is the opiate of the masses invented to serve the ruling cliques.

The characteristics of having "permanent realities" and fixed values in the Islamic system is a guarantee that the Islamic society will "move within a fixed orbit around a fixed axis" and that Islamic thought and action will be consonant with the system of the universe in general, thereby remaining immune to the evil perturbations of man's whims, which would destroy even the universe if it were to follow man's ever changing desires.

This characteristic of Islam keeps Islamic thought and Islamic society safe from the kind of madness that has gripped Marxist thought and socialist societies. Indeed, since the day they let themselves loose from the anchor of faith, Western thought and Western societies in general have been affected by this madness, even though they are opposed to Marxism on religious and political grounds.

The characteristic of "permanence" in the beliefs and values of Islam produces a deep sense of security in the conscience of the Muslim as well as in the Muslim society. This sense of security comes from the knowledge that the orbit and the axis of the Muslim's life are firm. A Muslim understands that his every step is a step forward, directed toward a goal; that his movements are connected in time, stretching from yesterday through today toward tomorrow; and that his action is purposeful, ascending sequentially toward spiritual heights, under the firm guidance of Allah's will.

Finally, the unchanging character of Islamic values guarantees for the Muslim certain inalienable rights and basic freedoms to which he and the judges and governors over him can and must refer. The governors are not free to change the constituents and the values of Islam, nor to lure the people toward lusts and physical pleasures in order to take their minds off the existing political oppression or financial ineptitude.

The Islamic concept stands firm on the basis of the policy that for the life of man there are but two states of being, and that these states are independent of time and place. Their respective values are intrinsic to them, because they are determined by Allah's just balance, which remains unaffected by temporal and spatial changes in man's condition.

There are only two possibilities for the life of a people, no matter in what time and place they live. These are the state of guidance or the state of error, whatever form the error may take; the state of truth or the state of falsehood, whatever may be the varieties of falsehood; the state of light or the state of darkness, regardless of the shades of darkness; the state of obedience to the Divine guidance or the state of following whims, no matter what varieties of whims there may be; the state of Islam or the state of *jahiliyyah*, without regard to the forms of *jahiliyyah*; and the state of belief or the state of unbelief, of whatever kind. People live either according to Islam, following it as a way of life and a socio-political system, or else in the state of unbelief, *jahiliyyah*, whim, darkness, falsehood, and error.

> The *din* of Allah is Islam (submission to His will) (*Ale 'Imran* 3:19).

> And if anyone seeks a religion other than *Al-Islam* (submission to Allah), never will it be accepted from him (*Ale 'Imran* 3:85).

> After the truth, what is there but error? (*Yunus* 10:32).

> And now We have set you on a clear way (*shari'ah*) of (Our) command; so follow it, and follow not the whims of those who do not know (*Al-Jathiyah* 45:18).

> This is My straight path, so follow it. Follow not other ways, lest you be parted from His way (*Al-An'am* 6:153).

> Allah is the Protecting Friend of those who believe. He brings them out of darkness into light. As for those who disbelieve, their patrons are false deities. They bring them out of light into darkness (*Al-Baqarah* 2:257).

> Then if any persons do not judge by what Allah has revealed, they are disbelievers (*Al-Mai'dah* 5:47).

> Do they desire [to be ruled by] the pagan ignorance? But for

people who have inner certainty, who could be a better lawgiver than Allah? (*Al-Ma'idah* 5:50).

And if you have a dispute concerning any matter, refer it to Allah and the Messenger, if you are believers in Allah and the Last Day (*Al-Nisa* 4:59).

When this framework is firmly in place, then life in its thought, concept, practice, and system, can move within clear boundaries freely and flexibly. Man can then respond to every natural and healthy development, directed by the Islamic concept, which itself remains firm and strong.

The great value of this state of guidance is that the root of all the Muslim's concepts and ideas are firmly planted in his soul so that the Islamic life and the Muslim society can stand on the framework of the *din* erect and firm. At the same time this framework leaves sufficient space for the natural growth and development of ideas and feelings and of methodologies and institutions. It neither puts an iron jacket around the Muslim society, which the Church intended for Christian society during the Middle Ages, nor does it free the society from every restriction so it can behave like a meteor in the sky or like a herd of stampeding buffaloes. This latter analogy fits the recent history of Europe, culminating in the chaotic Marxist way of thinking.

This state of guidance was the very characteristic that kept the Muslim society cohesive and strong for more than a thousand years, in spite of being shaken, beaten, and savagely attacked by all kinds of external and internal enemies in every time and place. The weakness and decline in the Muslim societies did not start until they began to lose confidence in the unchangeability and perfection of the fundamentals of Islam, so that the enemies of Islam could succeed in convincing the Muslims to set aside the Islamic ideas and replace them with Western ideas.[2]

No doubt, any society will be subject to violent swings from one extreme to the other if it has no firm roots in reality and follows ever-changing ideas and concepts originating in limited human understanding based on guess work, speculation, and false hypotheses. Such a society inevitably will set up this speculative knowledge or its own changing whim as a false god and derive its values and standards from this new idol. Such a society can only remain confused in ideas, disturbed in conscience, fatigued in nerves, and aimless in life, with its entire foundation resting on the shaky ground of illusion.

---

[2] Refer to Muhammad Qutb, *Are We Muslims?*

This is exactly what happened to European societies after they broke their ties with every firm principle, and this is exactly what is afflicting the whole of mankind today. Not only Europeans, but all the societies of the world today are lost in a wilderness.[3]

Such a concept with permanent constituents and fixed values, must come from a source with firm knowledge and will, which sees every area and every direction, and from which the curves of the road are not hidden. Such a source necessarily does not decide something today to find out the next day that it was faulty and in error, nor is it affected by lust, nor are its decisions influenced by whims and desires. Once such a concept from such a source is firmly established, then there is no harm in movement, change, development, growth, and progress, because all this becomes desirable, secure, and natural, based on the principle of movement within an orbit around a fixed axis. The movement will then be guided and enlightened, will aim at achieving a noble purpose, and will proceed with steady, straight, and firm steps. This guarantees that the society will have a long, purposeful, and harmonious life.

There is no need for us to state that all this does not mean that the Islamic society is frozen in a strait jacket. This is very remote from the Islamic concept and sense of purpose.

"The movement within an orbit around a fixed axis" is not a "frozen" movement nor is the life of such a society devoid of change and progress. The main principle here is the "movement," because this is the main principle in the pattern of the universe. The Universe does not freeze or become still. To the contrary, it is always moving, changing, developing, and at every moment taking new forms, but it moves while conserving its mass and energy as mentioned earlier.

When we study the Western schools of thought and find that they are dominated by the ideas of absolute "progress," without referring back to some fixed principle, we should be aware of the historical circumstances that propelled Western thought in this direction. We ought to be aware of the resulting enmity, both deep and hidden, against all religion, which has penetrated this thought and colored its entire concept.

It is wrong to apply the methodologies and philosophies of Western thought to Islam, or to seek from it any help whatsoever for the discussion of Islamic subjects and history.

Some of us take something from Western thought, sometimes its methodology, sometimes its conclusions, and sometimes just a worn-out piece of paper, and then intermingle it with a discussion of Islam,

---

[3] Refer to *Al-Islam Wa Al-Mushkilat Al-Hadarah*.

or of its society, or its way of thought and concept. This is pure ignorance, and arrogance to boot, if it is dressed up as "scholarship." Sometimes there is even malice behind this ignorance and triviality.

Muhammad Asad (Leopold Weiss) says in his book, *Islam at the Crossroads*: "History tells us that all human culture and civilizations are organic entities and resemble living beings. They experience all the phases through which organic life is bound to pass: they are born, they have youth, ripe age, and at the end comes decay, like plants that wither and fall to dust. Cultures die at the end of their time and give room to other, freshly born ones.

"Is this the case with Islam? It would appear so at a first superficial look. No doubt, Islamic culture has had its splendid rise and its blossoming age, and it had the power to inspire men to great deeds and sacrifice. It transformed nations and changed the face of the earth, and later it stood still and became stagnant. And then it became an empty word, so that at present we witness its utter debasement and decay. But is this all?

"If we believe that Islam is not a mere culture among many others, not a mere outcome of human thoughts and endeavors, but a Law decreed by God Almighty to be followed by humanity at all times and everywhere, then one's perspective changes totally. If Islamic culture is or was the result of our following a revealed law, we can never admit that, like other cultures, it is chained to the lapse of time and limited to a particular period. What appears to be the decay of Islam is in reality nothing but the death and emptiness of our hearts which are too idle and too lazy to hear the eternal voice. No sign is available that mankind, in its present stature, has outgrown Islam. It has not been able to produce a better system of ethics than that expressed in Islam. It has not been able to put the idea of human brotherhood on a practical footing, as Islam did in its supra-national concept of *ummah*. It has not been able to create a social structure in which the conflicts and frictions among its members are as efficiently reduced to a minimum as in the social plan of Islam. And it has not been able to enhance the dignity of man, his feeling of security, his spiritual hope, and last, but surely not least, his happiness.

"In all these things the present achievements of the human race fall considerably short of the Islamic program. Where, then is the justification for saying that Islam is "out of date?" Is it only because its foundations are purely religious, and religious orientation is out of fashion today? But if we see that a system based on religion in the Islamic sense of *din* has been able to evolve a practical program of life more complete, more concrete, and more congenial to man's constitution than any other thing the human mind has been able to produce by way of reforms and proposals, is not precisely this a very weighty argument in favor of the enlightened, religious outlook?

"Islam, we have every reason to believe, has been fully vindicated by the positive achievements of man and indeed pointed them out as desirable long before they were attained. Equally, it has been vindicated by the shortcomings, errors, and pitfalls of human development, because it loudly and clearly warned against them long before mankind recognized them as errors. Quite apart from one's religious beliefs, there is, from a purely intellectual view-point, every inducement to follow confidently the practical guidance of Islam.

"We need not 'reform' Islam, as some Muslims think, for it is already perfect in itself. What we must reform is our attitude toward religion, our laziness, our self-conceit, our shortsightedness, in one word, *our* defects, and not some supposed defects of Islam.

"Islam, as a spiritual and social institution, cannot be 'improved.' In these circumstances, any change in its conceptions or its social organization caused by the intrusion of foreign cultural influences is in reality retrograde and destructive, and therefore to be deeply regretted. A change there must be, but a change from *within ourselves*, and it should go in the direction of Islam, and not away from it." [4]

We assert that the loss from intermingling Islam with Western secular thought is not merely that of the Muslims, but of all humanity. Humanity will lose the only remaining source of guidance from Allah Most High, by confounding its teachings, and by polluting, or rather poisoning, the clear, clean spring of Divine revelation. The whole of mankind will lose by being deprived of the firm and reliable source of reference in a world shaking in the winds of random thoughts, and in which corruption has appeared in the land and sea by what men have wrought by their own hands. There is no refuge for mankind except in this preserved and pure source coming directly from the Creator Himself.

Those who are trying to undermine the last refuge, in the name of reform and progress, or in the name of getting rid of medieval heritage or in some other name, are indeed the real enemies of mankind. These are the people who should be rejected and thrown out, not only by us, but by every other member of the human race!

They imagine that they are speaking in the name of "progressive" versus "reactionary" ideas, while in fact they are picking up the intellectual crumbs from European thinkers of the nineteenth or even eighteenth century. They have not yet even reached the twentieth

---

[4] Mohammed Asad, *Islam at the Crossroads*, Ashraf Publications, Lahore (1955), pp. 150-155.

century! They are at least fifty years behind the times. Many do not know that while they are still in prostration before the Marxist philosophy of dialectic materialism and its derivatives, and the Darwinian theory of evolution and its implications, there have appeared, in Europe itself, ideas and tendencies that are in opposition to Marxism and Darwinism. These people themselves are "reactionaries" while claiming to be "progressive." Real progress today is possible only if we recognize our obligation to return to the truths of religion, seeking from them certainty, comfort, and spiritual solace, after three centuries of confusion, pain, and spiritual bewilderment. If we, whom Allah has saved from those historical forces that afflicted Western thought and led it into a wilderness of confusion, now jump into this wilderness without any historical or intellectual reason, we must be considered the worst of fools. Such an act of stupidity would not be a loss to ourselves alone, but would be a great loss for the whole of the human race, because we would have lost that source of reference to which we might return one day to find therein peace of mind and spiritual comfort after anxiety and fatigue.

In this serious situation confronting mankind today, we should recognize the great responsibility that rests on our shoulders, not only in relation to ourselves, but to the rest of mankind.

CHAPTER V

Comprehensiveness

"And all things We have kept in a clear register" (*Ya Sin* 36:12)

The third characteristic of the Islamic concept is its comprehensiveness. This characteristic also proceeds from its first characteristic, its Divine origin. It comes from the Creator Himself and not from any man, and comprehensiveness is a characteristic of what Allah has made.

When we look at a human being, we see that his existence is circumscribed by time and space. He comes into being from non-existence at some instant in time and then he perishes at a later instant. He occupies a limited amount of space. These limitations of time and space apply equally to a single human being, to a generation, and to the entire human species. Man is also limited in his knowledge, experience, and comprehension. As an individual he starts to learn from scratch after his birth, and the sum total of his knowledge and experience is limited by his life span and by the places he occupies. Man as a whole is limited in his knowledge and experiences by his sensory and mental apparatus, which are given to him for performing a certain task, that of being the vicegerent of Allah on this planet. In addition to this, he is subject to his inclinations, desires, and emotions.

When a human being tries to construct a metaphysical concept or a system of life through his own efforts, this concept or system cannot be comprehensive. It can only be partially valid, good for one time and place but not for other times and other places, and appropriate for one set of circumstances but not for another. Futhermore, even in tackling a single problem, he is incapable of looking at it from all possible sides and of taking into consideration all the consequences of this proposed solution, since every problem extends in space and

85

time and is connected with precedents and antecedents beyond the scope of observation and comprehension of human beings.

We therefore conclude that no philosophy and no system of life produced by human thought can have the characteristic of "comprehensiveness." At most, it can cover a segment of human life and can be valid for a temporary period. Because of its limited scope, it is always deficient in many respects, and because of its temporariness it is bound to cause problems that require modifications and changes in the original philosophy or system of life. Peoples and nations basing their social, political, and economic systems on human philosophies are forever confronted with contradictions and "dialectics." The history of European peoples is an example of such a process.

Allah Most High has ordained that this be so, and He took upon Himself the responsibility of providing mankind with the basis of true belief. Therefore, the belief system of Islam and the way of life that proceeds from it are free from the defects, contradictions, and confusions inherent in man-made philosophies and sytems. For the same reason, comprehensiveness is a characteristic of the Islamic concept.

In what follows, we provide a few examples of the teachings of Islam to illustrate the characteristic of comprehensiveness inherent in its concept.

First and most basic is the explanation of the totality of existence, including its beginning, its functioning after the beginning, the various changes that take place in it, its growth and development, and its administration, governance, and regulation. The Islamic concept ascribes all this to the Will of the Eternal, the Absolute, Divine Being, Who is All-Powerful and Absolutely Free. He is the Originator of this universe and everything in it, both animate and inanimate, and the Originator of every movement, change, and development that take place within the universe. These changes occur according to a measure determined by Him alone. This Divine Being then, the Originator and the Creator, Allah Most High, is the One Who originated the universe and it is He alone who brings into existence any change or any new thing as He deems proper.

The great truth of the Oneness of God (*tawhid*) is the primary and foremost constituent of the Islamic concept. A large portion of the Qur'an is devoted to the exposition of this sublime truth. We do not intend to discuss this subject here in any detail, because we will take it up again in the chapters entitled "Dynamism" and "Oneness." Here we will limit ourselves to a brief description of the significance and value of this belief.

Indeed, this concept not only provides us with an intellectually satisfying explanation of the origin of the universe and of its functioning and the new developments that take place in it, but also gives a reasonable explanation of the appearance of "life" in inert matter. No doubt, life is entirely different from dead matter, something great, something strange, and something planned and intended to be. The distance between inert matter and living matter is almost as great as the distance between nothingness and existence.

Man is first confronted with the existence of a universe that he feels the need to understand and explain. Next, the universe confronts him with its regularities, balances, and wonderful designs, which defy any hypothesis of chance. If one were to compute the probability of any of these harmonious and well-designed natural constructions, which are all around us, on the basis of pure chance, it would be negligible. If we were to further compute the probability of the regularities of all the things we perceive, the probability would be virtually equal to zero. Thus the universe, its existence, and its intricate harmonies and well-balanced designs, must be explained by a concept other than the concept of chance.

The presence of life raises some very deep questions that need to be answered by human beings in their quest for the knowledge of truth. Some of these questions are as follows:

How did life originate from dead matter? How has it continued to exist? How do all the delicate balances and harmonies, computed to the minutest degree, without which life as we know it cannot be supported, exist on this planet?

The Islamic concept alone possesses the capability to give satisfactory answers to all these questions and to explain the harmonies in the design of the universe. It has the capability to answer questions concerning the origin of this universe and of whatever takes place in it, as well as the origin of life in inanimate matter and its continued flourishing. We need not run away from any question raised, nor hide behind dogmatic assertions, nor need we dodge the question, nor take refuge in ascribing it to some undefined concept such as "nature."

Indeed, the distance between nothingness and existence is so great that it cannot be traversed by human intellect. How is it that there is a universe? How is it that "nature" exists, if by this term is meant the physical world? How can the human intellect traverse this vast distance, except by ascribing the existence of the universe to the will of the Creator Who says to a thing "Be" and it is? Anyone who would not acknowledge the will of the Creator as the sole agent of creation would be completely at a loss to find an explanation for the existence of this world.

The chaotic speculations of the philosophers throughout human history bear testimony to this elemental statement.

The distance between inert matter and the living cell is second only to the distance between nothingness and existence. Again, human intellect is not able to traverse this distance except by ascribing the origination of life to the will of the Creator, Who initiates what He desires and originates new creations. Yes, it is the will of Allah, ''Who gives to everything its form and thereafter guides it'' (*Ta ha* 20:50).

Human intellect, indeed the whole of human nature, finds this answer agreeable. There is no denying the fact that life came to inanimate matter from a source other than matter itself, since what was absent from matter could not have come from it. Nor is it possible to say that life is one of the properties of matter but was hidden within it. How is it that life remained hidden within matter for an uncountable number of years, only to appear at a known instant, without an outside agent, and without a purpose and a goal? We here close the discussion concerning the universe and life. This topic will be discussed, insha'Allah, more thoroughly in its proper place in the second volume of this work.

Let us return to the characteristic of comprehensiveness, which is manifested in the Islamic teaching that everything in this universe must ultimately be ascribed to Allah. In their relation to anything and everything, His will, His power, His administration, and His planning are comprehensive. Let us refer to some verses of the Qur'an that shed light on this topic.

We have created everything in due measure (*Al Qamar* 54:49).

And He created everything and determines its nature (*Al-Furqan* 25:2).

With Him everything is according to a measure (*Al-R'ad* 13:8).

Moses said: ''Our Lord is the One Who gave to each (Created) thing its form and nature, and, further, gives it guidance'' (*Ta Ha* 20:50).

Indeed, Our word to a thing, when We desire it, is that We say to it, ''Be,'' and it is (*Al-Nahl* 16:40).

Indeed, your Lord is Allah Who created the heavens and the earth in six periods, and is established on the Throne (of Sovereignty). He covers the day with night in swift pursuit. The sun, the moon, and the stars are subservient to His command. Indeed the Creation and the command are His. Glorified be Allah the Sustainer of the Worlds (*Al-A'raf* 7:54).

And a sign for them is the night. We withdraw from it the daylight, and behold they are in darkness. The sun runs toward its destination. This is ordained by the Almighty, the All-Knowing. As for the moon, We have assigned for it phases until it returns like an old date-stalk. Neither can the sun overtake the moon, nor does the night outstrip the day. Each one swims in its own orbit (*Ya Sin* 36:37-40).

It is Allah Who has created the animals out of water. Among them are such as crawl on their bellies and such as walk on two legs and such as walk on four. Allah creates what He wills, for verily, Allah has power over everything (*Al-Nur* 24:45).

We made every living thing from water (*Al-Anbiya* 21:30).

It is Allah Who splits the grain and the date-stone, brings forth the living from the dead and brings forth the dead from the living. That is Allah; then how are you deluded and led away from the truth? He makes the dawn appear, and has made the night for resting, and the sun and moon for the reckoning (of time). Such is the judgement and ordering of the All-Mighty, the All- Knowing. It is He Who has appointed for you the stars, so that by them you might be guided in the darkness, whether on land or on sea. We thus explain Our signs for a people who have knowledge. It is He Who produced you from a single person; and then there is a place of sojourn and a place of departure. We detail our signs for a people who understand. It is He who sends down water from the sky. With it We bring forth the shoot of every plant, and then We bring forth the green leaf of it, producing from it grain heaped up (at harvest); and out of the palm tree, from the sheaths of it, dates thick- clustered, hanging low and near; and gardens of grapes, olives, and pomegranates, each similar (in kind) and yet different (in variety). Look upon their fruits when they begin to bear fruit and ripen! Surely in all this are signs for a people who believe (*Al-An'am* 6: 95-99).

According to the Islamic concept, even for the events whose immediate causes are apparent the ultimate cause and agent is the will of
Allah Most High.

> We created you; therefore why will you not testify? Have
> you considered the sperm-seed you cast forth? Is it you who
> create it, or are We the Creators? We have decreed among
> you death; We shall not be frustrated in changing your
> forms and making you to grow again in a fashion you do
> not know. You have known the first form of creation, so
> why will you not think about this? Have you considered
> the seed you sow in the soil? Do you cause it to grow, or
> are We the growers? If We willed, you would be left to
> wonder (and lament): "Verily, we are ruined! We have been
> deprived (of our livelihood)!" Have you considered the
> water you drink? Do you bring it down from the cloud, or
> do We send it down? If We willed, We could make it bitter.
> Why, Then, are you not thankful? Have you considered the
> fire you kindle? Do you grow the tree that feeds it, or do
> We grow it? We made it to remind you (of Us) and as a boon
> to all who are lost and hungry in the wilderness (*Al-Waqi'ah*
> 56:63-73).

We will not go any further in discussing this characteristic of
comprehensiveness in respect to Allah's Oneness because it will be
discussed more thoroughly, in a second volume of this series. We
conclude this discussion by saying that the Islamic concept of *tawhid*
(Oneness of the Creator) brings deep satisfaction and comfort to the
human heart and intellect. This concept of *tawhid* connects man's
being with the real causes operative in this universe, thus freeing man's
intellectual energies from being wasted in fruitless speculations and
in postulating causes that do not exist such as "nature" or "the
intellect" or the mythical entities that have been conjured up by the
polytheists and by philosophers throughout history. In the Islamic
concept of *tawhid* all causes operational in this universe and in life
ultimately originate in the hands of Allah the Almighty and are under
His control and authority. We shall take up this topic again in the
chapter dealing with "Dynamism."

On the one side is the reality of the Divine Being and of His
attributes, works, and characteristics, and on the other side is the
reality of His creation, with its own characteristics and attributes. The
Islamic concept deals comprehensively with both realities, the reality

and Oneness of the Divine Person being the primary and greater of the two, since all creation proceeds from Him. Creation includes the universe, life, and the human being. The Islamic concept speaks comprehensively about the reality of the universe, the reality of life, and the reality of man, covering such aspects as their origin, nature, properties, and interrelationships, as well as their relationship with the greater reality, the Divine Being.

The Islamic concept connects all these realities in such a coherent, natural, and logical sequence as appeals to man's intuition and intellect, indeed to the total personality of man, in a deeply satisfying manner. These descriptions intuitively are perceived as self-evident truths, which penetrate the human heart in the easiest possible manner.

Furthermore, all these truths are presented so comprehensively, accurately, and in such depth and detail that they do not require any addition from any other source. Indeed, the Islamic concept cannot accept any additions to it from other sources, for it is vaster, more comprehensive, more accurate, deeper, and more harmonious and perfect than any other concept.

The Islamic concept first suffered major corruption and distortion when a group of individuals, known in history as "Islamic philosophers," decided to borrow ideas and terminology from the Greek philosophers, especially theologians, and introduced them into the Islamic concept.

Now, the *pure* Islamic concept, with its perfection and comprehensiveness, breadth and depth, and soundness and harmony, naturally rejects any foreign element, even though this foreign element may be merely a technical "term" borrowed from foreign modes of thought, because each term has a historical context, carrying within it meanings and associations appropriate to its history. It is not possible completely to eliminate the historical connotations from the use of a term and to force upon it an entirely new meaning. The Islamic concept has its own terminology, appropriate to its nature and its message, and its actualization in history. For a human mind to savor its delicate flavor and to understand and appreciate its full meaning, it is necessary that we present its teachings in its own original terminology.

The primary objective of the Islamic concept is to inform people about their Lord, and to inform them of Allah's Person, of His glorious attributes, and of what pertains to Him alone as distinct from what pertains to His creation. It also informs them concerning His relationship with the universe and with people, and with all the worlds and all the peoples of the earth. The Qur'an speaks about all these matters at great length and in such a vivid and forceful fashion as to make the Person of God interact with the human soul in a living, active, and concrete relationship, surrounding it from all sides. The human soul remains linked with Him, never forgetting His presence and deriving inspiration and power from Him.

All praise is due to Allah, the Lord of the worlds, the Compassionate, the Merciful; the Master of the Day of Judgement (*Al-Fatihah* 1:2-4).

Allah, there is no deity but He, the Living, the Eternal. Slumber does not overtake Him nor does sleep. To Him belong all things in the heavens and on earth. Who is there who may intercede with Him except by His permission. He knows what is before them and what is behind them, and they do not comprehend anything of His knowledge except as He wills. His Throne is as wide as the heavens and earth and preserving them does not weary Him. And He is the All-High, the All-Mighty (*Al-Baqarah* 2:255).

Allah, there is no god but He, the Living, the Eternal. He has sent down upon you the Book with the truth, confirming what was before it, and He sent down the Torah and the Injil earlier, as guidance to the people, and He sent down the Criterion. As for those who reject Allah's signs, for them awaits a severe punishment. Allah is Almighty, the Lord of Retribution. Indeed, nothing whatever is hidden from Allah in the earth or in the heavens. It is He who forms you in wombs as He wills. There is no deity but He, the All-Mighty, the All-Wise (*Ale 'Imran* 3:2- 6).

Say: "O Allah! Master of dominion, You give dominion to whom You Will, and You take away dominion from whom You Will. You exalt whom You Will and You abase whom You will. In your hands is all good. Verily, over all things You have power. You cause the night to gain on the day and You cause the day to gain on the night. You bring forth the living from the dead and You bring forth the dead from the living. And You give sustenance to whomever You will without measure" (*Ale 'Imran* 3:26-27).

Say: "To whom belongs what is in the heavens and in the earth?" Say, "It belongs to Allah. He has prescribed for Himself mercy. He will surely gather you on the Day of Resurrection, concerning which there is no doubt. But those who have lost their (own) souls do not believe. To Him belongs whatsoever inhabits the night and the day, and He is the All-Hearing, the All-Knowing." Say: "Am I to take for my master anyone but Allah, the Creator of the heavens and the earth, when it is He Who gives nourishment but Himself needs none?" Say: "I have been commanded to be the first of those who submit (to Allah), with the command: 'Do not be among the polytheists'." Say: "Indeed, I would dread, were I thus to disobey my Lord, the punishment on that awesome Day." Upon him who shall be spared on that Day, He will indeed have bestowed His grace. And this will be a manifest triumph. And if Allah touches You with affliction, none can remove it but He, and if He touches you with good, He has power over all things. He is the Omnipotent over His servants, and He is the All-Wise, and the All-Aware. Say: "What could most weightily bear witness to the truth?" Say: "Allah is witness between me and you, and this Qur'an has been revealed to me, so that thereby I may warn you and all whom it may reach. Can you possibly bear witness that there are other gods besides Allah?" Say: "I do not so bear witness." Say: "He is the One God, and I truly am innocent of (your blasphemy of) joining others with Him" (*Al-An'am* 6:12-19).

Allah knows what every female bears, and by how much the wombs fall short or exceed. Everything with Him is in due proportion. He is the Knower of the Unseen and the Visible, the Great, the Exalted. It is the same (to Him) whether any of you conceals his thought or brings it into the open or whether he seeks to hide [his evil deeds] under the cover of night or walks [boldly] in the light of day, [thinking that] he has hosts of helping angels before him and behind him that could preserve him from whatever Allah may have willed. Allah does not change the condition of a people until they change what is within themselves. If Allah desires to afflict a people, there is no turning it back. Apart from Him, they have no protector. It is He who shows you the lightning, for fear and hope, and He builds up the clouds heavy with rain. Thunder proclaims His praise, and so do the angels, who are in awe of Him. He sends the thunderbolts and strikes with them whomever He wills. Yet people dispute concerning Allah, Who is mighty in power, despite all the evidence that He alone has the power to

continue whatever His unfathomable wisdom wills! His is
the call of the truth, and those whom they invoke instead
of Allah cannot respond to them in any way, [so that he who
invokes them] is like the man who stretches out his hands
toward water [hoping] that it will reach his mouth, though
it never does. The prayer of the unbelievers goes nowhere
but astray. All who are in the heavens and on earth prostrate
themselves, willingly or unwillingly, as do their shadows in
the morning and evenings. Say: "Who is the Lord of the
heavens and the earth?" Say: "It is Allah." Say: "Do you
then take (for worship) protectors other than Him, such as
have no power either for good or for harm to themselves?"
Say: "Are the blind and the seeing equal? Or are the darkness and the light equal?" Or do they (really) believe that
there are, side by side with Allah, other divine powers that
have created the like of what He creates, so that this act of
creation appears to them to be similar (to His)? Say: "Allah
is the Creator of everything, and He is the One who holds
absolute sway over all that exists" (*Al-R'ad* 13:8-16).

To Him belongs whatever is in the heavens and the earth,
and those who are in His presence are not too proud to do
Him service, nor do they grow weary. They glorify Him by
night and by day, without intermission. Some people have
taken gods from among earthly things or beings or ideas
that allegedly can raise the dead? Had there been in heaven
or on earth any gods other than Allah, both would surely
go to ruin. So glory be to Allah, the Lord of the Throne, far
above all that men may devise by way of definition! He shall
not be questioned as to what He does, but they shall be
questioned, and yet they choose to worship (imaginary)
deities other than him? "Bring proof! This is a reminder by
those who are with me, just as it was a reminder (voiced)
by those who came before me." Nay, most of them do not
know the truth, and so they are turning away (*Al- Anbiya*
21:19-24).

All that is in the heavens and the earth glorifies Allah. He is
the All-Mighty, the All-Wise. To Him belong the sovereignty
of the heavens and the earth. He gives life and death, and
He is able to do everything. He is the First and the Last, the
Outward and the Inward, and He has full knowledge of all
things. It is He who created the heavens and the earth in six

aeons, and is established on the Throne (of authority). He knows what goes into the earth and what comes out of it, what descends from the sky and what ascends to it. He is with you wherever you are; and Allah sees all that you do. To Him belongs the dominion of the heavens and the earth, and unto Him all matters arc returned. He causes the night to gain on the day and He causes the day to gain on the night. And He knows what is in your hearts (Al-Hadid 57:1-6).

The Islamic concept also informs human beings concerning the nature of the universe in which they live, and its properties, and its connection with the Creator. It draws their attention to the signs of the Creator in the universe, to the possibility of the origination of life in it, and to the fact that it is made for their use and benefit by Allah's leave. It teaches them all this in a manner that appeals to human reason and to human nature, can intuitively be felt to be true, and can be verified in the natural events all around them. All this information is provided to them in some detail, and they are exhorted to study the universe, to discover its laws and its secrets, and to deal with it correctly, so that they may gain true understanding and knowledge.

O you people! Adore your guardian-Lord ... Who made the earth your couch and the sky a canopy, and sent down water from the sky, and brought forth therewith fruits for your sustenance. So do not set up rivals unto Allah, when you know (the truth) (Al-Baqarah 2:22).

All praise is due to Allah who created the heavens and the earth, and made the darkness and the light. Yet the un-believers hold (others) equal with their Lord (Al-An'am 6:1).

Allah is He who raised up the heavens without any pillars that you can see, and is established on the Throne. He has subjected the sun and the moon [to his law], each one running [its course] to an appointed term. He directs all affairs, explaining the signs in detail, so that you may believe with certainty in the meeting with your Lord. It is He who spread out the earth and set thereon firm moun-tains and rivers. And fruits of every kind He made in pairs, two and two. He draws the night as a veil over the day. Surely in that are signs for a people who think. And on the earth are tracts (diverse though) neighboring each other, and gardens of vines, and sown fields, and palms growing in clusters or singly, watered with the same water. Yet some of them We have made more excellent than others as food. Surely in this are signs for a people who understand (*Al-R'ad* 13:2-4).

It is He who sends down water from the sky; from it you drink and out of it (grow) the plants upon which you pasture your herds. And with it He causes crops to grow for you, and olive trees, and palms, and grapes, and all kinds of fruit. Surely in this is a sign for a people who think. And He has made the night and the day and the sun and the moon subservient for you, and the stars are subservient to His command. Surely in this are signs for a people who use their reason. And all the many things on this earth that He has multiplied for you in many hues! Verily, in this is a sign for a people who meditate on Allah and His bounties. And it is He who has made the sea subservient, so that you may eat from its fresh meat, and take from it gems to wear. And you see the ships plowing through its waves so that you seek His bounty. And perhaps you may be thankful. And He has placed firm mountains on earth, lest it sway with you, and rivers and paths, so that you may find your way, and means of orientation, and stars by which (men) guide themselves. Is, then, He who creates like the one who cannot create? Will you not then grasp the message? (*Al-Nahl* 16:10-17).

Are they who are bent on denying the truth not aware that the heavens and the earth were (once) a single entity, which We then separated, and (that) we made every living thing of water? Will they not then believe? And We set on the earth firm mountains lest it shake with them, and We set on it valleys to serve as roads in order that they might find their way. And We have made the heavens as a roof well-guarded. And yet they stubbornly turn away from the signs of this (creation) and (fail to see that) it is He Who created the night and the day and the sun and the moon, each one swimming along in its own orbit *(Al-Anbiya* 21:30-33).

Have you not seen how Allah has subjected to you all that is in the earth, and the ships to sail upon the sea by His command; and He holds back the heaven lest it should fall

upon the earth, except by His leave? Surely, Allah is All-
Gentle, All-Compassionate to people (*Al-Hajj* 22:65).

We have created above you seven paths, and never are we
unmindful of (any aspects of Our) creation. We send down
from the sky water in a measure and lodge it in the earth.
And most certainly We are able to take it away. And by
means of it We produce for you gardens of palms and vines,
wherein are abundant fruit for you, and of them you eat
(*Al-Muminun* 23:17-19).

Do you not see how Allah drives the clouds, then joins them
together, then piles them in a mass, so that then you see rain
coming from the midst of them? And He sends down from
the sky mountainous masses (of clouds) wherein is hail. He
strikes therewith whomever He pleases and He turns it
away from whomever He pleases. The flash of His lightning
almost blinds one's eyes. Allah alternates the night and the
day. Surely in that is a lesson for those who have vision
(*Al-Nur* 24:43-44).

Have you not turned your vision to your Lord, how He
lengthens the shadow? If He willed, He could make it
stationary. But then, We have made the sun its guide. And
then We draw it in toward Ourselves, a contraction by easy
stages. It is He who made the night as a garment for you and
sleep for a rest, and causes every day to be a resurrection.
It is He who sends the winds bearing good tidings, heralding His mercy, and We send down pure water from the sky
so that We may revive a dead land and quench the thirst of
what We created, animals as well as humans in great numbers (*Al-Furqan* 25:45-49).

A sign for them is the dead land, which We revive and from
it bring forth grain for them to eat. And We make therein
gardens of palms and grapes, and therein We cause springs
to gush forth, so that they might eat its fruits, though it was
not their hands that made it. Will they not then be grateful?
Glory be to Him who created pairs in whatever the earth
produces, and of themselves, and of what they have no
knowledge. And a sign for them is the night. We strip it of
the daylight and, behold, they are in darkness. The sun runs
toward its destination which is ordained by the All-Mighty,

the All-Knowing. As for the moon, We have assigned for it phases until it returns like an old date-stalk. Neither can the sun overtake the moon nor does the night outstrip the day; each one swims in its own orbit (*Ya Sin* 36:33-40).

Say: "What! Do you disbelieve in Him who created the earth in two aeons? And do you claim that there is any power that could rival Him, the Sustainer of all the Worlds?" And He set therein firm mountains and he blessed it, and equitably apportioned the means of subsistence to all who would seek it, making all this in four aeons. And He applied His design to the sky, which was (yet but) smoke (gas). And He said to it and the earth, "Come both of you, willingly or unwillingly," and both of them responded, "We come in obedience." So He decreed that they become seven heavens in two aeons, and imparted to each heaven its function. And We adorned the heaven nearest to earth with lights and made them secure. Such is the ordaining of the All-Mighty, the All-Knowing (*Fussilat* 41:9-12).

What, do they not look toward the sky above them, how We have built it and made it beautiful and free of all faults? And the earth We have spread out and set thereon firm mountains, and produced therein every kind of beautiful plants to be observed and thus offering an insight and a reminder to every human being who willingly turns to Allah. And We send down from the sky water rich in blessings and thereby We produce gardens and fields of grain, and tall palm trees, with shoots of fruit stalks, piled one over another — as sustenance for (Allah's) servants, and We give new life therewith to a land that is dead: thus will be the resurrection (*Qaf* 50:6-11).

The Islamic worldview tells human beings about life and the living, informing them concerning their respective sources. It describes some characteristics of life that can be understood and appreciated by the human mind. It informs people of the close ties they have with the animal world, for they and the animals are equally the creation of Allah and are His servants, all coming into existence by His will and sharing some characteristics that point to their common origin in the Divine will. It conveys a reminder of Allah's favor upon them in that He gave them authority and power over many of these animals.

And We brought every living thing out of water (*Al-Anbiya* 21:30).

It is Allah who has created the animals out of water. Among them are such as crawl on their bellies, and such as walk on two legs, and such as walk on four. Allah creates what He wills, for, verily, Allah has power over everything (*Al-Nur* 24:45).

No creature is there crawling on the earth, nor any bird flying with its wings, but are communities like yourselves. We have neglected nothing in the Book (*Al-An'am* 6:38).

No creature is there moving on the earth but its provision rests on Allah. He knows its lodging-place and its place of sojourn. All is in a clear record (*Hud* 11:6).

And how many are the creatures that do not carry their sustenance? (Yet) Allah feeds them and yourselves as well (*Al-'Ankabut* 29:60).

And you see the earth barren. Then, when We send down water upon it, it is stirred, and swells, and puts forth every kind of beautiful growth (*Al-Hajj* 22:5).

He brings forth the living from the dead and He brings forth the dead from the living, and He revives the earth after it is dead. In a like manner shall you be brought forth (*Al Rum* 30-19).

A sign for them is the dead land, which We revive and from it bring forth grain to eat. And We make therein gardens of palms and grapes, and therein We cause springs to gush forth, so that they may eat its fruits, although it was not their hands that made it. Will they not, then, be grateful? Glory be to Him who created pairs in whatever the earth produces, and of themselves, and of things they do not know (*Ya Sin* 36:33-36).

The Originator of the heavens and the earth has made for you pairs from among yourselves, and pairs among cattle, in order thus to cause you to multiply. Like Him there is nothing. He is the All-Hearing and the All- seeing (*Al-Shura* 42:11).

And it is He who sent down from the sky water in measure, and We revived thereby a land that was dead. Even so you will be brought forth. And it is He who created pairs in all things, and made for you ships and animals for you to ride on their backs. So remember your Lord's favor when you are seated on them, and say, "Glory be to Him who has subjected this to us for we could not have accomplished this ourselves (*Al-Zukhruf* 43:11-13).

Then let man consider his food. We pour out rain abundantly, and then We cleave the earth, splitting it, and therein We cause grains to grow and grapes and edible plants, and olives and palms, and gardens with dense trees, and fruits and pastures, for you and your animals to enjoy (*'Abasa* 80:24-32).

Glorify the name of Your Lord the Most High, who creates (everything) and forms it in accordance with what it is meant to be, and Who determines the nature (of all that exists) and guides it, and Who brings forth herbage and then turns it into blackened stubble (*Al-A'la* 87:1-5).

Before Allah prostrates all that is in the heavens and every creature moving on the earth, and the angels. They do not bear themselves with false pride, but fear their Lord above them and do what they are commanded (*Al-Nahl* 16:49-50).

Do you not see that it is Allah whose glory all who are in the heavens and earth extol, even the birds as they spread out their wings? Each knows how to worship Him and to glorify Him. And Allah has full knowledge of what they do (*Al-Nur* 24:41).

The Islamic concept also informs human beings about man, describing his origin and his source, his nature and his characteristics, his place in this existence, the purpose of his existence, his position of servitude to his Lord, and the requirements of this servitude. It then tells us the strengths and weaknesses of the human being, and his responsibilities and obligations, in fact, everything small or great related to his life in this world and concerning his destiny in the hereafter.

In making this statement, we intend to do no more than describe the characteristic of comprehensiveness in the Qur'anic concept, rather than describe the fundamental constituents of this concept. This, insha'Allah, will be the topic of the second volume of this work. We confine ourselves here to quoting some verses describing the attributes of the Divine, the nature of the universe, and the nature of life.

> Surely We created man out of clay, of moulded mud, whereas the jinn We had created before that out of scorching fire. And your Lord said to the angels, ''Behold, I am about to create a mortal man out of a clay of moulded mud. And when I have formed him and breathed into him of My spirit, then fall down before him in prostration.'' Then the angels prostrated themselves, all of them together except Iblis. He refused to be among those who prostrated themselves (*Al-Hijr*) 15:26-31).

> We created man out of the essence of clay. Then We set him, a sperm-drop, in a secure receptacle; then We created of the drop of sperm a germ-cell; then We created from the germ-cell a lump; then We created within the lump bones; then We clothed the bones with flesh; and thereafter We brought him into being as another creature. Glorified, therefore, be Allah, the best of creators. Then, after that you will surely die, and shall surely be raised up on the Day of Resurrection (*Al-Muminun* 23:12-16).

> I have not created jinn and mankind except to worship Me. I desire of them no sustenance, nor do I desire that they feed Me. Indeed Allah is the Provider, the Possessor of Strength, the Firm (*Al-Dhariyat* 5:56-58).

> And when your Lord said to the angels, ''Behold! I am about to appoint a vicegerent on the earth,'' they said, ''Will You place on it such as will spread corruption and shed blood, whereas We extol Your limitless glory, and praise You, and hallow Your name.'' He said, ''Verily, I know what you do not know'' (*Al-Baqarah* 2:30).

> Indeed, We have honored the children of Adam, and have

borne them over land and sea, and provided them with good things, and favored them far above most of Our creation (*Al-Isra* 17:70).

We said, (to Adam and Eve), "Down with you all from (this state). Yet there shall come to you guidance from Me, and for whomever follows My guidance there shall be no fear nor shall they grieve. As for those who disbelieve and reject our signs, those shall be the inhabitants of the fire, to dwell therein (*Al-Baqarah* 38-39).

Consider time! Verily man is bound to lose himself, unless he be of those who believe and do good deeds and counsel each other to truth and to patience (*Al-'Asr* 103).

We indeed created man and We know what his soul whispers within him, and We are nearer to him than his jugular vein (*Qaf* 50:16).

We created man to toil and struggle (*Al-Balad* 90:4).

Did man not see how We created him of a sperm-drop, whereupon he shows himself endowed with the power to think and to argue (*Ya Sin* 36:77).

Man is in most things contentious (*Al-Kahf* 18:54).

Truly man was created restless, impatient when evil visits him, and grudging when good reaches him, except those who are constant in prayer (*Al-M'aarij* 70:19-221).

Allah desires to lighten things for you, for man was created weak (*Al-Nisa* 4:28).

When affliction visits a man he calls us on his side or sitting or standing, but when We have removed his affliction from him, he passes on as if he never called Us during his affliction (*Yunus* 10:12).

If We give man a taste of mercy from Us and then withdraw it from him, he is desperate and ungrateful. But if We let him taste prosperity after hardship that has visited him, he is sure to say, "The evils have gone from me," and he is joyous and boastful (*Hud* 11:9-10).

Man prays for evil, as he prays for good. Man is ever hasty (*Al-Isra* 17:11).

Nay, but man becomes insolent, for he thinks himself self-sufficient (*Al-'Alaq* 96:6-7).

Consider the human soul and how it is formed in accordance with what it is meant to be, and how it is imbued with moral failings as well as with consciousness of Allah! Assuredly he who purifies it is successful, and he who buries it (in darkness) is truly lost (*Al-Shams* 91:7-10).

We indeed created man in the best of molds, and then We abase him to the lowest of the low, except those who believe and do good deeds, for they shall have a reward unfailing (*Al-Tin* 95:4-6).

Thus, in the numerous verses of the Qur'an, covering a variety of aspects of these fundamental realities, a person finds their definition and a comprehensive description of their nature and characteristics.

These are the mortar, the bricks, and the foundations of the independent structure of the Islamic belief system, a system whose elements as well as total design come from the Divine source. This guarantees its truth and accuracy and its perfection and comprehensiveness, so that it needs no addition from any other source. All other sources, having only partial and speculative knowledge, are lost in a wilderness and are themselves in need of a guide.

We turn now to another aspect of the Islamic concept's comprehensiveness. In ascribing everything that exists, things, life, animals, and human beings, to an all-inclusive Will, and by presenting all the fundamental realities, the reality of the Divine Being which is the greatest and the most fundamental reality, the reality of the universe, the reality of life, and the reality of man in this comprehensive manner, that is by presenting everything comprehensively, the Islamic concept addresses the human being from all sides, responds to all his needs and aspirations, and makes him turn his face in one direction, namely, the direction of the One who is the Creator, Owner, and Governor of everything. Then he will ask what he wants only from Him, seek only His pleasure, fear only His anger, and turn to Him alone with hope and with fear and with all his being.

Thus man, in his entire being, is directed to one Source, so that he will receive from that Source all his concepts and ideas, his values and standards, and his rules of conduct and laws of behavior.

He will find a satisfactory response to all his questionings and yearnings from this Source alone, whether they relate to the origin of the universe and of life and man, or to his own life situations.

Man's personality is thereby integrated. His concepts and ideas, behavior and responses, beliefs and actions, ways of learning and receiving, attitude toward life and death, efforts and activities, concerns about his health and provision, and his life in this world and his desires for the Hereafter are all tied together. He need not seek solutions to various problems from different sources, nor face opposing challenges, nor run on diverging paths. Human personality, thus integrated, attains its highest station, the station of "unification." For, indeed, the Creator is One, and existence, with all its diversity of forms, shapes, and phenomena, is a *uni*-verse. The essence of life, with all its varied species, is one, and the essence of man, with all man's individual variations and potentialities, is one. And so, likewise, the purpose of man's existence, which is to worship his Creator in spite of a variety of forms of worship, is one. An integrated human personality thus becomes harmonious with the rest of existence.

At this stage of harmony with "the Reality" in all its aspects, the human personality attains to the highest power of which it is capable. The human personality, being in perfect harmony with the universe with which it interacts, and with everything that influences it and is influenced by it, becomes capable of marvelous achievements and of great deeds. A glorious example of integrated personalities was the community of the first generation of Muslims, through whom Allah brought about tremendous changes on the face of the earth with lasting effects in the life and history of mankind.

Whenever such a group of people appears again — and by Allah's permission it will reappear some day — Allah will bring about great changes through it, no matter what obstacles are placed in its way, because the phenomenon of the unification of all human faculties is an irresistible force, a force coming from the very core of this universe, from the direction of the Originator of this universe, and against which no obstacle can stand.

Another expression of the integration of the human personality is the movement of all human actions in one direction toward the purpose of human existence, which is worship, namely, worship embracing all the activities of man in the service of Allah alone as Allah's vicegerent on earth.

This integration of personality and of all activity is a distinctive characteristic of Islam. Islam, on the one hand, offers an explanation of all the realities of existence that face a human being, and on the other, gives direction to all human activity. Only in Islam does a person live for the Hereafter while living in this world, engage in the service of Allah while working to earn his sustenance, and attain human perfection, which is the aim of his religion, while being engaged in the day- to-day affairs of the world, because this is his function as the deputy of Allah on earth. Islam demands only one thing from him: that he be sincere in his commitment to Allah in whatever he does, whether it be formal worship or the deeper prayer of worldly activity. The sincerity of man toward Allah means that he turns toward Him in all his actions, intentions, and pursuits, while taking care not to transgress the limits of what is permissible. It should be mentioned here that the circle of things and actions that are permissible is very wide and includes all that is good, because Allah has created man with needs that are to be fulfilled and with faculties that are to be used. Through the operation of these integrated faculties, man realizes the purpose of his existence in comfort and ease, in peace of mind, and in the total freedom that comes through a total commitment to Allah alone. This characteristic of comprehensiveness makes Islam a complete system of life, consisting of a heart-felt faith and of a way of life that is not in contradiction to this faith but proceeds from it. Unification of belief and practice is the nature of the Islamic *din* and any separation between the two rends and corrupts it.

The division of human actions into "worship" or *ibadat* and "human affairs" or *mu'amalat*, which we find in the books of Islamic jurisprudence, was introduced in the beginning merely for technical reasons in order to present different topics in a systematic manner. Unfortunately, with the passage of time, this produced the erroneous impression in people's minds that the term "worship" applies only to those actions that are included under the title "jurisprudence of Worship." The application of the term "worship" to "human affairs" gradually faded in their thought. Undoubtedly this was a grave distortion of the Islamic concept, which eventually resulted in producing deviations in the Muslim society.

In the Islamic concept there is not a single human act to which the term "worship" is not applicable or in which this property is not desired. Indeed, the Islamic way of life is nothing but the realization of the meaning of worship from beginning to end.

The ultimate aim of the Islamic way of life is not a system of justice, or a system of economics, or a system of legislation concerning criminal, civil, or family affairs, or any other of the rules and regulations that are part of this way of life. The only aim of Islam is the

establishment of the meaning of "worship" in human life, as, according to the Qur'an, it is for the worship of Allah that man was created.
No human action can be called worship of Allah unless it is done for
the sake of Allah alone, and with a recognition that He alone deserves
to be worshipped. Either this is the case or the act is not worship, and
hence not in the service of Allah, and in fact, is therefore a rebellion
against the *din* of Allah.

If we refer to the Qur'an concerning the acts that our scholars have
called "worship," we find that such acts are not discussed separately
from the other acts that they have termed "human affairs." Indeed,
both kinds of activities are intimately connected in the text of the
Qur'an, as both form parts of the "worship" that is the purpose of
human life, worship signifying total submission and commitment to
Allah Most High alone and the ascription of divinity and sovereignty
to Him alone.

As a result of this classification in the scholarly books, with the
passage of time people came to understnd that they could be "Muslims" if they performed "the acts of worship" in accordance with
what Islam prescribes, while in "human affairs" they could follow
other systems not necessarily coming from Allah but from some other,
little "deity" who legislates for them in secular affairs in contradiction
to Allah's commandments.

This is a great illusion, for Islam is an indivisible unity, and any
person who divides it into two parts, in the manner mentioned above,
is a rebel against this unity and therefore against this *din*.

This is a great truth, and any Muslim who wishes to practice his
religion faithfully, and thus wishes to realize the purpose of his
existence, must turn his full attention to it. The objective should be to
correct not merely one's belief, although the correction of Islamic
belief is an extrememly important matter in itself, since the whole
system of life depends on it. The importance of *tawhid* and an
integrated life is also manifested in one's very style of life, which
attains the highest rank of perfection and greatest value when it
becomes entirely dedicated to the worship of Allah, and when every
action, whether small or great, becomes a part of this worship. When
we consider the great meaning hidden in the concept of worship,
which is to ascribe divinity to Allah Most High alone and to acknowledge that He alone deserves our servitude, we realize that to be a
committed servant (*'abd*) of Allah Most High is the highest position a
man can attain and that without this commitment human perfection
is not possible. This was the station that the Messenger of Allah, may
peace be upon him, attained during his most exalted moments, while

receiving the revelation from Allah and during the Night Journey and Ascension.

> Glorified be He who has sent down the Criterion upon His servant so that he may be a warner to the worlds (*Al-Furqan* 25:1).

> Glory be to Him who carried this servant by night from the Sacred Mosque to the Further Mosque, the precincts of which We have blessed, so that We might show him some of Our signs. He is the All-Hearing, the All- Seeing (*Al-Isra* 17:1).

In this regard, Muhammad Asad (Leopold Weiss), in his book *Islam at the Crossroads*, presents some profound ideas concerning the differences between the Islamic concept and other concepts, and explains how the Islamic concept takes human beings to the highest level in the life of this world. In the chapter entitled "The Open Road of Islam," he says: "Thus, the conception of 'worship' in Islam is different from that in any other religion. Here it is not restricted to the purely devotional practices, for example prayers or fasting, but extends over the whole of man's practical life as well. If the object of our life as a whole is to be the worship of God, we necessarily must regard this life, in the totality of all its aspects, as one complex moral responsibility. Thus, all our actions, even the seemingly trivial ones, must be performed as acts of worship, that is, performed *consciously* as constituting a part of God's universal plan. Such a state of things is, for the man of average capability, a distant ideal; but is it not the purpose of religion to bring ideals into real existence?

"The position of Islam in this respect is unmistakable. It teaches us, firstly, that the permanent worship of God in all the manifold actions of human life is the very meaning of this life, and, secondly, that the achievement of this purpose remains impossible so long as we divide our life into two parts, the spiritual and the material. They must be bound together, in our consciousness and our action, into one harmonious entity. Our notion of God's Oneness must be reflected in our own striving towards a co-ordination and unification of the various aspects of our life.

"A logical consequence of this attitude is a further difference between Islam and all other known religious systems. It is to be found in the fact that Islam, as a teaching, undertakes to define not only the metaphysical relations between man and his Creator but also — and with scarcely less insistence — the earthly relations between the individual and his social surroundings. The worldly life is not regarded as a mere empty shell, as a meaningless shade of the hereafter that is to come, but as a self-contained, positive entity. God himself is a Unity not only in essence but also in purpose; and, therefore, His creation is a Unity, possibly in essence, but certainly in purpose.

"Worship of God in the wide sense just explained constitutes, according to Islam, the meaning of human life. And it is this conception alone that shows us the possibility of man's reaching perfection within his individual, earthly life. Of all religious systems, Islam alone declares that individual perfection is possible in our earthly existence. Islam does not postpone this fulfilment until after a suppression of the so-called "bodily" desires, as the Christian teaching does; nor does Islam promise a continuous chain of rebirths on a progressively higher plane, as is the case with Hinduism; nor does Islam agree with Buddhism, according to which perfection and salvation can be obtained only through an annihilation of the individual Self and its emotional links with the world. No, Islam is emphatic in the assertion that man can reach perfection in his earthly, individual life and by making full use of all the worldly possibilities of his life."[1]

This comprehensiveness of the Islamic concept — in all its forms — is very pleasing to human nature because it integrates it into a unified personality, neither taxing it nor tearing it apart. This characteristic also protects man from turning to anyone other than Allah, in any condition or at any moment, and protects him from accepting the domination of anyone who does not derive his authority from Allah within the limits of His *shari'ah* (Divine Law) in any field of life. Command, Dominion, and Authority belong to Allah alone, not merely in the sphere of "worship," or only in some other sphere, but in all spheres, in this life and in the life of the Hereafter, in the heavens and on earth, in the visible and in the unseen worlds, in prayer and in action, and this is true for every soul in its every movement, every step, and every direction:

It is He who is God in heaven and God on earth (*Al-Zukhruf* 43:84).

---

[1] Muhammad Asad, *Islam at the Crossroads* (1955), Arafat Publications, Lahore, Pakistan, pp. 17-20.

CHAPTER VI

Balance

"You do not see in the creation of the All-Merciful any imperfections"(*Al-Mulk* 67:3).

The fourth characteristic of the Islamic concept is balance, balance in its constituent elements and balance in its teachings. And this characteristice is closely connected with its characteristic of comprehensiveness, which is a balanced comprehensiveness. This distinctive characteristic protects the Islamic concept from fanaticism, contradictions, and foreign intrusions, while all other concepts are afflicted by such troubles, whether they be philosophical concepts or religious concepts that have been distorted by the addition or subtraction of human ideas or through wrong interpretations of the originally correct beliefs.

We present a few prominent examples from the Islamic teachings to illustrate their manifest quality of balance.

Some aspects of the Islamic concept we accept by immediate recognition of their self-evident truth, and the matter ends there. Other aspects need to be understood, discussed, researched, and applied to the actual circumstances of life. And there is a balance between these two types of aspects. Human nature is happy with both because both of them are as they ought to be. Indeed, Allah knows that the human intellect cannot compass all the secrets of existence, nor can it fully comprehend them. He therefore conditioned the human intellect to be happy with what it can know and with what it cannot know. And there is a balance between the satisfaction of knowledge and the curiosity about the unknown in the personality of man, reflecting the same kind of balance between the knowable and the unknowable in the nature of existence. A belief system in which there is no element

109

of the unknown nor anything greater than the limited understanding of man can hardly be called a belief. The human soul can find little appealing in such a system, because there would be little to excite its curiosity or satisfy its sense of mystery. On the other hand, a belief system that is self-contradictory or so steeped in mystery that it baffles the human intellect is also not a belief. The human personality requires something illuminating yet not contradictory or puzzling, because it also needs something that can be understood, translated into action, and be applied in life situations. A comprehensive belief system must contain both aspects in the right proportion so that human nature may find in it a correspondence with its own desires and potentialities. On the one hand, the essence of the Divine Being, the connection between the Will of the Creator and the creation, and the nature of the soul are some of the aspects of the Islamic faith that are beyond human comprehension, while on the other hand there are attributes of Allah, such as His existence, His Oneness, His power, His will, His creativity, and His knowledge, that are within the grasp of human thought. In fact, human reason insists that the Creator must have these attributes, and Islam gives convincing proofs of them.

Similarly, there are teachings in Islam concerning the universe, its origination in the Divine Will, its subservience to Allah's commands, its potentiality to welcome life, its relationship with man and man's relationship with it, and there are teachings concerning life, its varieties and ranks, its connection with the rest of the universe, and with its Originator, and there are teachings also concerning man and his nature, his origin and characteristics, and the purpose of his existence, and a system for his life. All these teachings are presented in a clearly understood, logical fashion, which appeals to the intellect and to the heart because these teachings are supported by arguments readily accepted by human intuition.

> Were they created of nothing? Or are they the creators? Or did they create the heavens and the earth? Nay, they have no certainty (*Al-Tur* 52:35-36).

> Some people have taken gods from among earthly things or beings or ideas that allegedly can raise the dead? Had there been in heaven or on earth any gods other than Allah, both would surely go to ruin. So glory be to Allah, the Lord of the Throne, far above all that men may devise by way of definition! He shall not be questioned as to what He does, but they shall be questioned. And yet they choose to worship (imaginary) deities) other than Him? Say, ''Bring proof!

This is a reminder by those who are with me, just as it was a reminder (voiced) by those who came before me." Nay, most of them do not know the truth, and so they are turning away (*Al-Anbiya* 21:21-26).

Is not He who created the heavens and the earth able to create the like of them? Yes, assuredly! He is the Supreme Creator, the All-Knowing. Indeed, when He desires a thing, His command is "Be" and it is (*Ya Sin* 36:81-82).

Who is it that created the heavens and the earth, and sent down for you water from the sky? For it is by this means that We cause gardens full of loveliness to grow, whereas it is not in your power to cause trees to grow. Could there be any divine power besides Allah? No, they (who think so) are people who swerve. Who is it that made the earth a place of rest and a fitting abode, and made rivers in its midst, and set upon it firm mountains, and placed a partition between the two bodies of water. Is there a god besides Allah? No! Most of those (who think so) do not know. Who is it that answers the distressed when he calls out to Him and removes the suffering, and has made you inheritors of the earth? Is there a god besides Allah? How seldom do you keep all this in mind and meditate on it! Who is it that guides you in the darknesses on the land and sea, and sends the winds bearing glad tidings of His coming mercy and grace. Is there a god besides Allah? Exalted is Allah above anything to which men may ascribe a share in His divinity. Who is it that originates creation, then repeats it, and gives you sustenance from the sky and the earth. Is there a god besides Allah? Say, "(If you think so,) produce your evidence, if you truly believe in your claim!" (*Al-Namal* 27:60-64).

Among His signs is that He created you from dust, and then, behold, you become human beings ranging far and wide. And among His signs is that he created for you spouses out of your own kind so that you might dwell with them in tranquillity, and He engenders love and tenderness between you. Surely in this are signs for a people who reflect. And among His signs is the creation of the heavens and the earth, and the variety of your languages and your colors. Surely in this are signs for all who are endowed with knowledge. And among His signs is your sleep during the night or day and your quest of some of his bounties. Surely in this are signs for a people who listen! And among His signs is that he shows you lightning, causing both fear and hope, and that He sends down rain from the sky and with it revives the earth after it is dead. Surely in this are signs for a people who use their reason. And among His signs is that the heaven and the earth stand firm by His command. (Remember all this, for) in the end, when He will call you forth from the earth by a single call, you will emerge (*Al-Rum* 30:20-25).

Among all these descriptions of the signs or messages of Allah visible in the universe and in their own selves, human beings can find a multitude of things to observe, ponder, and discuss, and everything is obvious and at every person's level of understanding.

Thus, within the Islamic concept is everything for which human nature yearns: the known and the unknown, the Unseen, which cannot be comprehended by one's intellect or seen by one's eyes, and the Visible, amidst which the reason delights to wander and hearts find many things upon which to dwell. Of all the earth's creatures, only man can even begin to comprehend the realms of the majesty of the magnificent Creator, which can be felt by intuition but are beyond human perception, as well as the realms of mundane activity in which man has the free will and responsibility to realize his potentialities and attain to the value and dignity bestowed upon him by Allah. And the human personality finds a balance between the great unknown and great known by believing in the one and enjoying the other.

There is a balance between the freedom of the Divine Will and the constancy of the laws of nature. The Divine Will is absolutely free, and one cannot conceive of any restrictions on it. It originates anything by merely desiring its being, with no necessary rule of operation governing it. Allah Almighty does what he desires and when He desires it.

Indeed, Our word to a thing when We desire it is that We say to it, "Be," and it is (*Al- Nahl* 16:40).

"Lord," said Zakariyyah, "how shall I have a son since I am an old man and my wife is barren?" "Even so," was the answer, "Allah does what He wills" (*Ale'Imran* 3:40).

"Lord," said Mary, "how shall I have a child when no mortal (man) has touched me?" (The angel) answered:

"Thus (it will be). Allah creates what He wills. When He decrees a thing, He says only 'Be,' and it is" (*Ale 'Imran* 3:47).

And his wife was standing by and she laughed. We then gave her the glad tidings of Ishaq, and after Ishaq, of Y'aqub. She said, "Woe to me! Shall I bear a child, when I am an old woman, and this my husband is an old man? This surely would be a strange thing!" They said, "What! Do you marvel at Allah's command?" (*Hud* 11:71-72).

Truly, the likeness of Jesus in the sight of Allah, is like Adam. He created him of dust and then he said to him, "Be," and he was. The truth is from your Lord, so do not be of the doubters (*Ale 'Imran* 3:59-60).

And [the angels said to Mary that Allah will make Jesus] a messenger to the Children of Israel, (who will say): "I have come to you with a sign from your Lord. I will create for you from clay the form of a bird. And then I will blow into it, and it will become a bird, by Allah's permission. I will also heal the blind and the leper, and bring to life the dead, by Allah's permission. I will also let you know what you may eat and what you should store in your houses. Surely in this is a sign for you, if you are truly believers" (*Ale 'Imran* 4:49).

Or like the one who passed by a town with its roofs caved in. He said, "How shall Allah bring this back to life after its death?" Thereupon Allah caused him to be dead for a hundred years, and then raised him up and asked, "How long have you tarried?" He answered, "I have remained thus a day, or part of a day." He said, "No you have remained thus for a hundred years. But look at your food and your drink. It has not spoiled. And look at your donkey. And We would make you a sign for the people. And look at the bones, how We put them together and clothed them with flesh." So, when it was made clear to him, he said, "I know that Allah has power over everything" (*Al-Baqarah* 2:259).

They said (to each other), "Burn him (Abraham) and help your gods, if you would do anything." (But) We said, "O

fire, be cool and safety for Abraham." Although they
desired to do him evil, we caused them to suffer the greatest
loss (*Al-Anbiya* 21:68- 70).

When the two hosts sighted each other, the companions of
Moses exclaimed, "We have been overtaken!" He replied,
"No, indeed. Surely my Lord is with me. He will guide me."
Then We revealed to Moses, "Strike the sea with your
staff," and it parted, and each part appeared as a huge
mountain (*Al-Shu'ara* 26:61-62).

You do not know it, after that, Allah may cause something
new to come about (*Al-Talaq* 65:1).

These examples amply illustrate the absolute freedom of the Divine
Will. Accordingly, anything that human imagination may think of as a
necessary law or as a logical necessity does not apply to the Will of
Allah Most High.

At the same time, it is also a part of the Divine Will that there be
some customary ways for Divine operation that appear to the people
as regular, which they can observe, and formulate as natural laws, and
according to which they can regulate their lives and interact with the
universe around them. All the while it remains firm in their thoughts
and feelngs that, in spite of this, Allah's will is absolutely free and can
originate anything he desires. Allah Almighty does what he pleases,
and it pleases Him to establish certain rules of operation to which they
can get accustomed, though, in spite of all these customary laws of
nature, His will remains absolutely free. Accordingly, Allah calls attention to His rules of operation within the universe as proof of His
control and administration of the universe, so that man, as much as
he can understand these rules, may apply them to his life-situations.

Said Abraham, "Allah makes the sun rise from the east, so
you bring it from the west." Then the unbeliever was
confounded (*Al- Baqarah* 2:258).

Neither can the sun overtake the moon nor does the night
outstrip the day (*Ya Sin* 36:40).

Such has been Allah's way with those who passed away
before. And you shall find no changing in Allah's way
(*Al-Ahzab* 33:62).

Many ways of life have passed away before you. Travel in
the land and behold how was the end of those who denied
the truth (*Ale 'Imran* 3:137).

Is it not a guidance to them (to contemplate) how many
generations We destroyed before them in whose dwelling
places they now walk? Surely in this are signs. What! Will
they not listen! (*Al-Sajdah* 32:26).

Indeed, We sent Messengers, each one to his own people,
even before you, and they brought them clear evidence of
the truth. And then We inflicted retributions upon those
who did evil, for We made it incumbent upon Us to help
the believers (*Al-Rum* 30:47).

We destroyed the generations before you when they did
evil. Although Messengers came to them with clear proofs,
they would not believe. Thus do we requite people who
persist in sinning (*Yunus* 10:13).

Had the people of the cities believed and remained conscious of Allah, We would have opened upon them blessings from the sky and the earth. But they denied the truth,
and so We took them to task for what they had done
(*Al-A'raf* 7:96).

Between the constancy of Allah's ways and His Free Will, the
conscience of man remains on solid ground. Through experimentation and observation man discovers the laws of nature and rules of
life, learns the nature of the earth on which he lives and the treasures
hidden in it, and finds the purpose of striving and the reward of action.
At the same time, he lives with his spirit and soul close to Allah, with
his heart always immersed in the Will of Allah, for which nothing is
too great or impossible. The difficulties of life, however great they
may be, cannot make him despondent. He lives free in his concepts,
not constrained in iron molds, with the consciousness that his soul is
enveloped by Allah's Will. And so his senses do not become dull, and
his hope does not fade. He lives in anticipation of new happenings,
taking nothing for granted.

The believer uses the laws and patterns of the universe as means
because he is commanded to do so, and he acts according to these
established patterns, because he is commanded to benefit from them.
Never for an instant, however, does he believe that these instruments

and means are the real causes or originators of their effects. Indeed, after fulfilling his duty of using the means, doing the best he can and striving in obedience to Allah's command, he ascribes every affair to the Creator of causes and connects himself to Him alone beyond all apparent causes.

Thus the Muslim benefits from the constancy of the natural laws, which can be discovered through scientific experimentation and practical experience in his interaction with the universe, and benefits from its secrets, forces, and treasures. He does not neglect any of the fruits of experiments in various sciences or any knowledge gained through practical experience. At the same time, his heart remains connected with Allah, and this connection keeps his heart and conscience alive to the sensitivities of high morals and good manners, which raise his humanity to the highest level of perfection possible during his sojourn on this earth.

There is a balance between the domain of free Divine Will, and the domain of limited wills of human beings. This is the famous dilemma that has appeared, in one form or another, among all religions, all philosophies, and all mythologies, the dilemma between freedom of choice and determinism, "the Divine decrees and their fulfillment."

Islam affirms that the Divine Will is absolutely free, that it is the active agent, and that there is no other active agent, as we explained in the chapter entitled "Comprehensiveness" and will explain further under the heading "Dynamism." At the same time Islam assigns a positive role for man's will as we will explain later under "Dynamism," and gives man the highest role on earth, the vicegerency of Allah. This is a great responsibility, which makes man's position in the universe very distinguished and central and grants him a wide field of activity and effectiveness. But all this is in perfect accord with Allah's Free Will, the real active agent beyond the apparent causes, of which man's activity is only one such cause. At a deeper level we see that the very existence of man, his freedom of choice and his power to do things, and his movements and his acts are all according to the all-encompassing Divine will. We read in the Noble Qur'an:

> No affliction can ever befall earth or yourselves unless it is in our decree before we bring it into being. This is easy for Allah (*Al-Hadid* 57:22).

> Say, "Nothing befalls us except what Allah has prescribed for us. He is our Protector. In Allah let the believers put all their trust" (*Al-Tawbah* 9:51).

If something good happens to them, they say, "This is from Allah," but if something bad reaches them they say, "This is from you." Say: "Everything is from Allah." What is wrong with this people? They scarcely understand a single fact (*Al-Nisa* 4:78).

Say: "Even if you had remained in your homes, those (of you) whose death had been ordained would have gone to the places where they were destined to lie down" (*Ale-'Imran* 3:154).

Wherever you may be, death will overtake you, even though you may be in high towers (*Al- Nisa* 4:78).

We also read the following in the Noble Qur'an:

Verily, Allah does not change the condition of a people unless they change what is in their selves (*Al-R'ad* 13:11).

That is, because Allah would never change the blessings with which He has favored people unless they change what is in their selves (*Al-Anfal* 8:53).

Nay, but man shall be an eye-witness against himself, even though he offers excuses (*Al- Qiyamah* 75:14-15).

Consider the soul and how it is formed in accordance with what it is meant to be, and how it is imbued with moral failings as well as with consciousness of Allah! Assuredly he who purifies it shall attain a happy state and he who seduces it shall fail (*Al-Shams* 91:7-10).

For he who commits a sin, commits it only against himself (*Al-Nisa* 4:111).

We also read in the Noble Qur'an the following verses:

Nay, this is an admonition, and whoever wills may take it to heart. And they will not take it to heart unless Allah so wills, for He is Lord of Righteousness, and the Lord of Forgiveness. (*Al-Muddaththir* 74:54-58).

Verily, this is a Reminder, so that whoever wishes may find

a way unto his Lord. But you cannot will it unless Allah so wills, for indeed Allah is All-Knowing, All-Wise (*Al-Insan* 76:29-30).

Now that a calamity has befallen you after you had inflicted twice as much (on your enemy), why did you say, "How is this?" Say: "This is from your own selves." Verily, Allah has power over everything. And all that befell you on the day when the two hosts met in battle happened by Allah's permission (*Ale 'Imran* 3:165-166).

When a person reads these verses describing the three elements (Divine Will, human Will, and the connection between the two), he begins to understand the scope of the meaning of the "Divine decree" in the Islamic concept, and thus understands the boundaries of the field of action of human will within the scope of the Divine decree.

Philosophers and the theologians of distorted religions are lost in the wilderness of confusion and wonderment when dealing with this issue. Even some of the Muslim scholastic thinkers were puzzled over this issue, because they followed the method of Greek philosophy, rather than following the Islamic method in dealing with it.

From the point of view of the correct Islamic concept this issue poses no problem, either in its meaning or in its message.

It is clear that Allah creates what He will and originates what He will of events, things, animals, human beings, and the circumstances of their lives, because they form a part of the total creation. Furthermore, all changes and new occurrences in His creation are according to His decrees. Allah's decree operates among a people, however, through the will of individual members and through their actions within their own selves.

Verily, Allah does not change the condition of a people unless they change what is in their selves (*Al-R'ad* 13:11).

This does not contradict the assertion that everything is ultimately referred back to the Divine Will. In the third group of verses quoted above, the human will and the Divine Will are mentioned together in a single sentence.

If we look at the issue of the relationship between the all-encompassing Divine Will and human actions by the dim light of man-made concepts, we must presume that there is a dilemma and a contradiction. But this is not the correct approach. Issues such as this, concerning Allah Most High, His attributes, and His decisions, cannot be dealt

with by using man-made rational categories. We must develop new
categories of thought in the light of what Allah Most High has informed
us in the text of the Qur'an. Other than this we do not have any reliable
source of knowledge, and speculation in these matters is no guide.

Allah said, ''So whoever wishes may find a way unto his Lord,'' and
then He said, ''But you cannot will it unless Allah so wills,'' and He
also said, ''Nay, but man shall be an eyewitness against himself, even
though he may offer excuses.'' And He said:

> Whomever Allah desires to guide, He opens his breast wide
> toward Islam; and whomever He wills to let go astray, He
> causes his breast to be tight and constricted as if he were
> climbing up to the sky (*Al-An'am* 6:125).

And He said:

> And your Lord is not in the least unjust to His creatures
> (*Fussilat* 41:46).

The only way the Muslim can reconcile the concept of the comprehensiveness of Allah's Will with his concept of Allah's justice in
judging human beings and rewarding and punishing them, is by
assuming that in Allah's reckoning some proportion of freedom has
been allotted to man's will, which makes him responsible for his
actions and hence liable for punishment and deserving of reward,
without permitting this allotted freedom to conflict with the comprehensive Divine will, which dominates all people, things, and
events.

How?

''Hows'' are entirely the work of Allah. ''How'' is the connection
between what He wills and the way it comes into being, that is, the
connection between Willing and Originating. The ''hows'' are beyond
human comprehension. The Islamic concept suggests that we leave
such matters to the One with absolute knowledge and absolute power
of planning, by placing complete confidence in His justice, His wisdom, His bounty, and His mercy. Indeed man's power of reasoning is
limited by time and space and by immediate influences and
psychological conditioning. Man is not destined to understand such
proportions and the ''how'' behind them. His task is not to judge the
connections and relationships between the Divine Will and human
actions. This is left entirely to the all-encompassing, all-planning Will,
and to the absolutely perfect Knower, that is to say, to Allah Almighty,
who knows the nature of man, the composition of his personality, his

natural capacities, his real work or contribution to the world, the exact extent of his choice in this work within the all-encompassing Divine Will, and the recompense for the actual amount of choice involved.

Only in this way can we attain right balance in our concept and in our understanding, so that we can work with confidence in accordance with the prescribed way of Allah, looking forward to a good ending.

The same is the case with what is called, "the problem of the existence of evil and suffering." From the Islamic point of view, this poses no problem.

The basic Islamic teachings are that this world is a place for trial and action, and the Hereafter is the place for accounting and compensation. Life on this earth is but a sojourn of short duration and is a stage in a long journey. What happens to a man in this life does not close his accounts nor is it the end of his journey. Indeed, this is a prelude to what comes later, and is a test that determines his grade on the Day of Reckoning.

The conscience of man is satisfied and content with this explanation. Furthermore, the suffering that befalls a good person because of the operation of evil in the world is balanced by the joy and comfort that also come to him. The Will that controls the two sides of the balance is a single Will, and the Source of both suffering and joy is a single Source, and no one can share His knowledge or His decision.

The message of Islam also addresses the deeper levels of human conscience. A sincere believer, striving to realize the way of Allah in his life and to establish it in society at large, is always consciously pleased and happy in this world, even before receiving the reward promised him in the Hereafter, and even while he is enduring suffering caused by evil people. This consciousness springs from his feeling that he is seeking the pleasure of Allah in whatever he does, and that Allah is pleased with his striving. Human nature is so constituted by Allah that it enjoys the thrills of doing battle against evil and falsehood and helping the cause of good and truth. Indeed, the enjoyment of this struggle is an ample reward in itself, even at the very moment a person is facing the assaults from evil and falsehood and countering them with all his power.

In the nature of this struggle there is a hidden recompense and also an inner peace coming from the consciousness that Allah will reward one both in this world and the next. This contentment of the heart lasts one until the Day of Reckoning.

But He guides to Himself those who turn to Him in

penitence, those who believe and whose hearts find rest in the remembrance of Allah; for verily in the remembrance of Allah are hearts at rest (*Al-R'ad* 13:28).

Is one whose heart Allah has opened wide to Islam, so that he walks in a light from his Lord (no better than the blind of heart)? Woe, then, to those whose hearts are hardened against the remembrance of Allah! They are in manifest error (*Al-Zumar* 39:22).

On those who have said, "Our Lord is Allah" and then have followed the right way, the angels descend, saying, "Neither fear nor grieve but be joyful about the Paradise promised to you. We are your friends in the life of this world and in the hereafter, therein shall you have all that your soul desires, and in it you shall have all that you call for, as hospitality from the All-Forgiving, All-Compassionate" (*Fussilat* 41: 30-32).

Do not lose heart, or grieve, for you are bound to rise high if you are truly believers (*Ale 'Imran* 3:139).

Say: "Are you waiting for something to happen to us? But except one of the two best things (victory or martyrdom). But we are waiting hopefully for Allah to inflict chastisement upon you either from Himself or by our hands. So wait, and we shall wait hopefully with you" (*Al-Tawbah* 9:52).

As to evil itself, which is not necessarily accompanied by suffering in every case, the question is raised why does evil exist, when Allah has the power not to have introduced it from the very beginning. He could have guided all the people, or in fact, could have created them guided? This question actually has no place in the Islamic concept.

Of course Allah is able to change human nature to fit the way of Islam or fit some other way, or He could have created man with an altogether different nature. But it pleased Him to create man with his existing nature and to create the universe as we see it. Should any creature play God, when it does not have and can never have the knowledge needed to comprehend the entire system of existence, and the natures of all the creatures, and their individual needs and requirements, and the wisdom behind the specific nature given to each creature? Allah is the only One who knows, because He is the One who created the world and whoever and whatever is in it, and He is the only One who determines the best nature and form for His creatures in the universe that He created for them.

So glory be to Allah the best of creators (*Al-Muminun* 23:14).

Moses said, our Lord is the One who gives to each thing its form and nature and then guides it (*Ta Ha* 20:50).

And if Allah had so willed, He would have made you one nation. But (He willed it otherwise) in order to try you in what has come to you. So, compete with one another in doing good works. Unto Allah shall you return all together, and then He will make you truly understand everything about which you used to differ (*Al-Ma'idah* 5:48).

Had Allah not driven back the people, some by means of others, the earth would have been corrupted, but Allah is bounteous toward all creation (*Al-Baqarah* 2:251).

We try you with evil and good as a test, and then unto Us you shall be returned (*Al-Anbiya* 21:35).

"Why is it so?" Such a question is raised neither by a sincere believer nor by a serious atheist. The sincere believer does not ask this question because he is too respectful of Allah Most High. He knows from the Islamic teachings the attributes of Allah, and knows perfectly well that the human intellect cannot operate in these realms. And the serious atheist is not concerned with this problem, because he does not believe in God to start with. If he would come to believe in God, he would also know that this is among the Divine prerogatives and that Allah's decisions are all according to His wise plan.

Only a hard-headed argumentative person or a light-hearted jester raises such questions. It is useless to try to answer him with rational arguments, since the question is on a plane higher than the sphere of human reason. To know the "why" of it, a man must become God. But man cannot become God. So, the only recourse left is to accept the given situation and all that it entails.

The forces of evil are similarly limited in knowledge and power. The one who urges toward evil through temptation and tries to push people toward sin and error, according to Islamic teachings has not been given decisive power over human beings. He can only tempt. In the conflict between man and Satan, strong shields against the power of Satan are faith, remembrance of Allah, and seeking Allah's help and protection.

> (Iblis) said, ''O My Lord! Since You have thwarted me, I shall make (all that is evil) on earth attractive to them, and I shall pervert them all, except such of them as are Your sincere servants.'' Said He, ''This is, with Me, a straight path. Over My servants You shall have no authority, except over those who are lost in error and follow you'' (*Al-Hijr* 15:39-42).

> Said He, (Allah to Adam and Eve), ''Down with you all from this and be enemies to one another. But guidance shall come to you from Me, and then whoever follows My guidance shall not go astray, and neither will he be unhappy. But whoever turns away from My remembrance shall have a life of narrow scope, and on the Day of Resurrection We shall raise him up blind.'' He will ask, ''O my Lord! Why have You raised me blind, whereas (on earth) I had eyes to see?'' (Allah) shall say, ''Thus it is: Our signs came to you but you were oblivious to them, and so today you shall be con-signed to oblivion'' (*Ta Ha* 20:123-126).

> And when everything will have been decided, Satan will say, ''Allah promised you a true promise, I also promised you, but I deceived you. Yet I had no power over you except that I called you and you answered me. So, do not blame me, but blame yourselves'' (*Ibrahim* 14:22).

> When you recite the Qur'an, first seek refuge in Allah from Satan, the rejected. He has no authority over those who believe and trust in their Lord. His (Satan's) authority is over those who take him as their friend and those who ascribe associates to Allah (*Al-Nahl* 16:98-100).

> Surely the guile of Satan is ever weak (*Al- Nisa* 4:76).

Still, the question remains: since Allah has created each human being with definite capabilities that incline him either toward good and guidance or toward evil and error, how can Allah punish the wicked and evil person and reward the rightly guided and good person, whether in this life or the next?

In this form, this is a misleading question. The Qur'an says in this regard only that Allah originally created man in the best of patterns, man does not lose his station except through his forgetfulness of Allah, that man is being tried through good and evil and has the power to choose, and that he is helped by Allah in his striving if he sincerely strives to please Allah.

> We indeed created man in the best of patterns. Then We reduced him to the lowest of the low, except those who believe and do good deeds, for theirs shall be a reward unending (*Al-Tin* 95:4-6).

> Consider the soul and how it is formed and is imbued with moral failings as well as with consciousness of Allah. Assuredly, he who purifies it will be successful, and he who seduces it will fail (*Al-Shams* 91:7-10).

> We created man of a drop of sperm intermingled, so that we might try him, and therefore We made him a being endowed with hearing and sight. Surely We have guided him to the way, whether he be thankful or unthankful (*Al-Insan* 76:2-3).

> Surely your striving is to diverse ends. As for him who gives and is conscious of Allah, and testifies to the best, We will indeed make smooth for him the path to the ultimate bliss. But he who is niggardly and thinks himself self-sufficient, and gives the lie to the best, We will indeed make smooth for him the path to the ultimate hardship (*Al-Layl* 92:4-10).

> But as for those who strive in Our cause, We shall certainly guide them to Our paths, for indeed Allah is with the doers of good (*Al- 'Ankabut* 29:69).

Thus, the Islamic concept deals with this issue in the correct perspective, whereby Allah's decree in human affairs works through the will of individual persons and through what they do to change themselves and to change the circumstances of their lives.

Furthermore, the Islamic concept teaches the Muslim that Allah has made obligatory on him some clearly spelled out duties, and similarly has forbidden him some clearly defined acts and things. These obligations and prohibitions are open to study and understanding, because there are no mysteries or unknowns among them. Allah will take account only of these matters. As to matters relating to the Unseen, to the Decrees of Allah, and to things beyond human perception, Allah does not make the Muslim responsible to investigate them. In fact, He does not command him to do anything in their regard except to believe that Allah decrees both the good and the evil.

Thus the path of the Muslim is clearly laid out and is straight. He is to fulfill the prescribed obligations, as much as he can; stay away from the clearly defined prohibitions; busy himself in acquiring the knowledge of Allah's commands and prohibitions; and avoid trying to go beyond the limited powers of man's comprehension in knowing the transcendent Unseen.

Indeed, Allah Most High did not intend to place any responsibility on us to know what is beyond our power or to do what is so difficult that it would be impossible to perform. Similarly, Allah Most High did not prohibit anything that would be beyond our power of abstention, or tempt us with a compulsion beyond our power of resistance.

> Allah does not charge any person beyond his capacity. In his favor shall be whatever good he earns, and against him whatever evil he does (*Al-Baqarah* 2:286).

> Whenever they commit an indecency they say, "We found our fathers practicing it, and Allah has commanded us to do it." Say: "Allah does not command indecency. Would you attribute to Allah something of which you have no knowledge?" Say: "My Lord has commanded you to do justice, and to put your whole being into every act of worship and to call on Him, sincere in your faith in Him alone" (*Al-A 'raf* 7:28-29).

Indeed, a person's faith in Allah is not complete unless he believes that Allah does not place a burden on him beyond his power to bear, or prohibit him anything beyond his power to renounce, and this is sufficient.

Through these teachings the right balance is achieved in belief and in understanding, as well as in work and activity. The Islamic concept gives an impetus to the conscience of every man to devote his energy to helping others by righteous deeds and to remaining active and dynamic in following the straight path by relying on the help of Allah in whose hands is everything. It also cuts the roots of lethargy, inaction, wishful thinking, and negativism, and blocks the temptation to transfer the responsibility for one's sins to the Will of Allah. Through these teachings it is made known that Allah is not pleased with unbelief and the rejection of truth, and that He does not want lewdness and indecency to spread among the believers. It is not pleasing to Allah if one leaves evil to itself without struggling against it, or leaves truth to itself without helping to support it, or abandons the earth to itself without the management of stewardship. It is also made clear that the present life is a trial, through the means of both good and evil, and a test in every action and circumstance; that man will be called to account on the Day of Reckoning and will be recompensed for his good and bad deeds; that man is the vicegerent of Allah on earth and has an honorable place in this universe, because he is to manage the affairs of the earth; and that if he does his task of vicegerency according to the way prescribed by Allah, he will be rewarded, and if he fails in this task he will be punished, even though this failure may be due to a lack of courage or to an attempted escape from responsibility.

There is a balance between man's absolute servitude to Allah and man's honorable position in the scheme of existence. The Islamic concept is completely safe and secure from the swings and oscillations that have plagued other religions, philosophies, and belief systems, between the two extremes of deifying man in various forms and degrading man to a level below other animals.

Islam makes a total distinction and separation between the essence of the Creator and the essence of the created, between the station of the Divine and the station of His servants, and between the attributes of the Deity and the attributes of His creatures, so that there remains no doubt or ambiguity about this clear-cut distinction.

Allah, "there is nothing like Him,"[1] means that nothing and no one can share with Him in His Essence or His Nature.

Allah, "He is the First and the Last and the Outward and the Inward,"[2] means that nothing and no one shares with Him in His being.

"All that is on earth will perish, but the Face of your Lord, majestic and splendid will abide,"[3] means that no one shares with Him in His eternity.

Allah, "He will not be questioned for what He does but they will be questioned,"[4] means that no one shares authority with Him.

"Allah is the Creator of all things"[5] means that no one has any share in His creating.

"Allah grants abundant sustenance or gives it in scant measure to

---

[1]*Al-Shura* 42:11
[2]*Al-Hadid* 57:3
[3]*Al-Rahman* 55:26-27
[4]*Al-Anbiya* 21:23
[5]*Al-R'ad* 13:18

whomever He wills"[6] means that no one participates in His sustenance of the world.

"Allah knows and you do not know,"[7] means that no one shares with Him in His knowledge.

"And nothing can be compared with him,"[8] means that no one shares His exalted station.

"Do they believe in forces supposed to have a share in Allah's divinity who enjoin upon them as a moral law something that Allah has never allowed?"[9] means that no one shares with Him in His lawmaking for the people.

The same is true for each and every attribute of Allah Most High.

In contradistinction to Allah, man is His servant, just like any other creature in existence. Man is a servant who has no share in Allah's essence or in any of His attributes. No finite being has anything in common with the Infinite, though the Christians say, depending on their denominations, that the nature of Jesus Christ, may Allah's peace be upon him, is purely Divine or is both Divine and human.

> (As for Jesus) he was nothing but a servant whom We had graced, and We made him to be an example for the children of Israel (*Al- Zukhruf* 43:59).

> Never did the Christ feel too proud to be a servant of Allah, nor do the angels who are near to Him (*Al-Nisa* 4:172).

> Not one of all (the beings) in the heavens or on earth appears before the All-Merciful other than as a servant (*Maryam* 19.93).

With this servitude to Allah, however, man has been honored, because Allah has breathed into him His spirit. Man is honored above all of Allah's creation, even to the extent that Allah commanded the angels, who are near to Allah, to prostrate before Him in respect.

> And when Your Lord said to the angels, "See, I am creating a mortal man from a clay of molded mud. And when I have fully formed him, and breathed My spirit into him, fall

---

[6] *Al-Zumar* 39:52
[7] *Al-Nur* 24:19
[8] *Al-Ikhlas* 112:4
[9] *Al-Shura* 42:21

down before him in prostration!'' Then the angels
prostrated all together, except Iblis (*Al-Hijr* 15:28-30).

Man is the deputy of Allah on this earth, with power over everything
in it and control over all its resources. This was man's role in the design
of the universe even before he came into existence.

> And when Your Lord said to the angels, ''I am setting in the
> earth a vicegerent,'' they said, ''What! Will you put in it a
> being who will spread corruption there and shed blood,
> while we proclaim your praise and sanctify You?'' He said,
> ''Assuredly, I know what you do not.'' And He taught Adam
> all the names. Then He presented them to the angels and
> said, ''Now, tell me the names of these, if you speak truly.''
> They said, ''Glory be to you! We know nothing except what
> You have taught us. Surely, You are the All-knowing and the
> All-wise.'' He said, ''Adam, tell them their names.'' And
> when he told them their names, He said, ''Did I not tell you
> that I know the hidden reality of the heavens and the earth,
> and I know what you reveal and what you conceal'' (*Al-
> Baqarah* 2:30-33).

> And He has subjugated for you, from Himself, all that is in
> the heavens and on the earth (*Al-Jathiyah* 45:13).

> He has placed firm mountains on earth, so that it will not
> shake with you, and rivers and paths, so that you might find
> your way (*Al-Nahl* 16:15).

> Have you not seen that Allah has made subservient to you
> all that is on earth, and the ships that sail on the sea at His
> command, and (that it is He who) holds back the sky so that
> the celestial bodies will not fall upon the earth, except by
> His leave? Surely, Allah is All-Gentle with people and All-
> Compassionate (*Al-Hajj* 22:65).

The human being, as we mentioned earlier, attains to the
highest station and the best position for him when he
commits himself to the service of Allah alone, because at
this level of commitment he is completely in tune with his
nature, in perfect harmony with the rest of existence, and
at the pinnacle of his abilities. This station, which Allah
granted to His Messenger, peace be upon him, when he

received revelation and was taken on the Night Journey and
Ascension, is the highest worship of Allah and is the very
purpose for which man was created. As He says: "I have
created jinn and mankind only to worship me (*Al-Dhariyat*
51:56).

When people attain to this station of servitude exclusively to Allah,
they are protected from servitude to other servants, and every one of
them secures his or her human dignity, whatever worldly positions
and ranks each might have. This station raises their foreheads high,
because they do not bow down before anyone except Allah, and at
the same time it restrains them from false pride and from the haughti-
ness that leads to corruption and tyranny. And it puts in their hearts
the fear of Allah, before whom all servants stand equal. It holds back
any servant of Allah from claiming the Divine attributes for himself,
for example, by promulgating laws for people without authority from
Allah, as if one were a sovereign over people, with the right to make
one's decrees into binding laws for mankind!

Again, in the Islamic concept the dignity, sublimity, and greatness
of man, and his servitude to Allah Most High do not conflict with
reserving Divinity for Allah alone with all the attributes pertaining to
it. Hence, it is not necessary to negate a person's position of servitude
to Allah in order to honor him, nor to ascribe to any person Divine
attributes undeservedly in order to elevate his status, as was done by
the Fathers of the Church and its Councils. They deified Jesus, may
peace be upon him, when they felt the need to honor him and to
elevate his status.

They who say "Allah is the Messiah, Mary's son, have
rejected the truth." For the Messiah said, "Children of
Israel, serve Allah, my Lord and your Lord. Verily if anyone
ascribes divinity to any being besides Allah, Allah will
prohibit him entrance to the Garden, and his abode shall be
the Fire, and such wrongdoers shall have no helpers." They
are unbelievers who say, "Allah is the third of three." No
deity is there but One God. If they do not desist from what
they say, a painful punishment shall afflict the disbelievers
among them. Will they not turn to Allah and ask for His
forgiveness? Indeed Allah is All-Forgiving, All-Compassionate. The Messiah, son of Mary, was only a Messenger.
There have been many Messengers before him. His mother
was a just woman. They both used to eat food. Behold, how

We make clear the signs to them. And then behold how they turn away from the truth" (*Al-Ma'idah* 5:72-75).

And when Allah said, "O Jesus son of Mary, did you say to the people, 'Take me and my mother as gods besides Allah?,' he said, "Glory be to you! It is not possible for me to say what I have no right to. Had I said this, You would have known it. You know what is in my mind, and I do not know what is in Your mind, for indeed, You are the Knower of the Unseen. I only told them what you commanded me, Serve Allah, my Lord and your Lord. And I was a witness over them as long as I dwelt among them, but when You took me to Yourself, you were yourself Watcher over them, for You are witness to everything. If You punish them, they are Your servants. If You forgive them, You are the All-Mighty, the All-Wise" (*Al-Ma'idah* 5:116-118).

Thus, there is no need to downgrade Allah the Exalted, however much one intends to honor man or to declare his high status and his dominance and authority on the earth, or however much Allah opens to him the secrets of matter and lets him have sway over the forces of nature.

Indeed, Allah Most High and man are not equals, nor rivals, nor combatants, and for this reason one does not have to be pushed down to lift the other, nor does one have to be defeated to make the other victorious. This type of ugly thinking among the Europeans is a heritage from Greek mythology and the Jewish tradition, which eventually found its way into Christianity and its secular successors.

Thus we have the story in Greek mythology about the chief deity, Zeus, who became angry at Prometheus for secretly stealing the light of the Sacred Fire (the secret of knowledge) and giving it to man. Zeus did not want man to acquire knowledge and thus vie with the "gods" and eventually depose the Chief god, so he severely punished Prometheus for this terrible crime!

And in Hebrew mythology ("Genesis" 3:22), God is afraid that if the man eats the fruit from the tree of life, i.e. after he had eaten from the tree of knowledge, he would become immortal like a god. So God drove man out of the Garden and stationed cherubim and a whirling and flashing sword to guard the way to the tree of life. And Nietzsche in his mythological work, *Thus Spake Zarathustra*, declares that god is dead and "Superman" is born.

A monstrous word it is, issuing out of their mouths. They say nothing but a lie (*Al-Kahf* 18:4).

In Islam, the human being accepts his true position calmly, contentedly, and with deep satisfaction that he is a true servant of Allah. And in this servitude to Allah he is the noblest of all creatures. He attains his highest position, his greatest happiness, and the best position when he becomes a willing and committed servant of Allah.

We must recognize that because such mythological concepts are hidden underneath European thought and indeed have penetrated deeply into its very heart, their philosophical systems, schools of thought, and indeed their very mode of thinking is in conflict, obviously or not so obviously, with the Islamic concepts and the Islamic mode of thinking. Any borrowing from the European concepts, or their way of thinking, or their schools and philosophical systems, is inherently inimical to the Islamic concept and the Islamic mode of thought. To take anything from European thought or to appeal to it can never be beneficial to Islam. On the contrary, it would act as poison in the body of Islam, paralyze its limbs, destroy its functioning and, if taken in large doses, ultimately kill it!

In the relationship between the servant and his Lord, there is a balance between the servant's attributes of fear, respect, and distance and Allah's attributes active in the universe. The life of people includes both aspects in a perfect balance.

The Muslim reads verses in the Qur'an that devastate his heart and shake his very being, for example:

> And know that Allah comes between a man and his heart, and that it is He to whom you shall be gathered (*Al-Anfal* 8:24).

> He knows of (the tricks) that deceive with the eyes, and all that the hearts conceal (*Ghafir* 40:19).

> It is We who created man, and We know what his soul whispers within him, for We are nearer to him than his jugular vein (*Qaf* 50:18).

> And be aware that Allah knows what is in your minds, so take heed of Him (*Al-Baqarah* 2:239).

> And fear Allah and know that Allah is strict in punishment (*Al-Baqarah* 2:196).

> We shall bring them low step by step without their perceiv-

ing how it has come about. I may give them rein for a while, for truly powerful is My plan (*Al-Qalam* 68:44-45).

Indeed, strong is the grip of Your Lord (*Al- Buruj* 85:12).

Allah is Exalted in Might, Lord of Retribution (*Ale 'Imran* 3:4).

And such is the grasp of your Lord when He takes to task any community given to evildoing. Grievous, indeed, and severe is His punishment (*Hud* 11:102).

And leave Me alone (to deal) with those in possession of the good things of life, but who deny the truth. And bear with them for a little while. With Us are fetters and a Fire, and a food that chokes, and a grievous punishment (*Al-Muzzammil* 73:11-14).

And there are descriptions of the varieties of punishments on the Day of Judgement that fill the heart with dread.[10] But then the Muslim can read about the attributes of his Lord that fill his heart with contentment and peace, and his soul with nearness and love, and his spirit with hope and expectation. Allah says:

When my servants ask you concerning Me, I am indeed near. I listen to the prayer of every supplicant when he calls on Me (*Al-Baqarah* 2:186).

Who is it that responds to the distressed when he calls on Him and who relieves the suffering and has made you inheritors of the earth? Could there be another god besides Allah? (*Al-Namal* 27:82).

Satan threatens you with the prospect of poverty and bids you to unseemly conduct. Allah promises you His forgiveness and bounty, and Allah cares for all, and He is All-knowing (*Al-Baqarah* 2:268).

And Allah will not let your faith be of no effect, for Allah is full of kindness toward man and Most Merciful (*Al-Baqarah* 2:143).

---

[10] See the author's book: *Mashahid Al-Qiyamah*

Allah wishes to lighten your burden, for the human being was created weak (*Al- Nisa* 4:28).

Why would Allah cause you to suffer if you are grateful and believe? Indeed Allah is appreciative of gratitude and He is All- Knowing (*Al-Nisa* 4:147).

Verily, those who believe and do good deeds will the All-Merciful endow with love (*Maryam* 19:96).

And He is Forgiving, and Loving (*Al-Buruj* 85:14).

And Allah is All-Kind to His servants (*Al- Baqarah* 2:207).

And give to the believers who do good works the glad tidings that theirs shall be a goodly reward, to live therein forever (*Al- Kahf* 18:2-3)

And there are descriptions of the varieties of pleasures and luxuries in the life of the Hereafter that fill the heart with joy.[11]

By considering both life and the afterlife and the rewards and punishments in each, the conscience of a person finds a balance between fear and hope, awe and love, and anxiety and contentment. Such a person continues his journey toward Allah with steady steps, open eyes, and a vibrant heart, full of hope, and aware of pitfalls, yet constantly climbing toward the bright horizon. Such persons neither overestimate nor underestimate the realities nor are heedless and forgetful of their responsibilities, yet are always aware that Allah Most Gracious is Forgiving and Forbearing, and Merciful and Full of Bounty, and that Allah does not intend evil toward them, and has not imposed hardships or searched for mistakes in order to inflict revenge. Indeed Allah Most High is far above such things.

We need only compare this concept with that of the Chief god of the Greeks, who is narrow-minded, jealous, sensuous, and malicious, or with the distorted concept of the Lord God of the Israelites who is jealous, partisan, vengeful and cruel. Or we might compare the Islamic concept of Allah, revealed in the Qur'an, with the abstract Divine Being of Aristotle, who is not even aware of the creation but only contemplates Himself, since he is the Most Sublime Being and nothing is befitting to such a god except thinking about the Most Sublime, or we might compare Allah with the concepts of the Materialists whose

---

[11] See the author's book *Mashahid Al-Qiyamah*

deity is "Nature," deaf, dumb, and blind. Then we can truly appreciate the beauty, the sublimity, and the balance of the Islamic concept, and its effects on the personalities and lives of human beings and on their mutual relationships as well as on their several and practical ways of dealing with each other. We will discuss this point in more detail in the chapter "Dynamism."

There is a balance between the sources of knowledge, between the Unseen and the observable in the universe, i.e. between the sources in revelation and scripture and the sources in the universe and life.

We have shown in earlier discussions how the European concept flip-flopped among three sources, emphasizing in turn Scripture (or Revelation) by itself, then reason on its own, and then sensory perception alone as the only valid source of knowledge. The partisans of one would reject the other sources entirely and deny their very existence.

Islam, on the other hand, with its comprehensiveness and balance and with its all-inclusive view of existence, and without any prejudice, whim, desire, ignorance, or deficiency holding it back, does not ignore any source of knowledge. Rather, it gives each source its proper place, neither exaggerating its importance nor down-grading it but assigning to it the place it truly deserves.

Islam refers the whole matter to Allah Most High and to His Will and Plan. Islam attributes the creation to His Will alone, and the creation includes this universe and what it contains, including every human being and his or her intellect and perceptions. It then follows that there cannot be any contradiction in whatever exists in the universe, or nature as is called by the Westerners, nor in life and its expressions, which include economics, the deity of Karl Marx. There cannot be any contradictions in what man observes and knows through his "intellect," because all objects of observation and intellect are made by Allah, and the human abilities to perceive them are also from Him, as is also the other source of knowledge, Revelation.

Islam considers Revelation (*Wahy*) the true source, because it is not touched by falsehood from any direction nor influenced by desire and hence is the highest source. At the same time Islam abolishes neither human reason, nor human powers of observation and sensory perception, nor what surrounds him waiting to be observed, because the physical universe is also an open book of Allah designed to provide knowledge to human minds just as does Revelation. The one difference between the two is that the knowledge man gets through his faculties of physical observation is subject to error and further verification, since it is a product of human effort, while what he learns from Revelation is true without doubt.

Indeed, Allah Most High has created man harmonious within himself and harmonious with the rest of the universe, both animate and inanimate. They are all created by Allah, and they all receive His guidance.

He (Moses) replied, ''Our Lord is the One who gives everything its form and nature and then guides it'' (*Ta Ha* 20:50).

Glorify the name of Your Lord Most High, Who creates (everything), then shapes it and determines its measure, and then guides it (*Al-A 'la* 87:1-3).

And of everything We have created pairs, so that you may receive instruction (*Al-Dhariyat* 51:49).

There is not an animal living on earth nor a bird flying on its wings but forms (parts of) communities like you (*Al-An 'am* 6:38).

(Moses replied) ''My Lord never errs, nor forgets, He who has made for you the earth like a carpet spread out and has provided you with means of communication to move on it and earn your livelihood'' (*Ta Ha* 20:52-53).

From it (the earth) We created you, and into it shall We return you, and from it shall We bring you out once again (*Ta Ha* 20:55).

Glory to Him Who created in pairs all things that the earth produces, as well as their own (human) kind and other things of which they have no knowledge (*Ya Sin* 36:36).

(He is) the Originator of the heavens and the earth, He has made pairs from among yourselves, and pairs among cattle (*Al-Shura* 42:11).

From the many verses in the Qur'an that mention the harmony, cooperation, and balance among all of Allah's creations, including the human beings, we mention a few here.

Have We not made the earth as a wide expanse and the mountains as pegs? And We have created you in pairs, and made sleep for your rest, and made the night as a covering, and made the day for livelihood. We have built above you seven firmaments, and have placed therein a lamp full of blazing splendor. And from wind-driven clouds We send down water in abundance so that We may produce therewith grain and vegetables and gardens dense with foliage (*Al-Naba* 78:6-16).

What! Are you more difficult to create than the heavens which He has built? High has He raised its vault, and then given it order and perfection. And He has made dark its night and brought forth its splendor with the light of day. And after that He spread wide the expanse of the earth and caused its waters to come out of it and its pastures, and has made the mountains firm. All this as a means of livelihood for you and your domestic animals (*Al-Nazi'at* 79:27-33).

Let man consider his food that We pour down water abundantly and split the earth in fragments and then cause grain to grow out of it and grapes and nutritious plants and olive-trees and date-palms and gardens dense with foliage, as well as fruits and herbage for you and your domestic animals to enjoy (*'Abasa* 80:24-32).

And Allah sends down rain from the sky and gives therewith life to the earth after its death. Indeed, in this is a sign for those who listen. And verily in cattle too you will find an instructive sign from what is within their bodies, between excretions and blood, for We produce, for your drink, milk, pure and agreeable to those who drink it. And from the fruit of the date-palm and the vine, you get wholesome drink and food. Behold, in this also is a sign for those who use their reason. And your Lord inspired the bee, ''Make for yourself dwellings in the hills and in trees, and in what (men) may build, and eat all kinds of fruit and follow humbly the paths ordained for you by your Lord.'' There issues from within their bodies a drink of varying hues, wherein is healing for people. Verily in this is a sign for a people who give thought (*Al-Nahl* 16:65-69).

It is Allah who has given you (the ability to build) your houses as rest for you; and has endowed you with (the skill to make) dwellings (tents) out of the skins of animals, which you find so light when you travel and when you camp, and (to make) furnishings and goods for temporary use out of their rough wool and their soft, furry wool and their hair.

It is Allah who made out of the things He created some things to give you as means of protection. Among the hills He made some for your shelter. He gave you (the ability to make) garments to protect you from extreme temperatures, and coats of mail to protect you from your (mutual) violence. In this way He bestows the full measure of His favors on you, so that you may surrender yourselves to Him (*Al-Nahl* 16:80-81).

The point we want to make is this: Islam is based on the premise that there is a fundamental harmony and unity between the universe and man. Within the universe, in life, and in animals there are sources of knowledge for the human being, beyond what he has received through Divine Revelation. Allah Most High exhorts man to receive knowledge of the truth first from the source of Divine Revelation, then from the open book of the universe which is His manifest creation, and also from within his own self. Indeed introspection and knowledge of one's self is a very important source of knowledge for man.

We first present textual examples that draw one's attention to the true and purest source of knowledge, which dominates and safeguards all the other sources:

Verily this Qur'an guides to what is most right (*Al-Isra* 17:9).

Finally We have set you on a way by which the purpose (of faith) may be fulfilled, so follow this way and do not follow the likes and dislikes of those who do not know (the truth) (*Al-Jathiyah* 45:18).

These are messages of a revelation clear in itself and clearly We have sent it down as an Arabic Qur'an from on high in order that you may learn wisdom. In revealing this Quran to you, We explain it to you in the best possible way, since before this you were among those who are unaware (of what Revelation is) *(Yusuf* 12:2-3).

(For although) We did say, "Down with you all from this (state)," there shall nonetheless most certainly come to you guidance from Me. And those who follow My guidance

need have no fear and neither shall they grieve. But those
who are bent on denying the truth and giving the lie to Our
Messages are destined for the fire, and therein shall they
remain (*Al-Baqarah* 2:38-39).

And then We made with you a covenant and caused the
Mount to tower above you, (saying), ''Hold fast by what We
have given you and remember what is therein (*Al-Baqarah*
2:63).

But we also find very many verses of the Qur'an calling our attention
to the open book of the universe, urging us to observe it, ponder upon
it, and learn from it.

And in the earth are signs for those who have sure faith, and
(also) in yourselves. Can you then not see? (*Al-Dhariyat*
51:20-21).

We shall show them Our signs on the horizons and within
themselves until it will be manifest to them that it is the
truth (*Fussilat* 41:53).

Do they (who deny resurrection) never gaze at the clouds
pregnant with water, (and observe) how they are created;
and at the sky how it is raised high; and at the hills, how
firmly they are set up; and at the earth, how it is spread out?
Remind them, for you are only to exhort them (to remember their Lord). You cannot compel them to believe (*Al-
Ghashiah* 88:17-12).

Have they not seen birds obedient (to his laws) in mid-air?
None holds them up but Allah. Herein, indeed, are signs for
a people who believe (*Al-Nahl* 16:79).

In the creation of the heavens and the earth, and the
difference between night and day, and in the ships that sail
upon the sea with what is useful to man, and in the water
that Allah sends down from the sky to revive the earth after
its death and cause all manner of living creatures to multiply
on it, and in the change of the winds and the clouds that
follow their appointed courses between the sky and earth,
are signs for a people who use their reason (*Al-Baqarah*
2:164).

On the role of reason in the service of knowledge, whether in contemplating the signs in the physical world or reflecting upon the truths of Divine Revelation or the realities of life, we find in the Qu'ran various texts.

> Say, "I counsel you one thing only: that you do stand up before Allah — (it may be) in pairs, or (it may be) singly — And reflect (within) yourselves): your companion is not possessed. he is no less than a warner to you, in face of a terrible penalty."(*Saba* 34:46).

> Will they not then ponder on the Qur'an? If it had been from other than Allah, they would have found therein much incongruity (*Al-Nisa* 4:82).

> Do they not travel through the land, so that their hearts (and minds) may thus learn wisdom and their ears may thus learn to hear? Truly it is not eyes that go blind but hearts, which are in their breasts (*Al-Hajj* 22:46).

> In the creation of the heavens and the earth, and the alternation of day and night, there are indeed signs for men of understanding, those who remember Allah standing, sitting, and lying down on their sides, and (thus) reflect on the creation of the heavens and the earth: "Our Lord You have not created this without meaning and purpose. Glory to You!" (*Ale 'Imran* 3:191).

> It is He who brought you forth from the wombs of your mothers and you knew nothing. And He gave you hearing and sight and minds, so that you may be grateful (*Al-Nahl* 16:78).

Thus all sources of knowledge, according to their relative importance, are emphasized in the balanced view of the Islamic concept. None of them is downgraded nor is anyone raised to the level of a deity. In the Qur'anic method of training and education, a great deal of emphasis is placed on directing the human mind toward the study of natural phenomena and of the human self, so that people may know their Creator by knowing His creation, may appreciate His greatness by looking at the greatness of His handiwork, and may love Him by delighting in His favors. Moreover, above all this, the Qur'an is designed to impress upon the human mind the characteristics of

Allah's creation, namely perfection, order, harmony, and beauty without any defect, conflict, or disturbance, just as it also is designed to impress upon the human mind the established laws, rules, and principles that govern creation. And again, by drawing attention to the constantly changing phenomena and events of the universe, and the changing conditions of people, and of constant tides of change in the ideas and feelings within human minds, the Qur'an is designed to engrain upon the human consciousness that Allah alone does not change for He is the One Who causes change but Himself is unchanging. Everything decays and perishes except the Living and Eternal, who does not die. Furthermore, the Qur'an functions to imprint on the human mind and character an awareness of the constancy of the natural laws that govern these changes, and the fixity of the fundamental principles operational in the universe, which show that events do not happen randomly, that life is not purposeless, and that man has not been left alone to his own resources. There is order and measure, trial and reward, and a delicate balance and precise justice in all that takes place.

Much emphasis is placed on sources of knowledge external to the Qur'an, namely, on observation of the phenomenal world and on contemplation of the self. Islam encourages people to learn from Allah's open book, the Qur'an, as well as from all other sources, because there is perfect harmony and balance among all these sources of knowledge, without conflict or contradiction, and without one disparaging the other. Alas we see such conflicts galore in the history of European thought!

To say that Divine Revelation is the fundamental source of knowledge does not imply the cancellation of man's faculties of perception and reasoning, just as the existence of the universe does not imply the non-existence of the human mind or of the Creator. Exalted is He above all these devious concepts followed by the West and the slaves of the West!

There is a balance between man's role and the role of the rest of the universe, and between the position of man and the position of the universe. The Islamic conception of these roles is sound and safe from the deviations and reversals that have afflicted other concepts whenever they have deviated from Allah's guidance.

The straightness of the Islamic concept in respect to man and the universe, becomes crystal clear when we look at the trash heaps of man-made philosophies and belief systems.

In Plato's view, matter was at the lowest level in value and estimation.

''In Plato's philosophy existence is divided into two opposing categories: Absolute Intellect and Matter or Substance. Power belongs entirely to Intellect, while Matter is powerless. Between these two are things ranked according to their proximity to Matter or to Intellect. The higher the Intellectual content in an object the higher its rank in the scheme of the universe.

"Substance is in opposition to the abstract Intellect, but it was not created by the will of the Intellect."[12]

"Plotinus, pursuing the line of thought Plato had set forth, held that matter cannot be the true reality. The true reality is the One from whom the intellect emanates. From the Intellect emanates the Soul, and from the Soul emanates the rest of the existing objects in a descending order until we reach the lowest level in the hierarchy of beings, the material world which is the farthest removed from the One."[13]

Christianity, as formulated by the Church, taught that the world of bodies, or the physical world, is the representation of all that is evil, while the good is in the world of spirit. Thus, whatever is physical must be shunned in order to attain salvation from evil and sin. Similar was the view of Hinduism before that.

While this was the view of the physical world in some philosophies and religions, a reversal of outlook took place during the nineteenth century in European thought. In the positive science of Comte and Fichte "nature" was the originator of life and the human intellect and was looked upon as god. In the formulation of Marx, the material world, in the form of economic activity, became the creator of morals, manners, minds, religions, and philosophies. In comparison with these gods of material order and economic force, an individual human being is worth very little, because he is a passive recipient and his mental activity is merely a secondary by-product of matter!

Among all these philosophies which go to one extreme or another, the Islamic concept stands out because it stands on a firm and fixed foundation. Allah is the Creator, the Originator, the Guardian, and the Ruler of the universe. Both man and the physical world are His creation and between these two elements of creation there is a relationship of harmony and cooperation.

In the Islamic concept man is more honorable in the sight of the Creator than other creatures. He is given dominance over matter, so that he may find its secrets, use it, mold it for his own purpose, change it, and transform it. Yet, his knowledge of the secrets of matter teaches him humility and fills his mind with awe and wonder.

---

[12] Al-Akkad, *Allah*, p. 137.
[13] Ibid, p. 188.

Honoring the human being, without at the same time degrading the physical world, guarantees for man his noble place in the scheme of things, bestows upon him dignity, and makes his life more valuable than anything material, all without underestimating the worth of material things and of human effort to enhance his material prosperity.

These are some aspects of the characteristics of balance in the Islamic concept. Following these examples the reader can pursue the subject further on his own.[14]

---

[14] See Muhammad Qutb's *Manhaj Al-Tarbiyat Al-Islamiyah*.

CHAPTER VII
Dynamism

Say: "Do good works! Allah will surely see your deeds, and (so will) His Messenger and the believers" (*Al-Tawbah* 9:105).

The fifth great characteristic of the Islamic concept is "dynamism." Dynamism is expressed in the active and ongoing relationship of Allah Most High with His creation, with the universe, life, and man. And dynamism is expressed also in the activities of man himself in his own sphere.

In the Islamic concept, the attributes of Allah are not negative attributes, and the perfection of Allah is not expressed in negative terminology, as is the case in Aristotle's concept; nor are His attributes deficient in some aspects of creation and planning, as is the case with the Zoroastrian concept of dualism, whereby Ahura Mazda, the god of light and goodness is equal to Ahriman, the god of darkness and evil; nor are Allah's attributes, according to the Islamic teachings, limited by necessity, as is the case with the God of Plotinus; nor is He confined to the concerns of a single tribe, as is the case with the Lord God of Israel; nor are His attributes mixed and mingled with the attributes of some nature other than Him, as is the case with the Godhead of some Christian denominations; nor are they completely non-existent, as is presumed by atheists who deny the existence of the Living and Purposeful Creator; and so on, down to the bottom of the heap of such nonsensical concepts.

Before we present the clear Islamic concept of the Divine Being, we should have a basis of comparison by considering the man-made alternatives.

"In Aristotle's thought God is everlasting, absolutely perfect, with no will and no action, because action is due to a desire of some object and God is independent of any desire, and because willing means choosing between two courses, while God is the most good and most perfect, and is in no need of choosing between good and bad, or good and better. Aristotle says that God is incapable of initiating action in time because, being self-sufficient and eternal, there is nothing that could persuade Him to action. Furthermore, God must be a self-sufficient Mind, for if it needed any external object to be the object of its thought, it would have in it an element of incompleteness. In fact, as it is a pure Mind entirely active in a single activity of thought, the only object of thought that it can have is itself. It would seem to be Aristotle's final conclusion that the Divine Mind has no knowledge of anything outside itself, and no activity except thinking about itself throughout all eternity.

"The perfect God, therefore, had no idea or will to create the world or pristine matter — the 'substance.' There is, therefore, according to Aristotle, only one way by which it can cause existence and motion, and that is by being the object of love and desire. This 'substance' had the potentiality of existence and a desire for existence made actuality. In other words, God the existent became the desired and the loved of the potential material world, and this desire brought it into actual existence. Similarly, the world desires the absolute perfection of the Unmoved Mover and this desire impels it from deficiency toward perfection, and this process of upward movement continues everlastingly. One cannot then say that God created the world, unless this process is termed creation."[1]

"The Persians, prior to Islam, believed in two gods: a god of good called Ahura Mazda, whose authority and power were limited to the world of goodness and light, and a god of evil called Ahriman, whose authority and power were specific to the forces of evil and darkness. These primal beings were twins and, according to one sect of Zoroastrians, were the 'sons' of the ancient god, Zurvan."

"They believed that before the creation of this world the two dominions were separate. Ahura Mazda then created the material world filling it with mercy and goodness. When Ahriman came to know about his brother's creation, he, together with his evil forces, who were devils, attacked it, marring its perfection, destroying its beauty, and filling it with evil and pain."[2]

"Plotinus, who lived in the early part of the third century after Christ, purified the concept of God to such an extent that it went

---

[1]Abstracted from Al-Akkad, *Haqaiq Al-Islam wa Abatil Khasumihi*, pp. 33-34.

[2]Al-Akkad, *Allah*, p. 188.

beyond all understanding. While Aristotle thought that God's perfection prevented Him from thinking about anything but Himself, and that He knew nothing of other things in existence, Plotinus went further and claimed that the perfection of the Pure Being prevented Him from knowing even Himself. He is exalted even above this knowledge.''

"Out of this One Being all existence comes, losing something of goodness as it is separated from the One, in a chain, each of whose links is farther and farther away from the Pure Being, on to the last link which consists of the material world and animals with their physical bodies.''

"Thus Plotinus says: the One engendered Intelligence, which created Soul; Soul, the offspring of Divine Intelligence, created the rest of the world in a sequence of descending order of beings reaching to the bottom of existence, the world of matter and motion.''[3]

Thus, in Plotinus' view, the only role of the One was to create Intelligence. After that there was nothing for Him to do!

As to "YHWE", the Lord God of Israel, He is the special God of Israel, who demands from the Israelites that they turn away from other gods and worship Him alone. He has anthropomorphic attributes. He can become wrathful and vengeful, but, when His people return to Him, He becomes pleased with them, desists from His intention to destroy them, and becomes extremely sorry for His intentions and actions.

We need not repeat our comments about the varieties of Christian concepts. Their mixing of the nature of man and the nature of God in Jesus, may peace be upon him, and whatever absurdities follow from such contradictions, have been discussed in Chapter I, entitled "The Wilderness and Intellectual Rubbish.'' Similarly, we discussed the various concepts of the Objective Materialists earlier and need not repeat them here.

From this wilderness of murky concepts let us turn now to the clear, straight, and appealing Islamic concept.

In the Islamic concept of God we are dealing with a living Creator and Administrator, an All-knowing God who is active and able to do anything He desires. The Ultimate authority is His. The universe came into being when He willed it to be, and whatever has happened within it and is happening now, including every movement and every change, originates in His will. Nothing takes place in this universe except by His will, knowledge, decision, and action. And He, the Glorious, is directly in touch with every single person, as well as with every animal and every single thing, through His knowledge, His will, and His plan.

---

[3]*Ibid*, p. 188.

The Qur'an presents this fundamental and grand reality of the Islamic concept in great detail by explaining its various aspects and forms, and by detailing the happenings and events that take place in this universe in all their innumerable varieties:

Indeed, your Lord is Allah who created the heavens and the earth in six periods, and is established on the Throne of Sovereignty. He covers the night with the day in rapid succession. The sun, the moon, and the stars are subservient to His command. Indeed, His is all creation and all command! Glorified be Allah, the Sustainer of the Worlds (*Al- A'raf* 7:54).

Allah can never be foiled by anything in the heavens or in the earth. Nothing escapes Him. He is the Knowing, the Able (*Fatir* 35:44).

Say: "O Allah! Master of dominion, You give dominion to whom You will, and You take away dominion from whomever You will. You exalt whom You will and abase whom You will. In Your hand is all good. Verily, over all things You have power. You cause the night to gain on the day and You cause the day to gain on the night. You bring forth the living from the dead and You bring forth the dead from the living. You give sustenance to whomsoever You will without count (*Ale 'Imran* 3:26-27).

He is Omnipotent over His servants, and He is the All-Wise, the All-Aware (*al An'am* 6:18).

Allah knows what every female bears, and by how much the wombs fall short [of their time] or exceed [it]. Everything with Him is in due proportion. He is the Knower of the Unseen and the Visible, the Great, the Exalted. It is the same (to Him) whether any of you conceals his thought or brings it into the open or whether he seeks to hide under the cover of night or walks in the light of day, [thinking that] he has hosts of helping angels before him and behind him that could preserve him from whatever Allah may have willed. Allah does not change the condition of a people until they change what is within themselves. If Allah desires to afflict a people, there is no turning it back. Apart from Him, they have no protector. It is He who shows you the lightning [a cause] for fear and hope, and He builds up the clouds heavy with rain. Thunder proclaims His praise, and so do the angels, who are in awe of Him. He sends the thunderbolts and strikes with them whomever He wills. Yet people dispute concerning Allah, Who is mighty in power, despite all the evidence that He alone has the power to continue whatever His unfathomable wisdom wills! His is the call of the truth, and those who they invoke instead of Allah cannot respond to them in any way, [so that he who invokes them] is like the man who stretches out his hands toward water [hoping] that it will reach his mouth, though it never does. The prayer of the unbelievers goes nowhere but astray. All who are in the heavens and on earth prostrate themselves, willingly or unwillingly, as do their shadows in the morning and evenings. Say: "Who is the Lord of the heavens and the earth?" Say: "It is Allah." Say: "Do you then take protectors other than Him, such as have no power either for good or for harm to themselves?" Say: "Are the blind and the seeing equal? Or are the darkness and the light equal?" Or do they believe that there are, side by side with Allah, other divine powers that have created the like of what He creates, so that this act of creation appears to them to be similar (to His)? Say: "Allah is the Creator of everything, and He is the One who holds absolute sway over all that exists" (*Al-R'ad* 13:8-16).

If Allah touches you with affliction, there is none who can relieve it except Him, and if He touches you with good, He is able to do all things (*al An'am* 6:17).

To Allah belongs the sovereignty of the heavens and the earth. He creates what He wills. He bestows female (offspring) upon whomever He wills and bestows male (offspring) upon whomever He wills or He mingles them, males and females, and He makes barren whomever He wills, for He is All-Knowing, All-Powerful (*Al-Shura* 42:49-50).

Allah takes souls at the time of their death, and (He takes) the one that has not died during its sleep. He keeps back that (soul) for which He has decreed death, but dismisses the rest until an appointed term (*Al-Zumar* 39:42).

There is no secret conference of three without His being

their fourth, nor five without His being their sixth, nor of less than that or more without His being with them wheresoever they may be. And afterwards, on the Day of Resurrection, He will inform them of what they did. Truly, Allah is the Knower of all things (*Al-Mujadilah* 58:7).

The consciousness of this intimate connection of the Creator with His creation is the foundation on which the edifice of faith is erected, the conscience of man is sharpened, moral feelings are enhanced, and standards of behavior are established.

Indeed, there is a vast gulf between a creed that proclaims a dynamic and continual relationship between Allah and His servants, and another that considers the Deity to be remote and uncaring. The faith that inculcates such a positive attitude toward Allah brings human activity into line with human nature, while a negative attitude toward the Deity separates day-to-day life from the spiritual aspects of human nature.

As a matter of fact, a man's concept of his Creator, and his concept of Allah's attributes and their connection with human life, define the value of Allah to him as well as the nature of the man's relationship with Allah.

There is a great difference between a person who thinks that Allah does not care about him or that He does not even know about him, as some philosophers have said, and the person who knows that Allah is his Creator, his Provider, and the Master of his affairs here and in the Hereafter.

Similarly, there is a difference between a person who is to deal with two quarreling gods, as the Persians thought, or a multitude of deities, as other polytheists presumed, and a person who looks toward Allah, Who has One Will, the One who reveals to people in precise terms what actions of theirs are pleasing to Him so that they may do them, and what actions are evil so that they may refrain from them.

Imagine the predicament of a polytheist who may have to deal with a god who is lustful, tyrannical, capricious, and willful, such as the chief god of the Greeks, Zeus or Jupiter, whom, in the words of Al-Akkad, they imagined to be "malicious, fierce, and fond of eating, drinking, and of amorous escapades. He did not care a bit about the affairs of other gods or of human beings except as they affected his sovereignty or interfered with his tyranny. He became angry with the "god" of medicine, Aesculapius, because he treated the sick, and he forbade Aesculapius from levying a tax on the souls of the dead who were transferred from the surface of the earth to the Underworld. He also became furiously angry with Prometheus, who, according to the

Greeks, was the god of knowledge and industry, and who stole the radiant light of all-consuming fire and gave this blessing to humanity. To punish him, Zeus ordered Hephaestus to chain Prometheus to a high crag of the Caucasus mountains where an eagle would eat out his liver all day long. During the night the liver would become whole again for the eagle to feast upon the next day, and so the torment would continue without healing and without pity."[4]

"Zeus, the chief god, who resided on Mount Olympus, had many affairs behind the back of his wife, Hera. Once he sent Hermes to the palace of Helios, the sun god, to tell him not to drive his chariot the next day so that he, Zeus, might have ample time for adultering with someone else's wife."[5]

There is a vast difference between a person who is to deal with such a god, learning from him indecent and immoral behavior, and the one who deals with Allah the Just, the Generous, the Merciful, who forbids indecent deeds, open or secret, and who loves those who are pure and clean and turn to Him in repentance.

Worse still is the case of a person who supposes that dumb, blind "Nature" is his creator, demanding from him neither belief nor faith, nor a way of life, nor morals and manners, nor conscience and good behavior. Such a "god" is entirely unaware of his existence, and, in fact, is devoid of any perception and knowledge. Obviously an entity that has no sense, no vision, and no perception of good and evil is incapable of taking account of good or evil behavior. There is then a vast difference between a person who takes "Nature" as his creator, and the one who recognizes Allah as his Creator, One who is Living and Eternal, Who responds to the needs of His creatures, Who is never absent and is a reckoner and never forgets, Who is just and never oppresses, and Who is merciful and responds to the call of those in distress.

Indeed, the whole way of life is entirely different, and consequently this characteristic of the Islamic concept has deep significance and great value in the life of a Muslim. It is a great blessing of Islam that it impresses upon the minds of the Muslims the living presence of Allah and the dynamic relationship of Allah with His creation. The first generation of Muslims lived in the shade of Divine Revelations, which were very closely related to the events in their lives and with what troubled their hearts, thus providing a concrete example of this characteristic. We have seen how the hand of Allah Most High operated in their lives and how they were able to see its operation very clearly.

---

[4]Al-Akkad, *Haqaiq Al-Islam wa Abatil Khasumihi*, pp. 40-41.
[5]*Ibid*.

We have witnessed how Allah's decision openly came down concerning a quarrel between an ordinary couple when the Messenger, may Allah's peace and blessings be upon him, did not find a solution to it:

> Allah has heard the words of the woman who pleads with you (Muhammad) concerning her husband and complains to Allah (about the unjust pre-Islamic custom of *zihar*). Allah hears what you both have to say. Surely Allah is All-Hearing, All-Knowing (*Al- Mujadilah* 58:1).

We have also witnessed how Allah addressed His Messenger, may Allah's peace and blessing be upon him, in connection with a poor, blind man, Ibn Umm Maktum:

> He (Muhammad) frowned and turned away because the blind man approached him. Yet for all you knew (Muhammad), he might have grown in purity or have been reminded (of the truth) and helped by this reminder. But you gave your whole attention to the person who thinks himself self-sufficient. Yet it is not your concern if he does not attain to purity. But you paid no heed to the one who came to you with earnest purpose and in awe of Allah. Nay, indeed, these (messages) are a Reminder, so let whosoever wills, pay heed to them (*'Abasa* 80:1-12).

We also have seen how Allah intervened in the great events of early Islam. We saw this in the migration of the Prophet from Makkah to Madinah:

> If you do not help him, the Messenger, then (know that Allah will do so, just as) Allah helped him when those who disbelieved drove him out and (he was only) one of two, when these two[6] were in the cave, and he said to his comrade, ''Grieve not! Surely Allah is with us.'' Then Allah sent down on him His peace of reassurance and supported him with hosts that you did not see, and He humbled to the depths the cause of the unbelievers, but Allah's cause is exalted to the heights, for Allah is All-Mighty and All-Wise (*Al-Tawbah* 9:40).

---

[6] The Prophet and Abu Bakr

We also witnessed His intervention in the Battle of Badr, as mentioned by Allah Most High:

> And your Lord brought you forth from your house with the truth, and a part of the believers were averse to it and disputed with you concerning the truth after it had become clear, as though they were being driven to death with their eyes wide open. And when Allah promised you that one of the two bands (of the enemy) should be yours, you wished that one not armed should be yours, but Allah willed that the truth be triumphant by His words, and cut the root of the disbelievers, so that He might prove the truth and disprove the falsehood, however much the sinners might be averse to it. When you were calling upon your Lord for Help and He answered you, ''I shall reinforce you with a thousand angels, rank upon rank,'' Allah did so in order to give you good tidings so that your hearts thereby might be at rest, for there is no help except with Allah. Surely Allah is All-Mighty and All-Wise. (Remember how) He caused inner calm to enfold you as an assurance from Him, and sent down water from the sky to purify you thereby and to remove from you the fear of Satan, and to strengthen your hearts, and to make firm your steps. (And remember how) your Lord inspired the angels (to convey this message to the believers:) ''Surely I am with you.'' (And He commanded the angels:) ''So make the believers stand firm (with these words from Me:) 'I will instill terror in the hearts of the unbelievers. So strike their necks, (O believers), and strike off every one of their fingers''' (Al-Anfal 8:5-12).

And concerning the Battle of Uhud, Allah says:

> Allah has been true to His promise toward you when you were about to destroy your foes by His leave, until you lost heart and disagreed about the order and disobeyed, after He had brought you in sight of the (victory) that you longed for. Some of you desired this world, and some of you desired the Hereafter. Then He made you flee from them, so that He might try you, yet now He has forgiven you, for Allah is bounteous to the believers. (Remember) when you climbed (the hill) in flight and paid no heed to anyone, and the Messenger, in your rear, was calling you (to fight). Therefore He rewarded you with grief in return for (the

Messenger's) grief, so that (He might teach) you not to sorrow either for what you missed or for what befell you. Allah is aware of what you do. Then, after this grief, He sent down upon you a sense of security, an inner calm and self confidence, which enfolded some of you, while another party, who were anxious for themselves, entertained wrong thoughts about Allah, the thoughts of ignorance, saying, "Did we, then, have any power of decision (in this matter)?" Say, "Verily, all power of decision does rest with Allah." But they are trying to conceal in their hearts (a thought) that they did not reveal to you (O Prophet, by) saying, "Ah, if we had any power of decision in this affair, never would so many of us have been slain here." Say, "Even if you had been in your houses, those for whom slaying was appointed would have gone forth to the places where they were to lie." (All this befell you) in order that Allah might try what is in your breasts and render your innermost hearts pure, for Allah is aware of what is hidden in the hearts (of men) (*Ale 'Imran* 3:152-154).

We have observed Allah's direct intervention in all the important affairs of the early Muslims. This direct intervention was not confined only to the first generation of Muslims because this is Allah's way in every situation, in every affair, and at all times, whether we realize it or not. It was evidenced in the lives of all the Messengers of Allah, peace be upon them, as reported by Allah Most High in the Holy Qur'an.

In the confrontation of Moses, peace be upon him, with Pharaoh and his officials, Allah's direct intervention was unveiled to the beholders.

We narrate to you something of the story of Moses and Pharaoh, setting forth the truth for a people who believe. Now Pharaoh had exalted himself in the land and had divided its inhabitants into castes. One group among them he oppressed. He slaughtered their sons and spared only their women, for he was one of those who spread corruption. We desired to show favor to those who were oppressed in the land, and to make them forerunners in faith and heirs (to Pharaoh's glory), and to establish them securely on earth, and to show Pharaoh and Haman and their hosts what they were dreading from them. So We revealed to the mother of Moses, "Suckle him, and when you fear

for him then cast him into the river, and do not fear or
grieve. We shall bring him back to you and shall make him
one of Our messengers.'' And the family of Pharaoh took
him up, for (We had willed) that he might become for them
an enemy and a source of sorrow, because Pharaoh and
Haman and their hosts were indeed sinners. Pharaoh's wife
said, ''He will be a comfort for me and you. Do not kill him.
Perhaps he may be of use to us, or we will adopt him as a
son.'' And they were not aware (of his future). And the heart
of Moses' mother became empty and she would have
betrayed him if We had not fortified her heart, so that she
might keep alive her faith (in Our promise). And so she said
to his sister, ''Follow him.'' So she observed him from a
distance, even while they (who had taken him in) were not
aware of it. Now from the very beginning We caused him
to refuse the breast of (Egyptian) nurses. So (when his sister
learned this,) she said, ''Shall I direct you to a family that
might rear him for you and take good care of him?'' So We
restored him to his mother, so that she might be comforted
and not grieve, and so she might know that the promise of
Allah always comes true, even though most of them do not
know this (*Al- Qasas* 28:2-13).

And in the case of Noah, peace be on him, we read:

The people of Noah denied (resurrection) long before those
(who now deny it), and they denied Our servant and said,
''He is a madman,'' and he was rejected. So he called upon
his Lord, saying, ''I am vanquished! Help me!'' Then We
opened the gates of heaven so that water poured down in
torrents and made the earth gush forth with fountains, and
the waters met for a preordained purpose. But We carried
him upon a vessel well-planked and well-caulked, running
before Our sight, as a reward for him who was denied
(*Al-Qamar* 54:9-14).

And in the case of Abraham, peace be upon him:

They said, ''Burn him, and help your gods, if you would do
something?'' We said, ''O fire, be coolness and safety for
Abraham!'' They desired to outwit him, so We made them
the real losers. And We delivered him and Lot into the land
that We had blessed for all peoples. And We bestowed upon

him Isaac, and Jacob as a grandson. Each of them We made righteous and appointed them to be leaders guiding by Our command, for We inspired them to do good works, and to be constant in prayers, and to give charity, and they worshipped Us alone (*Al-Anbiya* 21:68-73).

We observe His actions in the entire universe and in both animate and inanimate creation.

Verily, it is Allah (alone) who upholds the heavens and the earth so they will not deviate, for if they should ever deviate, none could uphold them after He ceases to do so. Surely He is All-Clement, All-Forgiving (*Fatir* 35:41).

Have they not regarded the birds subject (to His law) in mid-air? None holds them but Allah. Surely in this are signs for a people who believe (*Al-Nahl* 16:79).

How many animals are there that are helpless in providing for their own sustenance! Yet Allah provides for them and for you (*Al- 'Ankabut* 29:60).

Have you considered the seed you sow in the soil? Do you cause it to grow or are We the growers? If We willed, We would crumble it to dry powder and you would be left to wonder (and lament): ''Verily, we are ruined! We have been deprived (of our livelihood)!'' Have you considered the water you drink? Do you bring it down from the clouds, or do We send it down? If We willed, We could make it bitter. Why, then are you not thankful? Have you considered the fire you kindle? Do you grow the tree that feeds it or do We grow it? We made it to remind you (of Us) and as a boon to all who are lost and hungry in the wilderness (*Al-Waqi'ah* 56:63-73).

Have they not seen how We visit the earth (with Our punishing), gradually depriving it of all that is best on it? For, (when) Allah judges, no one can postpone His judgment, and He is swift in reckoning (*Al-Ra'd* 13:41).

The Qur'an is full of descriptions of the dynamic and positive relationship of Allah with His creation, and this, together with the Oneness of Allah Most High, constitutes the basis of the Islamic concept. Indeed, Allah's Oneness is expressed through this dynamic relationship.

In the Islamic belief, Allah is active and participatory and not like the gods of Aristotle or Plotinus, which are passive and self-centered.

The first generation of Muslims, the generation of the Companions of the Prophet, internalized this reality and became without exception the most unique and the most distinguished community in the entire history of mankind. In their daily lives, morning and evening, day in and day out, they lived with Allah Most High, and felt His presence within their selves and all around them more deeply and more concretely than the senses of touch and sight. They lived in the shades of His mercy, under His watchful eyes, and saw His hand intervening in their affairs, big and small, obliterating their mistakes, guiding them, and supporting them. With this realization in their hearts, they were alert but contented, awake but at rest, active but relying on Allah, fearful yet hopeful, humble before Allah and dignified before others for the sake of Allah, subservient to Allah and eager to gain the upper hand over His enemies. Through these people Allah brought great reforms and constructive changes in the world, whereby they cleansed it and uplifted people to an extent unprecedented in human history.

Another aspect of the dynamism of Islam is manifested in the active role it assigns to man in general and to the Muslim in particular, in this world.

The nature of the Islamic concept is not to remain hidden in the human mind. It must be translated immediately into action and become a concrete reality in the world of events. The believer cannot be content to have his faith remain concealed in his heart, because he feels compelled to make his faith an effective force in changing his own life and the lives of the people around him.

Indeed, the Islamic concept is not like a theory, or an ideal dream, or spiritual mysticism, which may remain passively in the depths of the human heart. It is a practical "plan" designed to be implemented. As long as it is not implemented, its value remains purely academic, and that is not its intent. It keeps stirring in the heart of the Muslim, spurring him to work in order to realize its goals in the world of events.

Thus the Islamic concept keeps the mind of the Muslim restless, always calling him to action from the depths of his consciousness, telling him to get up and go out and actualize this concept in the real world. It refines his sensibilities in order to bring the entire power of his belief and will to bear upon the reconstruction of a society so that the Islamic faith may be realized in the lives of people.

Whenever the Qur'an mentions belief or the believers, it also mentions appropriate deeds that translate the belief into practice, because Islam is not just a matter of feelings but of feeling that moves people to action in accordance with the Islamic ''plan'' and the Islamic concept.

> The believers are only those who believe in Allah and His Messenger and afterward do not doubt, but strive with their wealth and their lives for the cause of Allah. Such are the sincere (*Al-Hujurat* 49:15).

> Allah has promised those of you who believe and do good works that He would surely cause them to gain power and security in the world, even as He caused (some of) those before them, and that surely He will firmly establish the religion for them that He has approved for them, and will give them in exchange, after their fear, security. They shall serve Me and not ascribe divine powers to anything beside Me. But those who disbelieve after (having understood) this are truly iniquitous (*Al-Nur* 24:55).

> You are the best nation ever brought forth for people, bidding what is honorable, and forbidding what is dishonorable, and believing in Allah (*Ale 'Imran* 3:110).

> And their Lord answers them, ''I shall not lose sight of anyone of you who labors (in My cause), male or female, in as much as one of you is like the other. And those who emigrated, and were expelled from their homes, or suffered torture in My way and fought and were slain, shall I surely forgive their bad deeds, and I shall admit them to gardens underneath which rivers flow, as a reward from Allah, for with Allah is the best reward'' (*Ale 'Imran* 3:195).

> Consider the flight of time! Surely man is bound to lose himself unless he is among those who believe and do good works and counsel each other to pursue the truth and to be steadfast (*Al-'Asr* 103:1-2).

So, faith is not merely feelings in the heart or ideas in the mind, with no application in life, nor is faith merely rituals of worship, without action in society and effort to establish Allah's legislation.[7] The Mus-

---

[7]Refer back to the chapter, ''Comprehensiveness,'' in this book.

lim, under the inspiration of the Islamic concept, feels personally responsible to be a witness to the universal and eternal *din* of Islam. He cannot rest, nor can his conscience be satisfied, nor does he feel that he has fully expressed his thanks to Allah Most High for His great favor in making him a Muslim, nor can he even hope to be saved from Allah's punishment here and in the Hereafter, unless he has given complete testimony to the truth of Islam through his life, effort, and wealth.

> Thus We have appointed you as a mediating, median, and justly balanced nation so that you might be witnesses to the people and so that the Messenger might be a witness to you (*Al-Baqarah* 2:143).

> And who does greater evil than the one who conceals a testimony received from Allah? (*Al-Baqarah* 2:140).

The first manifestation of this testimony is within one's own self. One must bring one's personal life, in every detail, in line with one's concept and belief. One's every movement must conform to the demands of this *din*, so that one is witnessing to the truth of Islam by action and not merely by the tongue or by the heart. One should become a living embodiment of one's faith and be visible to everyone by initiating action in the real world and in the affairs of mankind.

Secondly, one expresses one's testimony by inviting others to this way of life through clear exposition of the Islamic concept. There are a great many motives for this invitation and this exposition. One's foremost motive is to thank Allah Most High for the blessing of Islam. Secondly, this concept teaches us that all mankind is a single brotherhood, and our goodwill toward our brethren propels us to inform them about the truth to which we are guided, because this truth is not meant only for ourselves or our family, tribe, nation, ethnic group, or race, but is meant for all the people in the world. Thirdly, our consciousness of the responsibility, similar to the responsibility of the Messengers of Allah, to dispel others' ignorance and error, motivates us to convey this message to one and all. We know that we are successors to the Messengers of Allah, and their burden is now on our shoulders.

> We sent all those Messengers as bearers of good tidings and as warners, so that men might have no excuse before Allah after the coming of these Messengers (*Al Nisa* 4:165).

> We never chastise, until We send forth a Messenger (*Al-Isra* 17:15).

Lastly, one gives testimony through one's efforts to establish the way of life prescribed by Allah, to build the system that proceeds from the Islamic concept, and to organize the affairs of man, and of all peoples, on the basis of this system. This is so because this concept is the theoretical "plan" or "framework" for the real world and is intended to become the way of life for all the people on earth. Islam, which proclaims that Sovereignty over people belongs to Allah alone, cannot exist without a society that recognizes Allah as its Sovereign and builds its entire system of life on this fundamental principle. When Muslims dedicate themselves entirely to this collective effort, then and only then do they deserve the help of Allah promised to them. This condition is a very clear condition and there is no ambiguity about it.

> Assuredly Allah will help the one who helps Him for surely Allah is Most Powerful and Almighty and (well aware of) those who, (when) We establish them firmly on earth, remain constant in prayer, and pay the prescribed charity, and enjoin what is right and forbid doing wrong, but with Allah rests the final outcome of all events (*Al-Hajj* 22:40-41).

It is the very nature of the Islamic concept to encourage and urge the human being to do something positive and productive, because according to the Islamic concept man is an active agent and not a passive recipient on this earth. To begin with, he is the deputy of Allah on earth, and he has been made the deputy in order to actualize the way prescribed by Allah, which is to initiate, to build, to change, and to make developments in the land in reliance on the natural forces that Allah has created to be of use to human beings in their work.

> It is He Who sends down water from the sky; from it you drink and out of it (grow) the plants upon which you pasture your herd. And with it He causes crops to grow for you, and olive trees, and palms, and grapes, and all kinds of fruit. Surely in this is a sign for a people who think. And He has made the night and the day and the sun and the moon subservient for you, and the stars are subservient to His command. Surely in this are signs for a people who use their reason. And in all the many things on this earth that He has multiplied for you in many hues (of kind, quality, and

color), indeed, are signs for a people who meditate on Allah and His bounties. And it is He Who has made the sea subservient, so that you may eat from its fresh meat, and take from it gems to wear. And you see the ships plowing through its waves so that you seek His bounty. And perhaps you may be thankful. And He has placed firm mountains on earth, lest it sway with you, and rivers and paths, so that you may find your way, and means of orientation, and stars by which (men) guide themselves. Is, then, He Who creates like the one who cannot create? Will you not then grasp the message? (*Al-Nahl* 16:10-17).

The condition for deserving this vicegerency of Allah on earth is well-known to the Muslim:

(For although) We did say, "Down with you all from this (state)," there shall nonetheless must certainly come to you guidance from Me. And those who follow My guidance need have no fear and neither shall they grieve. But those who are bent on denying the truth and giving the lie to Our Messages are destined for the fire, and therein shall they remain (*Al-Baqarah* 2:38-39).

The Muslim's consciousness that he is obligated to work, and that he is helped in doing his work, makes him aware that in his relationship either to natural forces or to the Will of Allah Most High there is no place for negativism in the system of this universe. He has been given his capabilities and powers, and the natural environment and laws are all there to help him for a purpose. And, as we stated previously, there is a balance between the absolutely free Will of Allah and the positive actions of man. For this reason man's role in the universe must be dynamic, productive, and positive.

Once the negative attitudes are removed from a person's mind, he is impelled toward work and dynamic action. Islam is not satisfied merely with removing the negative attitudes, but rather reinforces positive attitudes by teaching that Allah's will, among human beings, works through themselves and through their actions.

Indeed, Allah does not change what is in a people until they change what is in themselves (*Al-R'ad* 13:11).

Fight them, and Allah will chastise them by your hands and bring disgrace upon them, and He will bring healing to the breasts of those who believe, and He will remove the anger within their hearts. And Allah will turn in His mercy toward whomever He wills, for Allah is All-Knowing, All-Wise (*Al-Tawbah* 9:14-15).

Now, if the hypocrites, and those in whose hearts is disease, and those who make commotion in the city by spreading false rumors, do not stop (their evil actions) We shall assuredly urge you against them and indeed give you (Muhammad) mastery over them, and then they will remain your neighbors there for only a little while (*Al-Ahzab* 33:60).

Had Allah not driven back the people, some by means of others, the earth would have been corrupted, but Allah is bounteous toward all creation (*Al-Baqarah* 2:251).

Corruption has appeared on land and sea because of what man's own hands have wrought, and so He will let them taste (the evil of) some of their doings so that they might turn back (to the right path) (*Al-Rum* 30:41).

Islam also teaches that Allah is not pleased with mere thoughts in the minds of men and words on their tongues. He does not let a people alone until they translate their faith into action, and he continues to show them His signs until their reward from Him comes in the form of clear guidance.

But those who strive in Our cause, surely We shall guide them in Our ways; and Allah is with the doers of good (*Al-'Ankabut* 29:69).

Or did you suppose you would enter Paradise without Allah determining which among you have striven hard and shown patience? (*Ale 'Imran* 3:142).

Say, "Do good Work! Allah will surely see your deeds, and (so will) His Messenger and the believers. And you will be returned to Him who knows the seen and the unseen, and then He will make you understand what you have been doing" (*Al-Tawbah* 9:105).

Contemplating all this, the Muslim realizes that his existence in the world is not a transitory, unplanned, or chance event, but has been foreordained with a definite purpose. He has been brought into being on this earth in order to work for his own sake and for the sake of others. This earth is his field of action, and in this universe of space and time his actions are recorded. He will be considered to have given proper thanks to his Creator for his existence and for His favor of bestowing upon him the true faith, and he may hope to attain salvation from Allah's accounting and chastisement, only by fulfilling certain conditions. He must fulfill his positive role as Allah's vicegerent on earth, obey His guidance, apply this guidance to his life and to the lives of others, and struggle to uproot corruption from the earth, especially the corruption that comes by not applying the way of life prescribed by Allah for every person and community of people. If such corruption occurs, part of the blame may be on his shoulders for not being a witness to Allah in his own life before others and before the entire world.

When the Muslim looks at the situation in this manner, his self-image is elevated and his ambitions increase in proportion to his perception of the responsibilities he is supposed to bear and the tasks he is to perform. His life focuses on meeting his Lord, and his fondest desires are to stand up as a witness to the truth, fulfill the trust laid upon him, complete his tasks to the best of his powers, and to remain close to Allah forever, far removed from the Fire.

CHAPTER VIII

Realism

Say, "Glory be to my Lord! Am I anything more than a mortal messenger?" (*Al-Isra* 17:93).

The sixth characteristic of the Islamic concept is its realism. This concept deals with objective realities whose existence is certain and whose effects are positive and concrete. Mere abstract ideas or unattainable ideals that are not functional in the real world are not its concern. The system of life that it delineates for mankind is realistic and eminently practical because it is designed by Allah to be implemented in human societies. At the same time, this system calls for a realistic idealism or an ideal realism because it demands a very high level of performance from the human beings and great perfection in conduct and behavior. Let us elaborate on these aspects of the Islamic concept.

The Islamic concept deals with objective realities whose existence is certain and whose effects are positive and concrete. These realities are the actions of the Divine Being as He manifests Himself actively and positively in the world of events, the reality of the physical universe as it is felt and seen, and the reality of man as manifested in individual persons throughout the world.

The Divine Being with whom the Islamic concept deals is Allah, Who alone possesses Divine attributes manifested in the real world. These attributes are not something abstract or relegated to the realm of metaphysics because their effects are concrete and observable in the physical universe, and because the human intellect is capable of recognizing these effects as the creation of Allah Most High.

Extol Allah's limitless glory when you enter upon the
evening hours and when you rise for morning prayers. To
Him is due all praise in the heavens and earth, so (glorify
Him) also during the sun's decline and at noon. He brings
forth the living from the dead, and brings forth the dead
from the living, and He revives the earth after it is dead. In
a like manner you shall be brought forth. And among His
signs is that He created you from dust, and then, behold,
you become human beings ranging far and wide. And
among His signs is that He created for you spouses out of
your own kind so that you might dwell with them in
tranquillity, and He engenders love and tenderness between you. Surely in this are signs for a people who reflect.
And among His signs is the creation of the heavens and
earth, and the variety of your languages and colors. Surely
in this are signs for all who are endowed with (innate
knowledge. And among His signs is your sleep during the
night or day, and your (ability to go about in) quest of some
of His bounties. Surely in this are signs for a people who
(are willing to) listen! And among His signs is that He shows
you lightning, causing both fear and hope, and that He
sends down rain from the sky and with it revives the earth
after it is dead. Surely in this are signs for a people who use
their reason. And among His signs is that the heaven and
earth stand firm by His command. (Remember all this, for)in
the end when He will call you forth from the earth by a
single call you will (all) emerge (for judgement). To Him
belongs every being in the heavens and the earth. All are
obedient to Him. And it is He Who originates creation, then
recreates it. And it is most easy for Him, since His is the
essence of all that is sublime in the heavens and on earth,
and He alone is the All-Mighty, the All-Wise *(Al-Rum* 30:17-
27).

It is Allah Who splits the grain and the date-stone, brings
forth the living from the dead and brings forth the dead
from the living. That is Allah; then how are you deluded
away from the truth? He makes the dawn appear, and has
made the night for resting, and the sun and moon for the
reckoning (of time). Such is the judgement and ordering of
the All-Mighty, the All-Knowing. It is He Who has appointed for you the stars, so that by them you might be
guided in the darknesses, whether on land or sea. We thus

explain Our signs for a people who have knowledge. It is
He Who produced you from a single person; and then there
is a place of sojourn and a place of departure. We detail our
signs for a people who understand. It is He Who sends
down water from the sky. With it We bring forth the shoot
of every plant and then We bring forth the green leaf of it,
producing from it grain heaped up (at harvest); and out of
the palm tree, from the sheaths of it, dates thick-clustered,
hanging low and near; and gardens of grapes, olives, and
pomegranates, each similar (in kind) and yet different (in
variety). Look upon their fruits when they begin to bear
fruit and ripen. Surely, in all this are signs for a people who
believe. Yet some (people) have come to attribute to the jinn
a place side by side with Allah, although He created them
(all). And in their ignorance they impute to Him sons and
daughters. Glory be to Him! Sublimely exalted is He above
what they ascribe (to Him). He is the Originator of the
heavens and the earth. How could it be that He should have
a child, since He has no mate and since He created all things
and He alone knows everything? Such is Allah, your Sustainer. There is no deity but He, the Creator of everything.
Worship then, Him alone, for He has power to dispose of
all affairs. No human vision can encompass Him, whereas
He encompasses all vision, for He alone is the Unfathomabe
(All-Subtle) and the All-Aware *(Al-An'am* 6:95-103).

Say, "All praise is due to Allah, and peace be on His servants
whom He has chosen." Is Allah better, or those to whom
they ascribe a share in His divinity? Who is it that created
the heavens and the earth, and sent down for you water
from the sky? For it is by this means that We cause gardens
full of loveliness to grow, whereas it is not in your power
to cause trees to grow. Could there be any divine power
besides Allah? No, they are people who swerve. Who is it
that made the earth a place of rest and a fitting abode, and
made rivers in its midst, and set upon it firm mountains,
and placed a partition between the two bodies of water. Is
there a god besides Allah? No! most of them do not know.
Who is it that answers the distressed when he calls out to
Him and removes the suffering, and has made you inheritors of the earth? Is there a god besides Allah? How
seldom do you keep all this in mind and meditate on it! Who
is it that guides you in the darknesses on the land and sea,

and sends the winds bearing glad tidings of His coming mercy and grace. Is there a god besides Allah? Exalted is Allah above what they ascribe as partners (to Him). Who is it that originates creation, then repeats it, and gives you sustenance from the sky and the earth. Is there a god besides Allah? Say, "Produce your evidence, if you are truthful" *(Al-Namal* 27:60-64).

The Originator of the heavens and the earth has made for you pairs from among yourselves, and pairs among cattle, in order thus to cause you to multiply. There is nothing like Him. He is the All-Hearing and the All-Seeing. To Him belong the keys of the heavens and the earth. He enlarges and restricts His provision to whomever He wills. Truly He has knowledge of everything *(Al-Shura* 42:11-12).

Verily, it is Allah (alone) Who upholds the heavens and the earth so that they will not deviate (from their orbit), for if they should ever deviate, no one could uphold them after He ceases to do so *(Fatir* 35:41).

This is how the Islamic concept deals with the "living God,"demonstrating His existence through His creation, and the "willing God," who does what He desires, demonstrating His Will and power through the movements and changes in the universe.

Indeed, there is a vast difference between the Islamic concept of Allah and the concept of God presented by such philosophers as Plato, Aristotle, and Plotinus. They describe an "abstract" god which is a creation of their intellect and a product of their logic. It is a god without will power and without any action, and this is because of its assumed "perfection." This assumption then forces them to invent a series of intermediaries or lesser gods between God and creatures, after the pattern of the hypothetical beings that were all too familiar in the pagan mythology of the Greeks.

Professor Al-Akkad points out that:

"In Plato's philosophy there are two levels of existence: the level of Absolute Intellect, and the level of matter or substance. Power belongs to the Intellect and submissiveness to substance. Things in the universe possess ranks, higher as they take more Intellect and lower as they take of substance.

"God, the Absolute Intellect, is entirely Good and only goodness proceeds from Him. He does not create the mortal existences Himself but delegates this task to lesser gods whom He creates for this purpose.

These lesser gods are then intermediaries between God and substance, and they are the cause of evil, sorrow, and imperfection.

"Physical phenomena are all illusory, because they change and transform, taking various shapes and forms. Only the abstract Intellect has permanence and reality; and this Intellect is the abode of Forms or Ideas, which are unchanging and eternal. Concrete objects are mere copies of these absolute Forms.

"These Forms are the only objects of true knowledge, the unchanging realities that our mind perceives when it arrives at a true universal definition.

"This would seem to imply that there is a Form corresponding to every universal or general idea that we can think of, a Form of Bed, a Form of Toenail, a Form of Tree, and an infinite number more. Thus, for example, the Form of Tree, which is a perfect Tree, free from the particularities and defects of individual trees, exists in the Absolute Intellect of God from eternity. The trees we see individually are defective copies of that Tree.[1]"

In Aristotle's view, God is the First Cause, or the Unmoved Mover. As Professor Akkad describes it:

"Every movement has a mover, and that mover in turn has a mover. The chain of movers must stop at that which is itself unmoved, since it is impossible to conceive of an infinite regress in the past. This unmoved mover by necessity must be eternal, without beginning or end, perfect in itself and needing no development (i.e., movement), simple without parts, One not many; and existing independently of all other existents.

"This Mover has priority over the world, logically as a cause but not in time, just as assumptions have logical priority over conclusions. This priority cannot be in any temporal sense because time is nothing more than the movement of the world, and cannot precede it. So it is said, 'The world was not created in time.'

"Thus Aristotle is inclined to the opinion that the world is eternal, this being more logical. He says in his book *Dialectics,* however, that the eternity of the world cannot be demonstrated.

"We summarize his arguments in this respect: the origination of the world implies a change in the will of God, and God is not subject to change. Supposing that God originated the world, there are then three possibilities after this origination: He remained the same, He improved, or He decreased; and, according to Aristotle, all these alternatives are impossible in relation to God. If, after the origination of the world, God remained the same, then it was a purposeless act, and

---

[1]Professor Al-Akkad, *Allah, p.137.*

God is exalted above purposelessness. If by originating the world He improved over what He had been before, then He was not perfect and there was room for Him to improve. That is impossible in respect to God. Similarly, it is inconceivable that God became less perfect by originating the world.

"Now, if we suppose that God's will is eternal and does not change, then it follows that the existence of the world is coeternal with His will because the will of God (and nothing else) is the cause of the existence of the world; thus the emergence of the effect (i.e., the world) is necessary when the cause is operative, and all causal conditions are complete. The postponement of the effects is impossible.

"In case of a man it is possible to suppose that he wishes something now but postpones its fulfillment until a later time because of a lack of means or because some conditions for the fulfillment of the wish are not present, or we may suppose that he changed his wish. In the case of God, however, such a supposition is impossible.

"Aristotle continued on this track to such an extreme that he said that the Perfect Being has no knowledge of what exists beyond Himself. God can think only of the best of existents and, as there is nothing better than Himself, He contemplates Himself. Thus God is the thinker, the mind, and the thought, and that is His perfection."[2]

Plotinus went a few steps further than Aristotle in exalting God. In his view, God is beyond things, beyond attributes, and beyond knowledge. Quoting Professor Akkad again: "Indeed God is beyond existence! This does not mean that God is non-existent or that He is nothing because nothingness is the absence of existence while God is above the attribute of existence in the sense that we can only say, "One," and cannot attribute anything to this One without destroying its Oneness. It is One, with nothing like it and nothing to be attributable to it.

"Plotinus reached the conclusion that the One has no knowledge of Itself, as It cannot look at Itself separate from Itself to know It. Therefore, It is purified of this distinction and of the knowledge.[3]

These are the best concepts concerning God's perfection and Oneness to be found among the concepts constructed by philosophers. But what is this? A God about whom nothing can be said and who has nothing to do with the real world! Obviously a purely intellectual approach, without reference to the created universe and without the benefit of Revelation, can succeed only in constructing such a pallid and abstracted God that it can have neither existence nor reality.

---

[2]*Ibid.*, pp. 139-140.
[3]*Ibid.*, p. 187-188.

When people get trapped in a purely intellectual approach to the idea of God's perfection, not based on the observation of the real world, they end up with a concept of Perfection that is negatively defined so that no positive attributes such as creating, knowing, willing, and loving can be ascribed to God without disturbing His perfection.

When we compare these concepts with the Islamic concept, the meaning of "realism" in the Islamic concept becomes very clear.

In the Islamic concept, the Divine Being is active and His Attributes are manifested in actual happenings in the universe.

This is how the Qur'an describes Allah's Attributes for human beings and brings them closer to their Lord by giving them a clear and deep understanding of His involvement in their lives and in their environment by using empirical evidence and practical logic.

The Islamic concept looks at the universe in the same realistic fashion as a universe composed of things and objects, bodies and forms, movements and forces, and plants, animals, and human beings. This universe is not an "idea" without body or form, or a "will," or "chaos" without form, or a collection of "forms" or "ideas" in the Absolute Intellect. Nor is the universe simply "Nature" as a substitute creator which imprints facts on human mind, nor is it "illusion," nor a "dream" or nonexistents, or any other such formulation that can have no counterpart in existence with which human beings can interact.

Allah created the universe with an objective existence which we can observe and toward which the Qur'an draws the attention of our minds and hearts. We are asked to contemplate the heavens and this earth, the stars and planets, this world of minerals, plants, and animals, the alternation of night and day and of light and darkness, the rain, lightning, and thunder, and all the phenomena and events that actually take place in a physical universe.

When Islam draws man's attention toward natural phenomena as a proof of the existence of the Creator, and of His Oneness, Power, Will, Knowledge, and Dominion, it mentions real objects and real events. It does not talk about the universe as "will" and "idea," or as a mere "form" in the Divine Intellect, or as a "substance" without organization, or about a universe that is a reflection of the human mind or even a creation of the human mind. Rather we are asked to look at the structure of the objective universe which exists outside the human mind.

In the Islamic concept the universe is Allah's origination.

He brought it into being by His command, "Be," and it was. The universe obeys His will because it was created as His obedient servant, and whatever He wishes to happen in it does.

> All praise is due to Allah Who created the heavens and the earth, and made the darknesss and the light. Yet the unbelievers hold (others) equal with their Lord. *(Al-An'am* 6:1)

> Verily your Lord is Allah, Who created the heavens and the earth in six periods and is established upon the Throne (of Sovereignty), governing all that exists. No one can intercede with Him except following His permission. This is Allah, your Lord, so worship Him alone. Will you not then keep this in mind? *(Yunus* 10:3)

> It is He who has made the sun a (source of radiant light and the moon a light (reflected), and has determined for it phases so that you might know how to compare years and to measure (time). None of this has Allah created without an (inner) truth. He details the signs to a people of knowledge. Surely in the alternation of night and day, and in all that Allah has created in the heavens and the earth are signs for a people who are conscious of Him *(Yunus* 10:5-6).

> Allah is He Who raised up the heavens without any pillars that you can see, and is established on the Throne. He has subjected the sun and the moon [to His law], each one running [its course] to an appointed term. He directs all affairs, explaining the signs in detail, so that you may believe with certainty in the meeting with your Lord. It is He who spread out the earth and set thereon firm mountains and rivers. And fruits of every kind He made in pairs, two and two. He draws the night as a veil over the day. Surely in that are signs for a people who think. And on the earth are tracts (diverse though) neighboring each other, and gardens of vines, and sown fields, and palms growing in clusters or singly, watered with the same water. Yet some of them We have made more excellent than others as food. Surely in this are signs for a people who understand *(Al-R'ad* 13:2-4).

We have set in the sky constellations and beautified them for all to behold *(Al-Hijr* 15:16).

And the earth We have spread out wide and placed on it firm mountains, and caused (life) of every kind to grow on it in a balanced manner, and made in it a means of livelihood for you as well as for all (living beings) whose sustenance does not depend on you. And there is not a thing in existence whose source is not with Us, and We bestow nothing from on high except in accordance with a well-defined measure. And We send the fertilizing winds, and send down water from the sky and give it to you to drink, although you do not dispose of its sources. It is We alone who give life and death, and it is We who are the inheritors *(Al-Hijr* 15:19-23).

It is Allah who made out of the things He created some things to give you as means of protection. Among the hills He made some for your protection *(Al-Nahl* 16:81)

Are they who are bent on denying the truth not aware that the heavens and the earth were (once) a single entity, which We then separated, and (that) we made every living thing of water? Will they not then believe? And We set on the earth firm mountains lest it shake with them, and We set on it valleys to serve as roads in order that they might find their way. And We have made the heavens as a roof well-guarded. And yet they stubbornly turn away from the signs of this (creation) and (fail to see that) it is He Who created the night and the day and the sun and the moon, each one swimming along in its own orbit *(Al-Anbiya* 21:30-33).

And you see the earth barren. Then, when We send down water upon it, it stirs and swells, and produces vegetation of every kind in beautiful paired growth. This is so because Allah is the Reality, and He gives life to the dead, and He is Able to do all things, and because the Hour is coming without doubt, and because Allah will raise those who are in the graves *(Al-Hajj* 22:6-7).

Have you not seen that Allah has subjected to you all that is on earth, and the ships that sail on the sea at His command and (that it is He Who) holds back the sky so that the

celestial bodies will not fall upon the earth, except by His
leave. Surely Allah is, All-Gentle with people and All-Compassionate, (especially since) it is He Who gave you life, and
then will cause you to die, and then will bring you back to
life. Truly, man is ungrateful (*Al-Hajj* 22:65-66).

And We have created above you seven tracts and We are not
heedless of creation. And We send down water from the
sky in accordance with a measure and then cause it to lodge
in the earth, but, behold, We are most certainly able to take
it away. And by means of this water, we produce for you
gardens of palms and vines in which you have abundance
of fruit and from which you eat *(Al-Muminun* 23:17-19).

Are you not aware that Allah sends down water from the
skies, whereby We bring forth fruits of diverse colors, just
as in the mountains there are streaks of white and red of
various shades, as well as (others) ravenblack, and as there
are among men and beasts and cattle, too, many hues. Truly,
only those with knowledge among His servants stand
(truly) in awe of Allah, (for they alone comprehend that)
Allah is truly All-Mighty, and All-Forgiving *(Fatir* 35:27-
28).

What, do they not look toward the sky above them, how
We have built it and made it beautiful and free of all faults?
And the earth We have spread out and set thereon firm
mountains, and produced therein every kind of beautiful
plants to be observed and thus offering an insight and a
reminder to every human being who willingly turns to
Allah. And We send down from the sky water rich in
blessings and thereby We produce gardens and fields of
grain, and tall palm trees, with shoots of fruit stalks, piled
one over another — as sustenance for (Allah's) servants, and
We give new life therewith to a land that is dead: thus will
be the resurrection *(Qaf* 50:6-11).

Blessed is He in whose hand all dominion rests, since He
has the sovereign power to will and do all things, He who
created death and life so that He might try you (and thus
show) which of you is best in works and (make you realize
that) He alone is the All-Mighty, and All-Forgiving. Blessed
is He Who created seven heavens in full harmony with one

another. You do not see in the creation of the All-Merciful any imperfections. Turn your gaze (upon it) once more. Can you see any flaw? Yes, return your gaze again, and again, and (every time) your vision will come back to you dazzled, weary. And We have beautified the lowest heaven nearest to the earth with lights and We have made them missiles for devils *(Al-Mulk* 67:1-5).

Have you not turned your vision to your Lord, how He lengthens the shadows? If He willed, He could make it stationary. But then, We have made the sun its guide. And then We draw it in toward Ourselves, a contraction by easy stages. It is He who made the night as a garment for you and sleep for a rest, and causes every (new) day to be a resurrection. It is He who sends the winds bearing good tidings, heralding His mercy, and We send down pure water from the sky so that We may revive a dead land and quench the thirst of what We created, animals as well as humans in great numbers *(Al-Furqan* 25:45-47).

The Islamic concept deals with the universe in this realistic fashion. The universe has an existence separate from Allah's existence, with its own physical and observable characteristics. Islam does not ascribe imaginary characteristics to the physical world, as, for example, is the case with Hinduism. In that religion only "Brahma," the Supreme Deity, has real existence, and in comparison to Brahma's existence this world is nothing, a mere illusion. Because "nothing" or illusion is pure evil and imperfection, man's salvation lies in annihilating this evil, which is the physical body, and returning to pure "existence," which has been polluted by intermingling with "non-existence" or illusion.

As another example, we mention Plato's concept of the world of Forms or ideas, which alone is real, while objects in the physical world are mere shadows of those Forms. Thus the tree we see over there is merely a shadow of the Form of the Tree concealed in the Absolute Intellect. Each tree, in imitation of the Ideal Tree, loses something and is therefore imperfect. Perfection and real existence are attributes of the Absolute Intellect and its Ideas, while material objects have only a shadowy existence in spite of the fact that we see and touch them.

Similarly, Plotinus hypothesized that there is the One, the Deity, from whom proceeds the Intellect. From the Intellect proceeds the Universal Soul. And from the Soul has originated the sensory world whose essence is matter. Matter occupies the lowest level of existence and is pure evil and corrupt.

These and similar concepts are the product of human fancy, and are armchair speculations without any basis in the real world of physical objects and observable events. When we compare such concepts with the Islamic concept embodied in the Qur'anic verses, some of which we have quoted above, we understand the meaning of that characteristic of the Islamic concept which we have called "realism."

In a similar fashion the Islamic concept treats "the human being" in a realistic fashion because it deals with the actuality of millions of persons scattered all over the world. The human being as a generic category has its own special human characteristics and nature. It is made of flesh and blood and muscles and bones, and of mind and personality and soul. Each human being has desires and needs, eats food and walks in the streets, is born and dies, and has a beginning in time and an end in time. Human beings influence and are influenced, they love and hate, hope and fear, ascend and descend, believe and deny, go straight and get lost, build and destroy, conquer and kill, and so on down to the lowest of human characteristics and distinctive features. The Islamic concept is cognizant of all this.

> O Mankind! Be conscious of your Lord, who created you from a single soul and from it created its mate, and from the pair of them spread abroad a multitude of men and women. And remain aware of Allah in Whom you claim (your rights) from one another, and of these ties of kinship. Surely Allah is ever watchful over you (*Al-Nisa* 4:1).

> O Mankind! We have created you all out of a single (pair)of a male and female, and made you into nations and tribes so that you may know each other. Surely the noblest among you in the sight of Allah is the one who is deeply conscious of Him. Allah is All-Knowing and All-Aware (*Al-Hujurat* 49:13).

> Glory be to him who created in pairs all that the earth produces as well as their own (human) kind and other things of which they have no knowledge (*Ya Sin* 36:36).

> We created man out of the essence of clay. Then We set him, a sperm-drop, in a secure receptacle; then We created of the drop of sperm a germ-cell; then We created from the germ-cell a lump; then We created within the lump bones; then

We clothed the bones with flesh; and thereafter We brought him into being as another creature. Glorified, therefore, be Allah, the Best of Creators! *(Al-Muminun* 23:12-14).

Was there (not) an endless span of time before man (appeared — a time) when he was not yet a thing to be thought of. We created man of a drop of sperm intermingled, so that We might try him, and therefore We made him a being endowed with hearing and sight. Surely We have guided him to the way, whether he be thankful or unthankful *(Al-Insan* 76:1-3).

Doomed is man; how ungrateful! Of what did He create him? Out of a drop of sperm He creates him and proportions him, then makes the way easy for him; then makes him to die, and buries him; and then, when He wills He shall raise him again to life *('Abasa* 80:17-20).

When affliction visits a man, he calls Us (lying down) on his side, or sitting, or standing, but when We have removed his affliction from him, he goes on as if he never called Us during his affliction. Thus do their own actions seem good to those who commit excesses *(Yunus* 10:12).

When We let people taste mercy after hardship has touched them, then they immediately turn to devising false arguments against Our messages. Say, "Allah is swifter (than you) at devising." Behold, Our (heavenly) messengers are recording all that you may devise *(Yunus* 10:21).

And if We let a man taste mercy from Us, and afterwards We withdraw it from him, he is desperate and ungrateful. But if We let him taste prosperity after hardship that has visited him, he will say, "the evils have gone from me," and he is joyous and boastful, except those who are patient and do good deeds. For them forgiveness and a mighty reward is waiting *(Hud* 11:9-11).

And some men have appealing views about (ethics in) the life of this world, and they call on Allah to witness what is in their hearts, and moreover are very skillful in arguing their views. But when such people prevail, they go about the world spreading corruption and destroying man's family life and

productive endeavors (causing moral decay and social des-
tintegration). Verily, Allah does not love corruption (*Al-
Baqarah* 2:205).

Thus, the Islamic concept views the human being as he actually is.
He has characteristics and personal whims, gives and receives, and
influences and is influenced. In short, he is not some abstraction or
something hypothetical without any basis in reality.

The Islamic concept does not deal with an abstraction called
"humanity," which in the philosophy of Objectivists becomes almost
divine, nor with a personified "Absolute Intellect," which one finds
in the idealistic philosophy represented by Fichte. The Absolute
Intellect does not have any real existence because there are only
individual intellects belonging to real persons. Similarly, there is no
such thing as an Intellect that created the Soul or created the universe,
as was assumed by Plotinus, the leader of Neoplatonism.

The Islamic concept differs from "Idealism," which deals only with
intellectual categories and has no connection with the actual forces
operating in the universe and in the lives of real persons. It also differs
from "Sensory Objectivism," which has made "nature" the creator
of the human intellect and all its perceptions. In the Islamic concept,
Allah is the Creator of "nature" as well as of "man." In the Islamic
paradigm of thought, the human intellect perceives natural
phenomena, discovers natural laws, understands the operation of
physical forces, receives sensory impressions from the physical world,
and influences the physical world, all according to a balanced and
harmonious Divine plan.

The perspective of Islam, because of its Divine origin, made it
possible from the very beginning to look telescopically through the
centuries and perceive all the calamities of speculative thought that
would afflict mankind, such as "Idealism," "Obiectivism," and
"Dialectic Materialism." The Islamic concept was formulated in
Quranic Revelation with such amazing balance, comprehensiveness,
and perfection that the human conscience can find solace in it during
any period and can return to it for inspiration and guidance at any
time, secure from all the babble in the toxic wastelands of human
thought. Allah, the Almighty, spoke the truth:

Verily this Qur'an guides to what is most right (*Al-Isra*
17:9).

And who could be better of speech than the person who
calls (his fellow-men) to Allah and does good deeds and

says, "Truly, I am of those who have surrendered themselves to Allah?" *(Fussilat* 41:33).

Another aspect of the realism in the Islamic concept relates to the nature of its methodology in the life of mankind and the way it deals with the actual situation of human societies.

As was mentioned earlier, the "human being" in the Islamic concept is the real human being made of flesh and blood and nerves, with a body, mind, and soul, and with needs and desires, and strengths and weaknesses. He is not some ideal or imaginary being, nor is he an abstract logical entity to be dealt with intellectually. Neither is he the lowest of the low, a product of dead matter, nor merely a creature of "economics."

Indeed, every human being is a creature of Allah Most High Who made him His deputy on the earth to manage its affairs. He is to be active and productive and is required to initiate new activities in order to fulill his duty toward Allah and toward Allah's creatures, whether they be animals, plants, other human beings, or the physical resources of the earth.

Islam is a way of life for this physical and spiritual human being, and its system is designed to suit him physically and spiritually, taking into account his biological as well as his mental and spiritual makeup. This system is dynamic, realistic, and natural, in complete accord with human nature.

The system of life that Islam desires, with its idealism, loftiness, spirituality, and God-consciousness, is never the less practical and earthy and is within the grasp of every human being. It is suited to man who has to live on this earth, who has to earn his living, walk in the marketplace, marry and have children, and work and play, and who may both love and hate, as well as hope and fear, which are all the human characteristics given to him by his Creator.

The system of life that Islam prescribes for man is in accordance with his nature, his capabilities and capacities, and his strengths and weaknesses. It does not denigrate man's role on earth. Muslims do not consider man naturally sinful or evil, nor do they raise him to the status of a god or of an angel, made of light and goodness and free of physical needs and desires. Yet, the humanity of man has a very high status and every man is potentially capable of reaching great heights of perfection at any time and place.

We present here, from the text of the Qur'an, a few quotations to illustrate how the Islamic system is suited to the nature of man, while always guiding it toward purity and cleanliness, and toward the highest horizons to which this nature is capable of rising.

They say, "What sort of a Messenger is this (man) who eats food and goes about in the market-places? Why has not an angel (visibly) been sent down to him, to act as a warner with him? Or why has not a treasure been granted to him (by Allah)? Or: "He should (at least) have a garden to eat from (without effort)!" These evildoers say (to each other), "If you were to follow (Muhammad, you would follow) a man bewitched!" See to what they liken you (O Prophet, simply) because they have gone astray and are unable to find a way (to the truth)! Glorified is He who, if He wills, give you something better than that (what they speak about), namely, gardens through which running waters flow, and palaces (*Al- Furqan* 25:7-10).

They say, "We will not believe you until you make a spring gush forth from the earth for us, or until you possess a garden of palms and grapes and you make rivers flow among them abundantly or until you make the sky fall upon us in smithereens, as you have threatened, or you bring Allah and the angels face to face before us, or until you possess a house of gold, or you ascend to heaven, and even then we would not believe in your ascension until you bring down to us (from heaven) a book that we (ourselves) could read." Say "Glory be to my Lord! Am I anything more than a mortal messenger?" (*Isra* 17:90-93).

Allah does not burden any soul except within its capacity; for it is what it has earned and against it is (only) what it has merited (*Al-Baqarah* 2:286).

They ask you concerning menstruation. Say, "It is a discomfort, so leave women alone (sexually) at such times and do not approach them until they are clean. When they have cleansed themselves, then go into them as Allah has bidden you to do." Truly, Allah loves those who turn to Him and loves those who keep themselves pure. Your wives are like irrigated cropland for you, so go into this bounty as you desire, and send (good deeds) before you for your souls, and remain conscious of Allah, and know that you are destined to meet Him. And give glad tidings to those who believe (*Al-Baqarah* 2:222-223).

Fighting is prescribed for you, although it may be hateful

to you. Yet it may happen that you hate a thing that is good
for you, and it may happen that you love a thing that is bad
for you. Allah knows and you do not know *(Al-Baqarah
2:216).*

Alluring to people is love of the joys (that come) from
women and children, and stored up heaps of gold and
silver, and branded horses, and cattle and land. This is the
enjoyment of the present life. But in nearness to Allah is the
best of all goals (to return to). Say, "Shall I tell you of
something better than that? For those who are conscious of
Allah, with their Lord are Gardens through which running
waters flow, to dwell therein forever, with spouses
purified, and Allah's good pleasure. And Allah sees all that
is in the hearts of His servants *(Ale-'Imran* 3:14-15).

And compete with one another for forgiveness from your
Lord, and for a Garden as vast as the heavens and the earth,
which has been prepared for those conscious of Allah who
act charitably in both prosperity and adversity and who
control their anger and pardon their fellow-men, because
Allah loves the doers of good. This garden has been readied
for those who when they have committed a shameful deed
or have (otherwise) sinned against themselves, remember
Allah and ask forgiveness for their sins — and who forgives
sins except Allah? — and (they) do not knowingly persist
in their trangressions. The reward of such persons will be
forgiveness from their Lord, and Gardens through which
running waters flow, where they will dwell forever. What
a bountiful reward for those who strive in life *(Ale-'Imran*
3:133-136).

Men shall take full care of women with the bounties that
Allah has bestowed more abundantly on men than on
women and with what they may spend of their own property
(for the support of women). So the good women are the
devoutly obedient ones, guarding in (the husband's) absence what Allah would have them guard (their own virtue
and the husband's reputation and property). As for those
whose ill-will and ill-conduct you have reason to fear,
admonish them (first), then refuse to share their beds, and
(finally) beat them (lightly). If they then obey you, do not

act with continued ill-will toward them. For Allah is Most Exalted and Most Great *(Al-Nisa* 4:34).

So let those fight in the cause of Allah who are willing to exchange the present life for the life to come, for We shall bestow a great reward on whoever fights in the cause of Allah, whether he is slain or is victorious. And how could you not fight for the cause of Allah and for the helpless men, women, and children who are crying, "Our Lord rescue us from this city whose people are oppressors, and raise for us, out of Your grace, a protector, and appoint for us, out of Your bounty, someone who will help us? Those who believe fight for the sake of Allah, and those who disbelieve fight for the sake of idols. So fight against the assistants of Satan. Surely the guile of Satan is ever weak *(Al-Nisa* 4:74-76).

O you who have attained to faith! Be always steadfast in your devotion to Allah, bearing witness to the truth in all equity. And never let hatred of people lead you into the sin of deviating from justice. Be just, for this is closest to being conscious of Allah. And remain in awe of Allah, for surely Allah is aware of all that you do *(Al-Ma'idah* 5:8).

O Children of Adam! Make yourselves (both physically and morally) beautiful for every act of worship, and eat and drink freely but do not waste. For, verily, He does not love the wasteful. Say, "Who has forbidden the beauty that Allah has brought forth for His servants, and the good things of His providence?" Say, "They are (lawful) in the life of this world for all who have attained to faith, and they shall be theirs alone on the Day of Resurrection." Thus do we clearly explain these messages for those of knowledge. Say, "What my Lord has indeed prohibited are shameful deeds, open or secret; and sins and trespasses against truth or reason; and the ascription of divinity to anything other than Allah, since He has never given any authority to worship false gods; and attributing to Allah anything of which you have no knowledge *(Al-A'raf* 7:31-33).

Many other verses of the Qur'an, prescribing certain obligations or prohibitions for Muslims, prove the realism of the Islamic system of life and its practicality. This system of life is eminently suitable for the nature of man because it takes into full consideration his capacities and limitations, and does not demand anything from him beyond his power or against his nature.

This point may be further clarified by contrasting the Islamic system with other systems of life, such as Hinduism. According to Hinduism, people should abstain from nourishing food and from what strengthens their bodies because the soul is imprisoned in the body and is unable to escape from this non-existent and entirely evil "illusion" of the material world, to the real good of perfect "existence" unless a person frees his soul from the prison of his body.

Similarly, when we look at the concepts of the Christian Church, we see that most Christians view the human being, a melding of body and soul, an evil combination. The soul is pure, while the physical body is impure, and a person is supposed to sublimate the soul from the lowly physical body. Furthermore, these concepts require actions from people beyond their power or which come in conflict with human nature. For example, in the Catholic Church there is no divorce except in the case of adultery, and even after divorce a second marriage is prohibited.

Surely Islam is a practical religion, a religion for this life, for action, for work, production, and progress, and a religion in accordance with man's nature and his role in life assigned by Allah. This *din* of Allah energizes all the potentialities and powers of the human being and directs them toward the ends for which they have been bestowed. At the same time, Islam establishes ideals of human perfection and motivates every individual to extend himself to the fullest, without impeding his action or denigrating his value and his needs and inclinations.

Thus, the Islamic concept's characteristic of realism applies both in the realm of belief concerning Allah, the universe, life, and man, and in the Islamic system of life. They are realistic, firmly founded on a realistic view of man and a realistic view of the circumstances of his life. And there is complete harmony between this Islamic belief and Islamic practice.

Thus, man is free, with all his capabilities, to explore this world as Allah intended, to multiply the bounties of this earth and to make changes, and to develop its resources and use them for his own advancement. Islam does not act as a barrier to his beliefs or to his actions because both its system of belief and its system for practical life conform to the system of the universe surrounding him. This is so because both systems of belief and action come from the same unique Source who is also the Source of man and the universe and who has equipped him with the optimum capabilities and capacities to prosper in it.

Thus, the man who has attained to faith, and who understands the nature of the Islamic concept and of the Islamic system originating in this concept, participates fully in activities on this earth by re-searching, investigating, and inventing new things, but always in accordance with high moral standards and lofty aims, and with all the characteristics inherent in this concept, namely, harmony, balance, comprehensiveness, dynamism, and realism.

> In accordance with the natural disposition that Allah has instilled into man, (because) not to allow any change to corrupt what Allah has thus created is the (purpose of the one) ever-true faith. But most people do not know this. (*Al-Rum* 30:30).

CHAPTER IX
The Oneness of Allah

We sent no Messenger before you without revealing to him, ''There is no god but Me, so worship Me (alone)'' (*Al-Anbiya* 21:25).

The Oneness of Allah, known as *tawhid*, is the first and paramount constituent of the Islamic concept, as it is the fundamental truth of the Islamic faith. It is also one of the chief characteristics of the Islamic concept because, among all the belief systems and philosophies currently prevailing among human beings, only the Islamic faith can be characterized as having a pure form of monotheism. This is why we have included ''The Oneness of Allah'' as one of the characteristics of the Islamic concept.

From the outset we state that the message of the Oneness of Allah has been the chief constituent and characteristic of all religions brought by the Messengers of Allah Most High, because every religion sent from Allah was nothing but Islam, which is submission to Allah alone by following the way prescribed by Him alone, receiving guidance in matters of faith and moral conduct from Him alone, purifying one's intention and worship for Him alone, and obeying His commandments and implementing His laws in human affairs as well as in worship. Unfortunately, after these Messengers passed away, interpolations and deviations were introduced into the pure *din* of Islam producing many impurities in these religions, so that no belief has been left in its correct and pure form apart from the concept brought by Prophet Muhammad, may Allah's blessings be upon him. Allah Himself has protected the principles of the Islamic faith so that no deviation has ever touched it nor has any impurity ever entered into its beliefs. This is why "the Oneness of Allah" has become the distinctive characteristic of this faith.

The Oneness of Allah is a characteristic of the Islamic concept because the truth of the Divine Oneness includes all aspects of the Islamic faith and practice. It permeates concepts, morals, manners, and all types of dealings among people in a truly Islamic community. The certainty of the truth that Allah is One dominates the Muslim's concept of the universe and of everything happening in it and his concept of the real, active power behind events in his own life and in the life of the community in which he lives. This certainty and conceptual conviction extend to all aspects of a Muslim's life, including what is hidden and what is apparent and what is significant and what is insignificant, and it applies to everybody he meets, the great as well as the lowly, to all customs, laws, beliefs, and actions, and to this life and the life-to-come, simply because not a single element of the Islamic system can escape from the all-inclusive belief in the Oneness of Allah. This point was earlier discussed in the chapter entitled "Comprehensiveness."

The Islamic concept rests on the principle that the Divine Being is distinct from His creation. Divinity belongs exclusively to Allah Most High, while creatureliness is common to everyone and everything else. Since Allah Most High is the only Divine Being, it follows that all the Divine attributes belong to Him alone. And since everyone and everything else is His creation, it also follows that they are all devoid of Divine attributes. Thus there are two distinct orders of existence, namely, the independent existence of Allah Most High and the dependent existence of all others as His creatures. The relationship between Allah and everything else is that of the Creator to His creatures and of the Lord to His servants.

This is the first principle of the Islamic concept and all other principles follow from it. Because the Islamic concept rests on this basic principle, the Oneness of God is its most important characteristic.

Earlier we said that all the Messengers of Allah Most High brought the message of the Oneness of Allah, so this was the characteristic of all the Divinely-revealed religions. Our assertion is derived from the Qur'an, which states this fact in relation to the earlier Messengers.

> We sent Nuh (Noah) to his people, and he said, "O my people! Serve Allah. You have no god besides Him. I fear for you the retribution of an awful Day (*Al-A'raf* 7:59).

> And to (the tribe of) 'Ad (We sent) their brother, Hud. He

said, "O my people! Worship Allah alone! You have no god besides Him. Will you not then be conscious of Allah?" (*Al-A'raf* 7:65).

And to (the tribe of) Thamud (We sent) their brother Salih. He said, "O my people! Worship Allah alone! You have no god besides Him. A clear evidence has now come to you from your Lord" (*Al-A'raf* 7:73).

And to Midian (We sent) their brother Shu'ayb. He said, "O my people! Worship only Allah! You have no god besides Him. Clear proof has now come to you from your Sustainer" (*Al-A'raf* 7:85).

And has the story of Moses ever reached you? He saw a fire, and he said to his family, "Wait here! I see a fire (far away). Perhaps I shall bring you a brand from it or may find guidance at the fire." But when he came close to it, a voice called out to him: "O Moses! I am your Lord! Take off your shoes, for you are in the hallowed valley of Tuwa. I have chosen you (to be My apostle), so listen to what is revealed (to you). Verily, I, and I alone, am Allah! There is no god but Me! So serve Me and be constant in prayer in order to keep Me in your remembrance" (*Ta Ha* 20:9-14).

And when Allah said, "O Jesus son of Mary, did you say to the people, 'Take me and my mother as gods besides Allah?,' he said, "Glory be to you! It is not possible for me to say what I have no right to. Had I said this, You would have known it. You know what is in my mind, and I do not know what is in Your mind, for indeed, You are the Knower of the Unseen. I only told them what you commanded me, 'Serve Allah, my Lord and your Lord.' And I was a witness over them as long as I dwelt among them, but when You took me to Yourself, you were yourself Watcher over them, for You are witness to everything. If You punish them, they are Your servants. If You forgive them, You are the All-Mighty, the All-Wise" (*Al-Ma'idah* 5:116-118).

We sent no Messenger before you without revealing to him, "There is no god but Me, so worship Me (alone)" (*Al-Anbiya* 21:25).

With the passage of time, however, this message brought by all the Messengers about the Oneness of Allah became distorted by the influence of diverse beliefs and myths. We have already discussed this point in some detail in the chapter entitled, "The Wilderness and Intellectual Rubbish," in relation to the revealed religions as well as polytheism and paganism.

Before we describe why the Oneness of Allah is one of the characteristics of the Islamic concept and how it permeates the entire life of the Muslim community, we should first briefly describe some other concepts dealing with the Divine, with the other-than-the-Divine, and with the Oneness of the Divine Being.

Hinduism, for example, acknowledges one Divine Being called Brahma, who alone is "existent" and who alone has the attributes of perfection, goodness, and perpetuity. Apart from this One Existent and Real Being there is nothing, which is to say, this universe and whatever is in it is non-existent.

On the other hand, Hinduism also says that Brahma, the real Being, who is entirely Good, is incarnated or diffused into the "non-existent," which is entirely evil. Thus Brahma is diffused into every part of this universe, including man, and thus is a compound of being and non-being, good and evil, perfection and defect, and eternity and mortality.

A believing Hindu, therefore, must continually strive to separate the existence, the perfection, the goodness, and the eternity in his make-up from the non-existence, imperfection, evil, and mortality, in order to free "the being" that is incarnate in his body. This is called "Nirvana" or becoming free of mortality and non-being and returning to the status of pure being, Brahma.

We note that Brahma is not the Creator of this world, which is non-existent, evil, and imperfect, but he is diffused in it. Moreover, He does not administer or manage the affairs of this universe, which have become manifest because of the diffusion of Brahma into non-existence.

Again, beyond this Oneness, and apart from this diffusion, Hinduism also has a "Trinity": Lord "Brahma" the Creator; Lord "Vishnu," the Giver of life; and Lord "Shiva," the Destroyer.

Over and above the universe and the gods rules "Karma" or "Fate." It is karma which determines the cycles of birth and rebirth and which creates and repeats cycles of Universes. Clearly, with the Hindu pantheon and the theory of impersonal karma ruling over gods as well as the world, including human beings, the concept of the Oneness of God is completely lost.

The Egyptian Pharoah, Akhinaton, believed in One God, whom he called "Aton," and he considered Him to be the Creator of the universe and its Ruler. Apart from the revealed religions, his was the noblest concept of God conceived by man. And it is quite possible that he was influenced by the teachings of some Messenger of Allah. There was in his concept, however, some influence of paganism, because he considered the sun to be the representation of Aton. He thus polluted the purity of his concept of God by this interpolation from paganism.

Aristotle made a distinction between the "Necessary Being" and the "possible being." God is the Necessary Being but He is devoid of will and action, and He did not create the universe, nor is He concerned with it. The universe, and whatever and whoever is in it, was a "possible being." Its desire to be like the Necessary Being brought it into "existence" from "non-existence."

Belief in the Oneness of Allah was the religion of Abraham, peace be upon him, and he imparted it to his sons, Ishmael and Isaac. Jacob, the son of Isaac, was also a believer in the Oneness of Allah and bequeathed this to his children at the time of his death, as is reported in the Qur'an.

> And who would turn away from the religion of Abraham, except him who is deluding himself? Assuredly We chose him in this world, and truly in the Hereafter he shall be among the righteous. When his Lord said to him, "Submit!" he said, "I have submitted to the Lord of the worlds." And this Abraham enjoined upon his sons and also upon Jacob, saying, "O my sons! Truly Allah has chosen for you the *din* therefore, do not die without having submitted yourselves to Him." Or, were you witnesses when death approached Jacob and he said to his sons, "What will you worship after me?" They replied, "We shall worship your God, the God of your fathers, Abraham, and Ishmael, and Isaac, the One God, and to Him we have submitted" (*Al-Baqarah* 2:130-133).

When Moses, peace be upon him, came as a Messenger to the children of Israel, he came with the message of the Oneness of Allah, but the children of Israel, before and after Moses, corrupted this concept and changed the meanings of the words from their intended meanings. They made Allah into a national deity of the Israelites, the Lord God of Israel, who helped them against the worshippers of other gods. Furthermore, they ascribed to "the Lord God of Israel" many falsehoods, for example, by claiming that they were the sons of God and His beloved, that He would not punish them for their sins, that

Ezra was a "son of God," that He had sons who took the daughters of men as their wives and that the children of these unions were giants, and that the Lord God was afraid they might become gods like Him, and consequently He came down and caused them to speak different languages in order to destroy their unity. They also alleged that Jacob once fought with the Lord, hitting Him on His thigh. And they claimed that He walked in the shade of the garden and enjoyed the coolness of the breeze, and so on. All of such tales, singly as well as together, corrupted the pure concept of the Oneness of Allah.

Jesus, peace be upon him, came with the message of the Oneness of Allah, but Christians ended up with a belief in the Trinity. They still claim that the Godhead is One entity divided among three persons: the Father, the Son, and the Holy Ghost, and they exhibit a variety of beliefs among various denominations concerning the nature of the person called the Son. In spite of their claim about the "Unity of the Godhead," the variety of concepts and interpretations prevailing among various denominations prove that their claim is false.

Thus we can safely state that the Islamic concept is the only concept resting on the foundation of a complete and pure belief in the Oneness of Allah, and that, among all the belief systems existing today, Islam and only Islam can be characterized by this distinction.

After elucidating this point, let us now describe briefly the nature and the definition of the Islamic concept of the Oneness of Allah.

As we stated earlier, the Islamic belief is based on the concept that there is Allah and there is His creation. Divinity belongs to Allah alone, whereas anything and anyone other than Him is His creature and servant. Each and every Divine attribute belongs to Allah, whereas no creature of Allah can possess any of these attributes. Human life, then, ought to be based on the implications and consequences of this pure and complete belief in the Oneness of Allah Most High.

Allah Most High is One in His Person and is Unique in His attributes:

Say, "He is Allah, the One; Allah the Self-Sufficient; He begets not, nor is He begotten; and there is nothing that could be compared with Him" (*Al-Ikhlas* 112).

There is nothing like Him (*Al-Shura* 42:11).

So do not make any analogy to Allah (*Al-Nahl* 16:74).

Allah is the Creator of all things (*Al-Zumar* 39:62).

Such is Allah, your Sustainer. There is no god but He, the

Creator of everything. Worship, then, Him alone, for He has everything in His care (*Al-An'am* 6:102).

And He created everything and determines its nature in exact measure (*Al-Furqan* 25:2).

Say, "Do you see what it is you invoke besides Allah? Show me what it is they have created on earth. Or do they have a share in (creating) the heavens? (If so) bring me a Scripture before this (Scripture), or any remnant of knowledge, if what you claim is true" (*Al-Ahqaf* 46:4).

Allah, the Almighty, is the Owner of everything:

Say, "To whom belongs all that is in the heavens and on earth?" Say, "To Allah. He has prescribed for Himself (the rules of) mercy" (*Al-An'am* 6:12).

To Allah belongs the dominion of the heavens and the earth, and all that is between them (*Al-Ma'idah* 5:17).

Hallowed is He...the One to whom belongs sovereignty over the heavens and the earth, and Who begets no offspring, and has no partner in His dominion (*Al-Furqan* 25:2).

Allah Most Great is the Provider for everyone and everything He has created:

O people! Call to mind the favor of Allah upon you! Is there any creator other than Allah that could provide for you sustenance out of heaven and earth? There is no god but Him. So where else can you turn to? (*Fatir* 35:3).

How many are the creatures that cannot provide their own sustenance! It is Allah who feeds them and you (*Al-'Ankabut* 29:60).

There is no creature on the earth without its sustenance depending upon Allah. He knows its time-limit (on earth) and its resting place (*Hud* 11:6).

Allah, the Glorious, is the Administrator of all things and the Guardian of all things:

> Allah holds the heavens and the earth so that they do not deviate, and if they were to deviate there is no one to hold them after Him (*Fatir* 35:41).

> And among His signs is that the heavens and the earth stand firm by His command (*Al-Rum* 30:25).

> For We take account of all things in a clear record (*Ya Sin* 36:12).

Allah Most High is the All-Powerful Sovereign, Who is omnipotent over everything:

> And He is Omnipotent over His servants. He sends forth heavenly forces to guard you. And when death comes to one of you, Our angels take his soul, and they never fail in their duty. Then they are brought before Allah, their Just Protector and Lord of Truth. Surely His is the judgment. And He is most swift in taking account (*Al-An'am* 6:61-62).

> Say, "He is able to send punishment upon you from above you or from beneath your feet, or to bewilder you with mutual discord and let you taste the fear of one another" (*Al-An'am* 6:65).

> Say, "Don't you see! If Allah took away your hearing and your sight and sealed up your hearts, what god other than Allah could restore them to you?" (*Al-An'am* 6:46).

All the creation of the Most Glorious Allah is obedient to Him and approaches Him in submission and servitude:

> Then He turned to the sky when it still consisted of gases, and He said to it and to the earth, "Come, both of you, willingly or unwillingly," and they responded, "We come obediently" (*Fussilat* 41:11).

> And among His signs is that the heavens and the earth stand by His command. Then, when He calls you by a single call

from the earth, you come forth. To Him belongs every being
that is in the heavens and on earth, and all are devoutly
obedient to Him (*Al-Rum* 30:25- 26).

And before Allah prostrates whatever is in the heavens and
every creature moving on the earth, and the angels. And
they are not proud (*Al-Nahl* 16:49).

And there is not a thing but celebrates His praise (*Al-Isra*
17:44).

What has been presented here should suffice to give a clear understanding of the Oneness of Allah in the Islamic concept, with emphasis
on the unambiguous separation of the Divine from the other-than-the-
Divine, and on the fact that the relationship between the servants and
the Lord is based only upon servanthood and not upon lineage,
marriage, partnership, or resemblance, because such relationships do
not pertain to Allah Most High.

Our description of the concept of the Oneness of Allah in Islam
would remain incomplete if we did not mention, at least briefly, the
far-reaching and all-encompassing consequences of this belief in the
life of mankind. In fact, these consequences are an embodiment of the
belief in the Oneness of Allah and a clear proof that this is the chief
characteristic of the Islamic concept.

One consequence of belief in the Oneness of Allah is that Allah Most
High is the Lord and Sovereign of men not merely in their beliefs,
concepts, consciences, and rituals of worship, but in their practical
affairs.

The Muslim believes that there is no deity except Allah, that no one
is worthy of worship except Allah, that no one is Creator or Sustainer
except Allah, that no one can benefit or harm oneself except Allah,
and that no one except Allah is in charge of the universe or even of
one's own affairs. Accordingly, the Muslim worships Him alone, and
turns to Him alone with hope and fear and with the sincerity of his
heart. In the same way, the Muslim believes that there is no true ruler
above him except Allah, no legislator for him except Allah, no one
except Allah to inform him concerning his relationships and connections with the universe, with other living creatures, and with one's
fellow human beings. This is why the Muslim turns to Allah for
guidance and legislation in every aspect of life, whether it be political
governance, economic justice, personal behavior, or the norms and
standards of social intercourse.

Turning toward Allah for guidance in forms of worship, in situations

of hope or fear, in developing legal and economic institutions for
society, and in establishing norms and standards of behavior, is an
inevitable consequence of the Islamic concept of Allah's Oneness and
of its all-encompassing impact on the conscience and life of the true
Muslim.

In the Qur'an we find that belief in the Oneness of Allah is very
closely connected with this impact on every Muslim's conscience and
practical life. Belief in the Oneness of Allah and in His sole Sovereignty
over the universe and over the life of every person places on the
shoulders of the Muslim certain responsibilities of an intellectual,
spiritual, psychological, as well as moral and practical nature. The
Qur'an sometimes links all such things in one sequence of verses,
designed to connect Allah's power and dominion in the universe, in
this world, and in the Hereafter logically and systematically with
man's obedience to His commandments and Law.

> And your God is One God. There is no deity but Him, the
> Merciful and Dispenser of Grace.
> Surely in the creation of the heavens and the earth, and
> in the alternation of the night and the day and in the ships
> that sail the ocean for the benefit of mankind and in the
> water that Allah sends down from the sky to revive the
> earth after its death and cause all manner of living creatures
> to multiply on it, and in the change of the winds and the
> clouds that follow their appointed courses between the
> earth and the sky, are signs for a people of intelligence.
> There are people who choose to believe in beings that
> allegedly rival Allah, loving them as (only) Allah should be
> loved whereas those who have attained to faith love Allah
> more than all else. If only those who do wrong could but
> see, as they indeed will when they are made to suffer (on
> Judgement Day), that all power belongs to Allah alone and
> that Allah is severe in punishment! (On the Day) those who
> are followed will disown those who followed them and the
> followers will behold the punishment (that awaits them),
> with all their means cut off. And the followers will say, "If
> we had one more chance, we would disown them as they
> have disowned us." Thus will Allah show them their deeds
> (in a manner that will cause them) bitter regrets, but they
> will not escape from the Fire.
> O people! Partake of what is lawful and good on earth,
> and do not follow the footsteps of Satan, for he is an open
> enemy to you. He bids you only to do evil and to commit

shameful deeds, and to attribute to Allah something about which you have no knowledge. When it is said to them, "Follow what Allah has revealed," they say, "No! We shall follow what we found our forefathers believing in and doing. What! Even though their forefathers did not use their reason at all and had no guidance? The parable of those who disbelieve is as if one were to shout like a goat-herd, to things that listen to nothing but calls and cries: deaf, dumb, and blind, they are without understanding.

O you who believe! Eat of the good things We have provided for you and give thanks to Allah, if it is He whom you worship. He has forbidden to you only carrion, and blood, and the flesh of swine, and that which has been consecrated to anyone other than Allah. But if one is in grave need, without coveting it or exceeding one's immediate requirements, then there shall be no sin on him, for, behold, Allah is Forgiving and Merciful (*Al-Baqarah* 2:163-173).

When we ponder this passage of the Qur'an, we note that it begins with the Oneness of Allah. Then follows the description of natural phenomena in which Allah's power is manifested, and then the description of the Day of Resurrection in which Allah's sovereignty, judgement, and exclusive authority are manifested. Then come verses describing various lawful and unlawful things, and commanding people to obey Allah's legislation and forbidding them to obey Satan and the customs of the Days of Ignorance, since nothing is to be followed except what Allah has legislated. The believers are then told to eat of the good things that Allah has made lawful, with the reminder that if they worship Allah alone they must follow His instructions about the lawful and the prohibited. Thus Allah alone is God, He alone is the Ruler of the universe, He alone is the Master of the Day of Resurrection, and He alone prescribes acts of worship, the norms of moral behavior, and what is lawful and what is prohibited.

In many other places the Qur'an describes the meaning of the Oneness of Allah with all its implications. We present another such text to throw more light on this subject, as well as to show how the Qur'an presents the characteristics and the constituents of the Islamic concept in a complete and comprehensive manner.

And thus We have made a Revelation to you in the Arabic tongue so that you might warn the Mother of Cities (Makkah) and all around her, and give warning of the Day of

Assembly, (the coming) of which is beyond all doubt, when some shall find themselves in Paradise and some in the blazing Fire. If Allah had willed, He could have made them all into a single nation, but He admits whom He wills to His mercy, whereas the wrong-doers shall have no protector or helper. Or (did they think they could) choose protectors other than Him? But Allah alone is the Protector, since He alone gives life to the dead and He alone has power over all things.

And on whatever you may differ, the decision is with Allah. (Say, therefore,) "Such is Allah, my Lord; in Him do I trust and to Him do I turn." (Allah), the Maker of the heavens and the earth, has made for you pairs from among yourselves and pairs among cattle, in order thus to cause you to multiply. There is nothing like Him. He is the All-Hearing and the All-Seeing. To Him belong the keys of the heavens and the earth. He increases provision to whomever He wills or restricts it. Truly He has knowledge of all things.

In matters of faith, He has ordained for you the *din* enjoined on Noah, knowledge of which We have given to you (Muhammad) through Revelation, and what We enjoined on Abraham, and Moses, and Jesus, namely, that you should be steadfast in upholding the (true) faith and make no division in it. The polytheists consider this unity of the *din*, to which you call them, an enormity, but Allah draws to Himself everyone who is willing and guides to Himself everyone who turns to Him.

And (the followers of earlier Revelation) broke up their unity, out of mutual jealousy, only after they had come to know the truth. Had it not been for a word that had already gone forth from your Lord (postponing all decision) for a term set (by Him), the matter would have been adjudged between them. And indeed those who inherited the Scripture after them are in hopeless doubt concerning it. Because of this, summon (all mankind), and stand firm as you are commanded, and do not follow their likes and dislikes, but say, "I believe in the Book that Allah has sent down, and I am commanded to dispense justice among you. Allah is my Lord and your Lord. For us are our works and for you your works. Let there be no contention between us and you. Allah will gather us together, for with Him is the end of every journey" (*Al-Shura* 42:7-15).

When we ponder this passage of the Qur'an, we find that it starts with revelation and messengership. It tells the Messenger to warn people of the Day of Assembly and of the judgment in the Hereafter, and describes the differing ends of the believers and of the wrong-doers in the Hereafter depending on their ways of living in this world. Then follows the exposition of Allah as the only Protector, who alone has power over everything, including the power to revive the dead. Then it emphasizes that Allah is the Ruler, and that true believers turn to Him alone and put all their trust in Him alone. Attention is then drawn to His creation and the phenomena of the physical world, such as the creation and sustenance of people and animals in pairs, followed by a renewed focus on the uniqueness of His Person, "There is nothing like Him," and the uniqueness of His Sovereignty, "To Him belong the keys of the heavens and the earth," and of His Providence, "He increases sustenance to whomever He wills or restricts it."

After these descriptions of the uniqueness of His Person, Sovereignty, and other Divine attributes, the Qur'an emphasizes in this passage that He alone is the Lawgiver, not only through this Messenger but through all previous Messengers, "In matters of faith He has ordained for you the *din* enjoined on Noah, knowledge of which We have revealed to you, and enjoined on Abraham and Moses and Jesus." This passage further commands the Prophet, may Allah's peace and blessings be upon him, to call people to this *din* of Allah and to the legislation inherent in it, and to stand firm on it, ignoring peoples' desires and opinions, and to exercise justice among people by judging in accordance with Allah's legislation. Finally, the text emphasizes that there is a complete separation between the believers who rule and judge according to what Allah has legislated and all others, and that the believers' final goal is Allah Most High.

We hope that these two examples from the text of the Qur'an are sufficient to elucidate the connection between the Islamic concept of the Oneness of Allah and the concept of Allah's sovereignty over people, and to explain the deep influence this belief exerts in the life of mankind, as well as to substantiate our claim that the Islamic concept is unique in being able to claim the Oneness of Allah as its most distinctive characteristic.

Belief in the Oneness of Allah deeply affects one's personal life because it affects both one's intellect and heart more markedly than any other concept possibly can, so much so that it can transform the total life of mankind.

Belief in the Oneness of Allah disciplines the mind and heart so that concepts, values, and morals are not shaken by changing conditions. For the person who believes in Allah in this manner and understands his position as a servant of the Almighty Lord knows his direction and knows his way. He knows clearly the answers to such questions as to who he is, what the purpose of his life is, and what the limitations of his power are. He also comprehends the nature of everything in this universe and the nature of the Active Power operating within it. With his correct understanding of the realities, he can deal with things and events in a correct manner without wavering and without hesitation. The accuracy of his conceptual framework produces in him a disciplined intellect with balanced standards as well as a disciplined heart with firm values. This helps him deal effectively with the "laws of nature" established by Allah Most High, which further increases his intellectual discipline and his firmness of character.

We can grasp this fact very clearly when we consider the Muslim, who deals with One Sovereign Lord and acknowledges Him alone as the Creator, the Provider, the Almighty, and the All-Knowing, and contrast the Muslim with believers in other concepts, such as those who have to contend with two adversarial gods, the god of good and the god of evil, those who have to struggle with an existent god diffused in non-existence, those who have to deal with a god who knows neither them nor the universe in which they live, and those who have to deal with matter as a god that does not hear or see or remain constant. Such myths deprive the intellect of anything firm and the heart of satisfaction.

The Islamic concept produces steadfastness in the heart and mind, because the man who understands his Lord and His sublime attributes and His relationship with the events occurring in the world can never be anxious or beset with worries.

By knowing the attributes of his Lord, the Muslim understands what is pleasing to Him and what is displeasing. He becomes firmly convinced that there is no way of gaining Allah's pleasure except through faith, through knowledge of His attributes, and by standing firm on His commandments and obeying His revealed Law. He understands that his relationship with Allah is not that of sonship nor of kinship, nor are there any intermediaries between himself and his Lord. Rather his relationship is that of a worshipper and an obedient servant who does what his Lord commands him to do, keeps away from what He forbids, and follows the way of life that He has legislated.

This insight gives steadfastness to his heart and intellect, clarity to his thoughts, and firmness to his conduct.

The clarity, simplicity, and straightforwardness of the Islamic concept and conduct can be appreciated most fully when we compare the concept of the Oneness of Allah in Islam with the concept of the Trinity in Christianity. According to "mysteries" in the Christian belief, there is One God but three Persons. Salvation can be attained only through the Person of the Son, and Original Sin, inherited by every human being, cannot be forgiven except through the sacrifice of the Son, who is Jesus Christ, may Allah's blessing and peace be upon him.

Or consider the individual who thinks of himself as the creation of "Nature," which neither hears nor sees, neither commands nor prohibits, neither encourages its creatures to action and noble conduct nor discourages them from meanness and indecency. How can the servants of such a deity be steadfast in any way of life or moral conduct? How can they be firm of heart and intellect when they do not know whether their god possesses anything absolute, or whether they may come across something new by chance or by experimentation.

Similarily, if we study all the concepts discussed above in the first chapter, entitled "The Wilderness and Intellectual Rubbish," and also in other chapters, we can see why, because of their confusion, complexity, and intricacy, they cannot produce firmness of concept and conduct in their followers.

When a sincere person first encounters the Islamic concept, its characteristics of straightness, simplicity, and clarity appeal to his or her heart and mind. This feature of Islam has attracted and still attracts both the less-sophisticated peoples of Asia and Africa as well as the more sophisticated persons in Europe and America, because this appeal to straightforward and simple truth is a part of human nature common to all peoples, both "primitive" and "civilized."

The concept of the Oneness of Allah integrates the personality of an individual just as it integrates the powers of a community, which is not the case with other belief systems. And this concept prevents disintegration of the individual personality and dissipation of community cohesion. In Islam the total personality of man, which has been created as an indivisible whole, is directed toward One Divine Being and deals with Him alone in all respects, in beliefs and concepts, worship and devotions, moral rules and social laws, and in the affairs of this world and of the Hereafter.

The Islamic belief is not refracted among numerous deities nor among numerous persons in the same deity, nor among various forces, some of which are divine while others are independent of divine power, nor among "natural" forces that cannot be defined uniquely or even considered as one entity.

Islamic teachings come from a single source, whether it concerns personal belief and worship or the system of life for an entire community or nation. This source is not divided between matters of faith and conscience and matters of practical life. Furthermore, the Law prescribed for human beings is the same Law that governs the entire universe. Accordingly, when human beings deal with each other and the universe in accordance with this one universal law, they achieve harmony and avoid conflict and division.

This integration of all human power generates such an invincible force that nothing can stand before it. That is why the great accomplishments of earlier generations of Muslims now seem almost supernatural. Indeed, such things were possible because the Islamic concept generates a unified force, which integrates the energies of both people and nature, prepares them to receive the blessing of Allah, and thereby makes them responsive totally to Allah so that both forces mutually reinforce each other in a single force dedicated to His service.

The Islamic concept, and especially the concept of the Oneness of Allah, has an electrifying effect on the life and conscience of the Muslim and on the internal organization and functioning of Islamic communities, whether at the level of the family or at the level of all mankind.

Indeed, the effect is no less than the liberation of man or rather the birth of man. To believe in the Uniqueness and Oneness of Allah and to understand His Divine attributes of divinity means that human beings must take the rules and laws for their lives from no one other than Allah, just as they take the rules for conducting their worship from Allah. Sovereignty is one of the most important attributes of Allah. The person who refuses to attribute sovereignty, either in theory or practice, to anyone besides Allah is a Believer, while the one who does so is an Unbeliever.

The text of the Qur'an is very clear about this, and there cannot be any doubt or controversy concerning this point.

> Judgement belongs only to Allah; He has commanded you not to serve anyone or anything but Him. This is the (one) ever-true faith (*Yusuf* 12:40).

> Or have they partners (for Allah) who have made lawful for them in religion that which Allah has not allowed? (*Al-Shura* 42:21).

> Whoever does not judge according to what Allah has revealed is a disbeliever (*Al- Ma'idah* 5:44).

> But no, by your Lord! They will not believe until they make you the judge regarding disagreements between them and

find within themselves no dislike of your verdict but surrender in full submission (*Al-Nisa* 4:65).

The Islamic concept does not differentiate between the rules of
conduct for private worship and the laws governing public life,
because the source of both is the same. There cannot be any differentiation between these two sets of rules, because the Oneness of Allah
and the Divine Sovereignty that belongs to Him alone demand that
there be no such differentiation. Anyone who differentiates one from
the other is completely estranged from Islam and has no belief in the
Oneness and Sovereignty of Allah Most High. This is made clear by the
Qur'anic passages cited above, as well as by the following.

They have taken their rabbis and their monks as lords
besides Allah, as well as the Messiah son of Mary, whereas
they were commanded to worship only One God. There is
no god but He! Glory be to Him, Who is far above anything
to which they may ascribe a share in His Divinity! (*Al-
Tawbah* 9:31).

The people of the Book, about whom this verse speaks, took Jesus
the son of Mary, as their Lord, in the sense that they worshipped him,
and took their rabbis and monks as their lords, not in the sense of
worshipping them, but in the sense that they took the rules and laws
of life from them. This verse combines these two aspects of lordship
by considering each aspect as the denial of the worship of One God.
It accuses them of ascribing associates or rivals to Allah because they
took Jesus as Sovereign Lord in worship and took monks and rabbis
as lords in legislation. The Messenger of Allah, peace be upon him,
gave such a clear-cut explanation of this verse that its meaning is
beyond all argument.

Imam Ahmad, Al-Tirmidhi, and Ibn Jarir have variously reported
from 'Adi bin Hatim, may Allah be pleased with him, that when the
Call of the Messenger of Allah reached him, he fled to Syria. He had
been a Christian in the days of pre-Islamic Ignorance, and some people
of his tribe, including his sister, fell prisoners of war to the Muslims.
The Messenger of Allah, peace be upon him, released 'Adi's sister and
gave her generous gifts. She returned to her brother, persuaded him
to accept Islam, and to visit the Messenger of Allah. 'Adi came to
Madinah as chief of the tribe of Tayy, and people talked about his
coming. He came into the presence of the Messenger of Allah, wearing
a silver cross around his neck, while the Messenger of Allah was
reciting the verse quoted above, "They have taken their rabbis and

monks as their lords beside Allah..." 'Adi reports that he said, "They do not worship them." The Messenger of Allah replied, "No, but they forbid to people what is permissible and make permissible what is forbidden (by Allah) and people follow them in this. This is their worship and servitude."

In this respect the Islamic concept is very sharp and clear by proclaiming the liberation of man, and indeed, the birth of man. Through this proclamation it brings mankind out of servitude to creatures into the servitude of the Creator. The "human being," in its full sense, cannot be found on this earth except when he is totally liberated from enslavement to servants, whatever be the form of this slavery, whether of belief and of conscience, or of rules of behavior and system of life. Only Islam refers back all legislative power and sovereignty to Allah and thereby brings people from servitude to the servants into the service of their Lord. In systems where legislative power and sovereignty belong to human beings, there is a kind of slavery of people to other people, but in Islam, and only in Islam, all people, without exception, are liberated from such slavery and serve their Creator alone. This is true "liberation of man" and this is the "birth of man," because before this man's true "humanity" had never come into existence in its complete and true form. This belief in the Oneness of Allah and in His Sovereignty over people is a Divine gift that guides all people on earth, and is the Divine favor referred to in the following verse:

> Today I have perfected your religion for you, and I have completed My blessing upon you, and I have approved Islam for your religion (*Al-Ma'idah* 5:3).

This gift the believers in the Oneness of Allah offer to all mankind, and this is the blessing they want to share with people, after benefiting from it themselves. They offer nothing less than the pleasure of Allah Most High. This is the new message that the believers in the Oneness of Allah can offer to mankind today, as their forefathers offered it in the past. Men and women receive it eagerly today. The attraction to this message is enormous because it offers mankind something it does not possess, something not contained in other concepts and beliefs, ideologies and philosophies, and systems and constitutions.

Before the battle of Al-Qadisyyah, Raba'i bin 'Amer came to Rustum, the commander of the Persian army, as a messenger from the Muslim army. Rustum asked him, "For what purpose have you come?" Raba'i replied, "Allah has sent us to bring whoever wishes from servitude to men into servitude to Allah alone, from the narrowness of this world into the vastness of this world and the Hereafter, and from the tyranny of religions into the justice of Islam.''

These few words convey the total message of Islam, namely the nature of this belief and of the movement produced by this belief, as well as the Muslims' understanding of this message and of their role in carrying this message to the entire world.

Indeed, Islam is a migration from the servitude of men toward the servitude of Allah, and a commitment to refer everything, whether it concerns this world or the next, to Him alone, and to ascribe every attribute of divinity to Allah Most High alone. Since sovereignty over people is a major attribute of divinity, the believer cannot divide his loyalty between Allah and something other than Allah. It follows that anyone who divides his loyalty in such a position is a disbeliever.

It is not possible to find liberation for the human being, or indeed, to find the "human being" at all except by purifying one's understanding that the attribute of Sovereignty belongs to Allah alone and by purifying one's loyalty exclusively to Him.

The believers in the Oneness of Allah Most High, by returning to this concept and raising its banner, are able to tell the whole of mankind what Rabi'i bin 'Amer told Rustum at a time when the state of mankind was similar to that of today. Mankind today is drowned in the servitude of servants, and only belief in the Oneness of Allah in its most comprehensive meaning can bring whoever wishes out of this enslavement into the servitude of Allah alone. Only in this way can any person liberate himself or herself and become a human being in the full sense of the word.

Moreover, believers in the Oneness of God, by returning to the system of life that this belief entails and calling others to it, are in a position to offer the whole world something possessed by no other religion, ideology, system, constitution, or philosophy. This is the grand opportunity for them to play a great and significant role in transforming the entire world. Their essential role will be to lead mankind in all important matters, just as the first generation of Muslims from the Arabian Peninsula led mankind 1400 years ago.

At present they are not in a position to offer mankind great scientific discoveries or dazzling cultural achievements, so that the people of the world would flock to them because of their superiority in science and culture. They can offer something else, however, something greater than all scientific discoveries and all cultural achievements. This is the "liberation of man," or greater still, the "birth of man" as intended by Allah.

In offering mankind this gift, they offer with it a complete way of life, a way of life based on the dignity of man and based on freedom of his person, his mind, his conscience, and his soul from all bondages. Freed from the shackles of human enslavement, he stands as the deputy of Allah on earth, strong and noble, just as Allah intended him to be. As the deputy of Allah, he can make splendid discoveries and open up great avenues of culture, remaining at the height of his freedom, noble and dignified, slave neither to any machine nor to any mortal.

If Allah has inspired us to say the right thing, all praise belongs to Him the Lord of all Being.

INDEX

BIBLIOGRAPHY

Abul Hasan Ali Nadawi, *Islam and the World*
Al-Akkad, *Allah*
Al-Akkad, *Haqaiq Al-Islam wa Abatil Khusumihi*
Al-Bukhari, *Sahih Al-Bukhari*
Al-Bahi Mohammad, *The New Islamic Thought and its Connection with Western Imperialism*
Alexis Carrel, *Man the Unknown*. New York: Harper Brothers, 1939.
Alfred Butler, *The Arab Conquest of Egypt*. Oxford: Clarendon Press, 1978.
Al-Kalabi, *Kitab Al-Asnam*
Arnold T.W. *The Preaching of Islam*
Dorner I.A., *A System of Christian Doctrine*
Draper, *History of Conflict Between Religion and Science*
Mohammad Iqbal, *The Reconstruction of Religious Thought in Islam*. London: Oxford UP, 1934.
Mohammad Asad, *Islam at the Crossroads*
Muhammad Qutb, *Manhaj Al-Tarbiyah Al-Islmaiyah*
Muhammad Qutb, *Are We Muslims?*
Nietzche, *Thus Spake Zarathustra*. New York: Heritage Press, 1967.
The Challenges of Modern Science to Human Action and Belief
The New English Bible. Cambridge, England: Oxford University Press, 1961.
Robertson, J.C., *Histroy of the Christian Church*
Sa'd, *Tabaqat Al-Umam*
Sayyid Qutb, *Al-Islam Wal Mushkilatal Hadarah*
Sayyid Qutb, *Mushahidil Qiyammah*